# CHILD PROTECTION: FAM
# CONFERENCE PROCESS

MW01233066

# Child Protection: Families and the Conference Process

MARGARET BELL
*University of York*

Routledge
Taylor & Francis Group

LONDON AND NEW YORK

First published 1999 by Ashgate Publishing

Reissued 2018 by Routledge
2 Park Square, Milton Park, Abingdon, Oxon, OX14 4RN
711 Third Avenue, New York, NY 10017, USA

*Routledge is an imprint of the Taylor & Francis Group, an informa business*

Publisher's Note
The publisher has gone to great lengths to ensure the quality of this reprint but points out that some imperfections in the original copies may be apparent.

Disclaimer
The publisher has made every effort to trace copyright holders and welcomes correspondence from those they have been unable to contact.

A Library of Congress record exists under LC control number: 99072841

ISBN 13: 978-1-138-31399-6 (hbk)
ISBN 13: 978-1-138-31402-3 (pbk)
ISBN 13: 978-0-429-45258-1 (ebk)

# Contents

# List of Tables

# Preface

*Evaluative Studies in Social Work* brings together research which has explored the impact of social work services in a variety of contexts and from several perspectives. The vision of social work in this series is a broad one. It encompasses services in residential, fieldwork and community settings undertaken by workers with backgrounds in health and welfare. The volumes will therefore include studies of social work with families and children, with elderly people, people with mental and other health problems and with offenders.

This approach to social work is consistent with contemporary legislation in many countries, including Britain, in which social work has a key role in the assessment of need and in the delivery of personal social services, in health care and in criminal justice. It also continues a long tradition which perceives an integral relationship between social work, social research and social policy. Those who provide social work services are acquainted with the complexities of human need and with the achievements and shortcomings of major instruments of social policy. This knowledge was exploited by, amongst others, Booth, Rowntree and the Webbs in their studies of poverty. Politicians and sociologists have also recognised that, together with the people they try to help, social workers can provide a commentary on the human meaning of public policies and the social issues that grow from private troubles.

This knowledge and experience of the recipients and practitioners of social work are not, of course, immediately accessible to the wider community. A major purpose of research is to gather, organise and interpret this information and, in the studies in this series, to evaluate the impact of social work. Here there are many legitimate interests to consider. First and foremost are direct service users and those who care for them. These are the people who should be the main beneficiaries of social work services. Also to be considered are the personnel of other services for whom liaison and collaboration with social work are essential to their own successful functioning. The needs and views of these different groups may well conflict and it is the researcher's task to identify those tensions and describe social work's response to them.

The problems which confront social work are often extremely complex. They may need to be tackled in a variety of ways; for example, through practical assistance, advocacy, counselling and supervision. Outcomes may be similarly varied and studies of the effectiveness of social work must demonstrate the different kinds of impact it can have. These may entail changes in users' circumstances, behaviour or well being. On these changes, and on the kind of help they have received, users' perspectives must be of great significance. Also of central interest to those who provide or manage services is an understanding of their form and content and the relationship between the problems identified and the statutory responsibilities of social workers and the help given. Social work researchers must therefore take care to study what is actually delivered through social work and how, as well as its outcomes, aspirations and objectives. For good and ill social work has an impact on a large and increasing number of citizens. A major aim of *Evaluative Studies in Social Work* is to increase well-informed understanding of social work, based on knowledge about its real rather than imagined activities and outcomes.

The identification of effectiveness, in its various forms, can also not be the end of the story. The costs of the associated services must be studied, set in the context of their effectiveness, to allow the most efficient use of resources.

These demands present major challenges to researchers who have to use, adapt and develop a wide range of research methods and designs. Ingenuity and persistence are both required if evaluative research in social work is to be pursued in contexts often regarded as beyond the scope of such enquiry. *Evaluative Studies in Social Work* intends to make widely available not only the research findings about the impact of social work but also to demonstrate and discuss possible approaches and methods in this important and developing field of enquiry.

The first volumes in this series described studies undertaken in the Social Work Research Centre at the University of Stirling. In 1997, we decided actively to seek proposals from major centres of research for future books in this series. It had become clear from the 1996 UK Higher Education Funding Councils' assessment of research in British universities that both the quality and quantity of social work research were increasing substantially. It was also clear that a priority for many researchers - in this strategic and applied field - is, quite appropriately, to publish digests of their work in books and journals designed particularly for busy practitioners and managers. A consequence of this is that the full context, content and methodology of the research may never enter the public domain. This is a loss for researchers and those with a specialist interest in the subjects under enquiry, especially so in a relatively new and complex field of research when methodological innovation and development are important. Ashgate provides an excellent context for books which can explore subjects in depth and also allow exploration of research design, method and technique.

Juliet Cheetham and Roger Fuller
University of Stirling

# Acknowledgements

I am grateful to the Nuffield Foundation for funding the research upon which this book is based. I am indebted especially to Ian Sinclair for his help and expertise in supervising the empirical work and the statistical analyses and for his challenges to my thinking. Mike Stein also deserves thanks for his helpful insights and for his encouragement and support. I am also grateful to Roger Fuller and Juliet Cheetham for encouraging me to complete this book for publication within their series of evaluative studies of social work. Barbara Dodds helped enormously with the typing. I would like to also thank my daughters, Harriet and Eleanor, who struggled with the Tables and Christopher and Martin for their enthusiastic support throughout. Finally and most importantly, thanks are owing to the Area Child Protection Committee and the local authority who enabled me to undertake the research and to the professionals in the city who so willingly gave of their time and expertise. In particular I owe thanks to the families who told me so cogently and courageously about their experience.

For giving copyright permission for some already published material to be adapted for use in this book, I have to thank the following: Blackwell Science, Bell, M. (1996), 'An account of the experiences of 51 families involved in an initial child protection conference', *Child and Family Social Work*, Vol.1, January 1996 and Bell, M. (1995), 'A study of the attitudes of nurses to parental involvement in the initial child protection conference, and their preparation for it', *Journal of Advanced Nursing*, 22, 250-257; Wiley and Sons, Bell, M. (1996), 'Why some conferences are difficult: A study of the professionals experience of some initial child protection conferences', *Children and Society*, February 1996, and Oxford University Press, Bell, M. (1999), 'Working in Partnership in Child Protection: The Conflicts', *British Journal of Social Work*, June 1999.

# 1 Introduction

## The aims of the book

This book is written at a time when there is general agreement that too much of the work undertaken for children in need in England and Wales comes under the child protection banner. The debate about the direction the child protection system has taken following the implementation of The Children Act, 1989, has preoccupied policy makers practitioners and researchers. The issues raised encompass philosophical discussions about the nature and morality of judgments about behaviour and standards of parenting, about conflicts of rights and about power and justice. Detailed questions are raised about practice, particularly with regard to the concept of working in partnership. And a raft of policy and procedural issues are raised which require responses at a national level, as well as for Area Child Protection Committees to address locally.

This book attempts to address some of these issues with reference to a research study undertaken at the same time as those summarised in Messages from Research (1995). The research evaluated the involvement of parents in eighty three initial child protection conferences in a northern city between 1991 and 1993 from the perspective of all the participants - the family members and the professionals. Further, it assessed the impact on the decisions made and the conference process and it explored the effects on the ongoing intervention. The study was comparative, comparing conferences and professional attitudes before and after families were included, and comparing conferences and family experiences at conferences with and without parents present. So, although the study reported here was carried out at a time when the policy of involving parents was new and some authorities have since experimented with less formal alternatives, such as family group conferences and mediation, the centrality of the child protection conference within the administrative system is the same, the procedures by which it is run are largely the same, the tasks and roles of social workers are the same and the difficulties they face are the same. Moreover, while the government is actively seeking a refocused children's service, the current consultation document, Working Together, 1998, reinforces the need for the existing child protection system - including the initial conference - to be kept in place.

In providing a comprehensive and critical account of what works well and what works badly for professionals and families involved in the existing child protection system this book furthers our understanding of the child protection process and so contributes to the refocusing debate. It provides information about what families value in the intervention, it quantifies and analyses the factors that contribute to the most difficult cases and it explores inter-agency process and training. I hope, also, that it will demonstrate the immensely challenging and often contradictory tasks the professionals face in setting up partnerships with families who may have abused their children. Social workers are expected to be all things to all men. As Cleaver and Freeman (1995) have suggested, they need "the skills of Machiavelli, the wisdom of Solomon, the compassion of Augustine, and the hide of a tax inspector". Generally they succeed, but moral panic and professional failure ensue when they do not. It seems timely, therefore, to examine further the rhetoric of partnership and optimism by reference to a research study which reveals that there are some child abuse situations where the procedures and the principles underlying them work well, but there are others where they do not. The detailed analysis that is presented here suggests the reasons why, and this can only be helpful to the debate.

## The structure of the book

The overall objective, then, is to build upon and augment other research in the area and to take forward the current debate about services for children in need of protection. The book begins by describing the background to the research study that was undertaken between 1991 and 1993. The history of the initial child protection conference and the involvement of family members is described and located within the context of the emerging concerns with civil liberties and increasing consumer involvement in social welfare that marked the 1980s. These principles were reformulated in terms of partnership and the concept of partnership has preoccupied developments in policy and practice throughout the 1990s. This book argues that the principles of consumer involvement and partnership which are then built into the Children Act 1989 create opportunities as well as difficulties for the professionals operating them. The moral and practice issues concern matters of rights and justice, power and conflict. My hypothesis is that these issues are inherent in the child protection system and are enacted in the conference arena. These themes are discussed and given more detailed attention in Chapter 2, preliminary to presenting the research findings. The study involved the collection of data from a variety of sources and using a range of methods, and the design and methodology for this is explained in Chapter 3. Essentially, the design was intended to facilitate the exploration of the issues identified above from the perspectives of all the participants. The subsequent five chapters report the empirical findings from the different aspects of the study. The first of these, Chapter 4, presents a study of the attitudes of the professionals at two points in time - before the implementation of the policy of parental involvement and after. It explores the perceptions that professionals have of each other and to the involvement of family members and describes the inter-agency training they received. This study of changing attitudes provides the backcloth to the analysis of the eighty three conferences, fifty involving parents and thirty three where they were not then invited. Chapter 5 describes and analyses information about the children and families conferenced, about the conference structures and about the decisions and recommendations made. This information provides the context for the more detailed presentation of the experiences of the professionals case by case. The analysis of this data, combined with the observation of twenty two of these conferences, enables the conferences to be grouped according to the degrees of difficulty experienced by the professionals. Certain features of the families and the conferences clustered in the more difficult cases, and this is analysed in Chapter 6.

Chapter 7 reports on the experiences of the parents. The research was designed to allow for a comparison to be made between two groups of families, one group who had been invited to the conference and a second group who had not been invited. The research is unique in having this comparative study, which enables clear conclusions to be drawn about the impact on the professionals and the parents and the decisions made following their involvement in the conference. The last of the data chapters provides a detailed account of the social work practice in twenty two cases where parents attended the conference. The difficulties for the investigating social workers of undertaking assessments for the conference and of managing conflicts of task and role are explored here. Some understanding is offered as to the reasons for the social workers sharp focus on procedural regularity rather than empathic involvement with the family. Finally, the book is concluded by drawing together and identifying the main findings and discussing them in relation to the themes of partnership, empowerment and the conflicts identified as being inherent to the conference task. Some implications for policy and practice are suggested with reference to the proposals in Working Together, 1998.

## The background

### The context

The principle of involving parents in decisions that are made about their children has fundamentally informed recent government policy on child care and is now a dominating principle in welfare provision underpinning a wide range of social policy legislation. The Children Act 1989 sets out a clear framework for services to be built upon the participation of all family members, requiring their involvement in the consultation and decision making processes at every stage of the child care work. Although the word partnership is not specifically used in the Act or the Guidance (it was used in the White Paper "The Law on Child Care and Family Services" and the Department of Health "Principles in Practice" in Regulations and Guidance, 1990), the emphasis is on the local authority supporting parents in caring for their children, rather than providing substitute care, "the State being ready to help, especially where doing so would lessen the risk of family breakdown" (Parton, 1991). The Challenge of Partnership in Child Protection (1995) spelt out in more detail ways in which partnership with parents should be managed, sustained and developed throughout the decision making processes and the provision of services for children in need. Most recently the consultation document, Working Together (1998), takes forward the process by reiterating that partnership is central to the child protection process, while sounding a cautionary note - that partnership with parents should not be "interpreted to mean that professionals should never engage in an analysis of a child's situation without the parents present" (p.49).

Previous Government documents have also required the involvement of parents, as in the Code of Practice (1983) governing the access of parents to children in care. Nor is this emphasis confined to social service provision. The Education Act 1981 requires local authorities to take into account the wishes of parents in determining services for children having special educational needs. The service framework of the NHS and Community Care Act 1990 and the Carers Act 1996 also lay substantial emphasis on strengthening users' rights to participate in decisions, for example by exercising choice in the package of services to be delivered. There is a strong emphasis in a wide range of welfare legislation on consulting users, on participation by users and carers in decision making and on promoting partnerships between users, carers and providers.

*Consumerism*

The requirement to promote parental involvement which permeates the legislation referred to above and its associated guidance, is part of a wider political movement toward strengthening civil liberties and increasing consumer involvement in social care - trends which have been encouraged by judgments in the European Court of Human Rights (1988). Concerns about citizenship and rights are also reflected in the legislation governing the computerization of records and access to personal files carried on computer, as required by the Data Protection Act 1984 and Access to Personal Files Act 1987. In the personal social services and in the health field open records are now the norm. In the Health Service the patient's right to see his/her records forms part of the citizen's charter, although some Doctors continue to maintain that the practice raises serious ethical and practice issues in their work. In the field of social work the principle is less controversial. Most practitioners agree that good practice requires them to be aware of and to promote their client's right to see their records, not only in the interests of natural justice, but also because they view the process of the client's involvement in record keeping as part of a therapeutic process which is empowering. Research on written agreements (Cordon and Preston-Shoot, 1987, Aldgate, 1990) suggests that successful participation in casework is facilitated by using records and written agreements. Nevertheless, in practice there are a number of situations where social workers find it very hard to put in writing opinions which may be perceived as derogatory by their clients. They need to be very clear indeed what the purposes of the record are for, and to be skilled in the art of shared recording.

*Values*

While the concepts of partnership, empowerment and advocacy that have emerged from the recent legislation feel new they have a long and respectable pedigree. The recent legislation can be seen as providing an operational framework for the traditional social work values of respect for persons, dignity and client self-determination as laid down by Biesteck in The Casework Relationship (1961), and encapsulated in the principles of the earliest caseworkers (Hollis, 1966).

> What we really mean by the concept [self-determination] is that self-direction, the right to make his own choices, is a highly valued attribute of the individual. The more he can make his own decisions and direct his own life the better, and the less the caseworker tries to take over these responsibilities the better (p.13).

So while new terms are now being used and their incorporation into the ideology underpinning the legislative framework may mark new ground, the value base of social work has not changed. A glance at reports such as the BASW Working Party Report "Clients are Fellow Citizens" (1980), at Berrys' work on complaints procedures (1988), and at the earlier research studies, such as that conducted by Stein and Ellis (1983) on the views of four hundred and sixty five young people in care demonstrate this point. Other studies have consistently found that both clients and practitioners have valued access to information and shared recordings (see Ovretiet, 1986; Shemmings, 1991). The work of Sainsbury (1989), Etherington (1986) and Banks (1995) furthered the growing preoccupation with the wider ethical formulations impacting upon practice, especially taking into account a user perspective, and suggested that practice was more likely to be effective when based upon an agreed perception of need and a negotiated contract.

Other research supported these findings. In this country the work of Mayer and Timms (1970) on differing perceptions between clients and workers suggested that clients and workers had their own agendas and that the goals of the intervention were commonly not shared. This finding was later replicated by Sainsbury (1982) and, again, by Lishman (1988). Themes running through key government publications, Social Work Decisions in Child Care (1985), and Patterns and Outcomes in Child Placement (1991) also relate clear and negotiated goals to better outcomes for children.

*User involvement*

User involvement in service provision and delivery is thus now not only a legislative requirement in many areas of social service provision but is also regarded as being an essential component of good practice. Beresford and Croft (1992) describe a number of ways in which better services result from the greater public accountability and democratization to which the involvement of users leads. They also argue that the process of involving users is empowering to them as individuals and to the groups and communities they represent. The theme of user involvement, especially in relation to the effectiveness of service provision and developing models of practice based on partnership principles, has been widely researched across a range of settings and with different client groups. For example, the

Economic and Social Research Council is currently funding a project on consumerism and citizenship amongst users of health and social care services in the fields of mental health and physical disability. A number of the research studies presented in Messages From Research (1995) include the views of families on the early stages of a child abuse investigation (see Farmer and Owen, 1995, Cleaver and Freeman, 1995, Thoburn, Lewis and Shemmings, 1995).

*Partnership*

> Once a jolly swagman camped by a billabong,
> Under the shade of a coolibah tree,
> And he sang as he sat and waited till his billy boiled,
> 'You'll come a-walzing, Matilda, with me.
> > Waltzing Matilda, Paterson, 1864.

The concept of partnership that emerged from The Children Act 1989 can thus be seen as deriving from the more traditional value base of practice and also as representing a more proactive model of practice based on the values of shared care, empowerment and advocacy for individuals and communities. As suggested above, there now seems to be widespread agreement that taking users views into account produces more effective services and that this requires social workers to develop and use particular practice skills. Marsh and Fisher (1993) have developed a list of practice skills which they regard as being fundamental to partnership practice. In their view:

> Goals should be negotiated, explicit and observable... Tasks should form the central working tool...active intervention should be brief...records should form the principal means of sharing the purpose of intervention (p.13).

This task centred approach, with its reliance on openness, clarity of mandate and negotiated agreement obviously addresses the issues raised by the research studies mentioned above regarding the need for clarity and negotiated agreement about the basis, purposes and methods of intervention. It is also helpful in pinning down some specific practice skills which enable practitioners to begin to find concrete ways of operationalizing a principle in which they believe, but are less sure how to operate. However, as Katz (1995) has observed, since the tasks are generally determined by workers rather than clients, client participation is no more likely to be guaranteed by the task-centred model than by other approaches. None really stand the acid test of being beyond the boundaries of manipulation, persuasion or coercion within the unequal balance of a relationship which inevitably has a power dimension (see Bell, 1993).

Some recent research studies (Thoburn et al., 1995, Farmer and Owen, 1995, Westcott, 1995) on practitioners' perspectives on their child protection work suggest that, while the principles of partnership have liberated social work thinking by providing a framework for practice which is participative rather than paternalistic, social workers are continuing to struggle with how to do it, and to define more accurately what it is. Reporting on a conference at Brunel University, Kaganas (1993) comments on the confusion arising from the multiplicity of perspectives:

> There is no consensus on precisely what [partnership] means in practice, whether it is desired and, indeed, whether it can be achieved...some thought it could never be more than a fond hope.

Delegates at the conference saw constraints upon partnership practice as including absence of cooperation between social services and departments such as housing, lack of resources, bureaucracy, the adversarial nature of the legal system and, most strikingly, the power imbalance between professionals and parents. More importantly, they did not know how to do it.

Whatever the professional's view on partnership, other research has suggested that clients have a different perspective altogether. A study by Barnado's (1993) found that, while their clients valued their relationship with their social worker and saw it as embodying friendliness and accessibility, staff viewed partnership as a strategy to empower users. This gap in perceptions puts flesh upon the distinction suggested by Daines (1990), who comments that the partnership process can be both instrumental, as judged here by the staff, and expressive, as judged by the users. Staff thus defined partnership as an end, something which led to an empowered client; whereas clients understood it to be a means, a quality of relationship. While this relationship was valued, what the families most wanted, but did not get because it was not within the power of social workers to provide, was "an adequate income, more skills and better housing" (1993). Further if, as Bradshaw (1972) has suggested, there is a relationship between assessment of need and available service provision, social workers assessments and interventions are more likely to reflect the available service provision and their own value position and favoured skills rather than the views of the client, or some agreed objective standard of 'good' child care. Clearly there are limitations to the ideal of partnership. Marsh and Fisher (1993) concede that where clients decide that "even 'minimal choice' is not relevant ... work will assume the characteristics of surveillance and maintenance without consent, with attempts to move back to partnership at appropriate intervals" (p.19). It has to be said, further, that not all practitioners would agree that their practice either does or should meet the requirements that Marsh and Fisher outline, or that these skills are an essential prerequisite to partnership practice. Social workers are required to perform a huge range of different tasks, to sustain relationships of differing duration and intensity with immensely different individuals and client groups and for very different purposes. For this they need a repertoire of skills and available resources which will enable them to establish the trusting relationships on which partnership work depends and which may or may not be task centred or based on negotiated agreement.

There are other difficulties with the concept of partnership. It seems that where clients are in agreement with social services that there is a problem - and about the cause - the opportunity exists to build a voluntary partnership based on their shared perception. However, Thoburn et al. (1995), in addressing parents' understandings of the requirements agreed at the initial child protection conference, found that many families did not understand that, technically, their cooperation was voluntary. If they had, they may well have withdrawn their cooperation. There are a number of situations where a social services intervention is not welcomed by families, or by one or more of the family members, but where the social worker is required by law to intervene. Further, these situations may involve a fundamental conflict of rights, for example the rights of children to be protected from further abuse may well conflict with the rights of parents to be self-determining. In these situations it can be extremely difficult to determine who the partnership and negotiated agreement should be with; the child, the non-abusing parent, other carers, let alone whether the partnership approach under discussion is the most appropriate intervention, or is possible or practicable.

The Challenge of Partnership (1995) has helped by providing more detailed guidance on how to implement the commitment to partnership with families. It sets out issues relating to the organizational framework as well as examining the concept of partnership in practice. The concept of partnership outlined in the document is similar to that constructed by Thoburn et al. (1995) in suggesting that partnership with parents takes place, essentially, on three levels; providing information, through a more active involvement such as consultation, to participation in decision making. However, while the optimistic tone of the government publication suggests that full partnership with parents is a realistic objective, Thoburn et al.'s recent study (1995) demonstrates that, in practice, it is extremely difficult to achieve. The conclusion of the researchers in the study of two hundred and twenty cases which reached child protection conferences in seven authorities, was that only 16% of the parents could be described as participating in an arrangement which could broadly be described as a full partnership. Of the remainder, 42% of the main parents and 10% of the non-resident parents were rated as being informed or consulted, and 13% were not involved at all.

The common theme emerging from the research is that practitioners are more likely than their clients to believe that their work is participative. Practitioners value the principle of partnership, but are not always clear how it can be operationalized. Clients are generally satisfied with their practitioners, but are unclear about the mandate for social work interventions. The balance of power within the relationship is uneven and clients do not feel powerful.

*Involving parents and family members in the initial child protection conference*

It is within this context that the inclusion of family members in child protection conferences was determined. There is now widespread agreement, in support of the basic premise in The Children Act 1989, that the interests of the child are best served when they remain within the family unit. Since children are, and wherever possible should be, looked after at home, their parents' knowledge and expertise should be acknowledged and built upon and their voluntary cooperation sought. The concept of "parental responsibility" is clearly intended to support this principle and the premise that each family is the expert on itself is now well established in the literature. The work of Malluccio (1986) in America, and Wilcox (1991) on family group conferences in New Zealand, strengthened the argument that families are experts on themselves and should be given more responsibility for the protection of their children. Reporting on the work in New Zealand on family group conferences, Wilcox writes:

> We found that [family] change could be dramatic when the professionals begin to grasp an understanding that while their training and expertise gives them general knowledge about children and families, it does not make them experts in specific families, other than their own. Wilcox et al.

Families should be regarded as the experts on themselves and as Jane Rowe (1991) suggests, their "potential as a resource" should be exploited. Further arguments in favour of parental involvement in the early child abuse investigation are provided by research undertaken by the Dartington team and other researchers from Bristol University. A number of their studies have provided evidence that the great majority of children who are case conferenced following an allegation of suspected abuse either remain at home or return to it. In Farmer and Owen's study (1995), two thirds of the children who had suffered from physical abuse, neglect and emotional abuse continued to live in the same household as the abusing parent. In March 1992 73% of children on child protection registers lived at home with at least one parent. Even in the most extreme cases, where children enter the care system, the most likely outcome at the point of separation is that the children will return home. Bullock and his colleagues (1993) suggest that 87% will return home within five years, and 92% eventually. Milham's research (1986) emphasized how quickly parents can be frozen out of the care process and feel disempowered when professionals take over. Milham identified the early stages of care as being crucial to the maintenance of contact between children removed from home and their parents. Such evidence suggests that parents have a continuing role to play and children, parents and professionals have to work together if a good outcome is to be achieved. Practitioners also argue that it is essential and, indeed, logical (with certain notable exceptions, such as in cases of sexual abuse) to involve parents in the treatment of their abused children. Effective child care practice is, on this account, seen as being built upon careful and sensitive family work which includes all members of the family in treatment choices and, where appropriate, in the intervention. Kempe and Kempe (1984), Tunnard (1983) and Dale (1986) are among a number of exponents of this position.

Underlying this practice development and research work, and a key to it as well as to the legislation, is a theme common to a number of the inquiry reports into the abuse of children. This is the extent to which parents should be included in the decision making process in child protection work. In the inquiry reports this theme can be traced as a swinging pendulum. The Maria Colwell Inquiry (1974) questioned the principle of parents' rights after Maria was returned to her parents against her will. In contrast, in Cleveland (1987), the concern was that parents' rights were being denied because the judicial system favoured the rights of the child. The Children Act 1989 can be seen as an attempt to manage the inherent conflict in child protection work between the rights of the parent to have a say in what happens to their children and the rights of children to be protected from the inherent harm in a firmly grounded social attitude that still regards children as the property of their parents (Aries, 1973, Archard, 1993).

To summarize, the three main strands making up the argument for the involvement of parents in conferences are that practice is more effective when parents are involved, that parents have a right to be present and it is unfair to exclude them and that the principle of natural justice requires them, as human beings, to be treated with respect. These arguments underlie much of the discussion in this book and will be the subject of more detailed consideration in the next chapter.

## The conference

Within this context and in response to the themes outlined above, the child protection conference has developed as the crucible of the child protection system. In this section, I chart in more detail the historical development of the conference and the involvement of parents up to the present day.

### *History and functions of the conference*

While case conferences in their present form were set up following the publication of the Maria Colwell Inquiry Report (1974), meetings convened for communicating interagency concern about neglected and maltreated children have been held for over fifty years. Stevenson (1980) points out that even before the 1950 Home Office circular ('Children neglected or ill-treated in their homes') recommended the establishment of children's coordinating committees to discuss children who had been ill-treated, conferences were held in clinical settings with the psychiatrist as 'the team leader' to discuss the diagnosis and treatment of children. The advent of Children's Departments in 1948 had the effect of bringing the case conference out of the medical arena and throughout the 1950s case conferences were increasingly used as a mechanism for improving inter-agency cooperation.

In 1974 the death of Maria Colwell focused attention more keenly on the inter-agency component of child protection work. Following the Inquiry Report, the DHSS (DHSS 1974 (a)) advised local and health authorities to form Area Review Committees (now Area Child Protection Committees) to oversee local policy and training arrangements, to ensure that case conferences were held after every suspected case and to set up central registers containing information about children considered to be at risk of abuse. As in 1950, the way forward was seen mainly in terms of ensuring better inter-agency collaboration.

The status of the register and its purposes were ambiguous. There was no legal duty to report cases and no requirement as to how authorities should operate and use the register. It was, therefore, hardly surprising that they were not widely used and had limited value in the identification of cases (ADSS, 1981, 1987, DHSS I, 1990). In addition, the inclusion of suspected cases raises issues of civil liberties and privacy. Issues of fairness and justice were highlighted further by the fact that different authorities operated widely differing criteria for registration, since there was no standardization of the criteria. Some writers suggested that the registers provide a 'gatekeeping' function for scarce resources (Corby and Mills, 1986; Jones et al., 1986). Others (Geach and Szwed, 1983) pointed out that the bureaucratic procedures associated with registration do not in themselves protect the child or ensure good social work practice.

Government circulars remained unclear as to the procedures that should be adopted for the holding and managing of case conferences until 1988. In 1988 Working Together made it clear that the protection of the child was the main purpose of the conference, again stressing its purpose as a 'forum for the exchange of information between professionals'. The guidance is developed in Working Together, 1991. Here it is made clear that the purpose of registers was not to measure the incidence and prevalence of child abuse but was a tool for case management within the child protection system. Essentially, the register was to provide a record of children needing an inter-agency protection plan:

> The purpose of the register is to provide a record of all children in the area for whom there are unresolved child protection issues and who are currently the subject of an inter-agency protection plan... The register will provide a point of speedy enquiry for professional staff who are worried about a child and want to know whether the child is the subject of an inter-agency protection plan.
>
> (Home Office et al., 1991, para. 6.37)

The name of the conference is changed to the child protection conference which is required to assess risk, decide whether the child's name should be put on the child protection register and devise a child protection plan. There are four categories to be used for registration: neglect, physical injury, sexual abuse and emotional abuse. Grave concern as a category was abolished in 1991, during the year of this research study.

> Before a child is registered the conference must decide that there is, or is a likelihood of, significant harm leading to the need for a child protection plan. One of the following requirements needs to be satisfied:
>
> i) there must be one or more identifiable incidents which can be described as having adversely affected the child. They may be acts of commission or omission. They can be either physical, sexual, emotional or neglectful. It is important to identify a specific occasion or occasions when the incident has occurred. Professional judgment is that further incidents are likely.
> or
> ii) significant harm is expected on the basis of professional judgment of findings of the investigation in this particular case or on research evidence.
>
> (Home Office et al., 1991, para. 6.39)

Gibbons et al. (1995) observe that the combination of a clearer definition of the register's purpose, with a better defined threshold and more specific categories will probably mean clearer evidence will need to be brought to the conference to demonstrate the need for a protection plan. However, while harm is defined under The Children Act 1989 as "ill-treatment or the impairment of health or development", the addition of the term significant introduces a higher threshold but without stipulating when this is reached. This, she claims, has wide reaching implications for the operation of the child protection system. If the threshold is set too high, some children will be unprotected; conversely, if too low, the system will become overloaded, failing to concentrate resources on children at risk.

As things stand there is little evidence of substantial changes in the ways in which the threshold criteria are being applied. The numbers of children on the child protection register declined and then stabilized after 1993, and the categories of neglect and emotional abuse are now more commonly used (Health and PSS Statistics, 1997).

*History of the involvement of parents*

Up to Working Together 1988 government guidance had been clearly against the attendance of parents at conferences. Thoburn et al. (1995) observe that in the early 1980s there was very little mention of parental participation in the literature on child abuse. In 1985 a BASW policy paper on the management of child abuse stated:

> Parents, however, should not attend entire conferences, which are basically meetings where professionals take information and advice from each other and form recommendations for action - some being related to statutory duties. It is most unlikely that the best interests of the child can remain the objective focus of a conference if the parents are present.
>
> (BASW, 1985)

However, the impetus in the late 1980s to include parents in decisions about their children came from a range of directions. Events in Cleveland acted as a major catalyst, placing parents' rights high on the agenda. Butler Sloss regarded parents' attendance as critical to child protection work:

> Parents should be informed of case conferences unless, in the view of the Chairman of the conference, their presence will preclude a full and proper consideration of the child's interests.
>
> (Report of the Inquiry into Child Abuse in Cleveland, 1987, p.246)

Some short time later, the Social Services Inspectorate at Rochdale (1991) expressed criticism of local authorities who had not developed a policy of inviting parents to the initial case conference. In many respects Working Together 1988 can be seen as an attempt by government to address the issue of rights and, to some extent, to circumscribe the powers of professionals by opening their workings to public scrutiny. Morrison et al (1990) suggested that the guidance was produced apparently in response to a ruling in the European Court of Human Rights (1988) about the lack of parental involvement in recent child care cases. It heralded a major change of policy.

> Parents should be invited wherever practicable to attend part, or if appropriate, the whole of the case conference unless in the view of the chair of the conference their presence will preclude a full and proper consideration of the child's interests.
>
> (Home Office et al., 1988, para. 5.45)

However, what is conspicuous by its absence from this paragraph is any reference to parental participation. Indeed, as Morrison et al. (1990) point out, the guidance goes on to talk about parents "being informed" of the inter-agency plan and the purposes of registration, and does not refer at any stage to their participation in the decision making process.

The publication of The Children Act 1989, with its wide ranging requirements for local authorities to work in partnership with parents, marked a shift in government philosophy to a more full blooded position. When the guidance was later produced, in Working Together 1991, it stated unequivocally that parents and children should have a seat at the conference table:

> This guide emphasizes the importance of professionals working in partnership with parents and other family members or carers and the concept of parental responsibility. These principles must underpin all child protection work. It cannot be emphasized too strongly that involvement of children and adults in child protection conferences will not be effective unless they are fully involved from the outset in all stages of the child protection process, and unless from the time of the referral there is as much openness and honesty as possible between families and professionals.
>
> (Home Office et al., 1991, para. 6.11)

Only certain criteria for exclusion were suggested, for example where there is risk of violence or where a potential participant is suffering from a mental illness. The guidelines are clear and detailed and have had considerable impact on local action even though they have no legal mandate. Allen (1991) suggested in his editorial in the contemporary Practitioners Child Law Bulletin that government had deliberately left the status of the conference and the rights of parents to attend on a non-statutory basis.  He observes that this does not seem to have been an oversight, but a deliberate effort to avoid statutory regulation.

> Detailed legislation, had it been put in place, would have meant an end to the degree of flexibility inherent in the present arrangements...and that flexibility is essential to allow agencies to deal with the infinite variety of situations that are brought to them (p.51).

I will discuss the significance of this point later, as I believe it is an important indicator of government thinking in relation to parents' rights. The lack of legal authority also marks the English system as being substantially different from other child protection systems in Europe, which Hetherington, Cooper, Smith and Wilford (1997) argue is disempowering for the social workers. Nevertheless, local authorities in England and Wales have treated these guidelines as if they were legally binding, and different models of family participation have evolved. Implementation was initially slow and patchy. Some areas encountered opposition to the policy from some of the workers involved. For example, in Rochdale, the police withdrew their support because they thought it improper to present a person's criminal record in public; in Newcastle the consultant paediatricians expressed grave doubts about the adverse affect on the assessment of risk, and the difficulties inherent in declaring information they regarded as confidential. Other professional groups, such as health visitors, feared that they would be denied access to the child if the parents heard what they really thought of them.  Teachers said it would interfere with their relationship with parents and so adversely affect the child's education (Wattam, 1989).

*Present situation*

Now many of these teething problems have been ironed out and it is generally agreed that levels of parental participation at conferences are an indicator of good practice (see Messages from the Research, 1995). Parents and, to a lesser extent, other family members are now routinely involved in the conference. In 1996, 75% of parents attended conferences (Messages from Inspections). Generally, parents are allowed to stay in the meeting for its duration but practice varies as to whether they are consulted about whether they wish their child to be registered. The inclusion of children continues to be rare and is thought to be appropriate only for some adolescents. Age plays a part but the literature reports general unease which goes beyond that and, as Stevenson (1995) points out, children themselves may not be keen to attend. Some authorities are using the more radical New Zealand model of family group conferences, where the families develop a protection plan with the help of the professionals, rather than the other way round. Working Together (1998) is suggesting that, while family group conferences serve a useful function in enabling families to participate in the decision making process, they should not take the place of the conference. Other areas are using 'core group' or 'strategy' meetings after the conference where parents and the key professionals agree on the detail of the child protection plan and how it will be resourced.

Thoburn et al. (1995) caution that the register is not a record of actual abuse as some children are registered because of concern about future abuse, whereas others who have been the victim of abuse may not have been registered because it was decided there was no need for a multi-agency child protection plan. Gibbons et al. (1995) have suggested that 160,000 children each year are subject to enquiries under Section 47 of The Children Act 1989. Most of the abuse is relatively mild, but within that group there are about 100 child homicides and 6,000 children who have to be looked after away from home. Only a quarter of these referrals result in a child protection conference.

For the year ending March 1st 1992 there were estimated to be 38,600 children and young people on child protection registers in England, representing 3.5 per thousand of the child population under the age of eighteen years. Between 1992 and 1993 the numbers of children registered fell, to 32,500, and have remained steady since. In 1997, 32,400 children were registered.

Regarding prevalence, according to Gibbons' research, there is significant regional variation in the rates of children on and added to registers, ranging from 2.1 (Thames Anglia) to 8.1 (Inner London). Categories of abuse also vary: for neglect, from zero to 38%; for physical abuse, from 7% to 64%; for sexual abuse, from 3% to 34%. Mixed categories are rarely used, so official records do not reflect the way concerns are clustered together. In cases of physical abuse a substantial minority of apparently serious and substantiated cases were not placed on the register, whereas few high risk sexual abuse cases were not registered. Although serious neglect cases were less likely to reach the conference, those that did were more serious. The numbers of children registered under the category of neglect and emotional concern is, in 1997, significantly higher whereas there has been a reduction in the categories, physical and sexual abuse (Health and Personal Social Service Statistics, 1997).

Are the registers used? In 1991, Gibbons et al. (1995) undertook a postal survey of one hundred and seven English registers. The conclusion was that 80% of the respondents in her sample considered the register to be an essential part of the system for improving the detection and prevention of child abuse. They found it was used for the purposes for which it was established. For example, the mean number of enquiries over six months in six authorities was two hundred and eighty one; it was used to support reviews in three-quarters of the authorities; and the number of enquiries to the central register was seen as reflecting high levels of inter-agency co-operation. Working Together, 1998, however, expresses concern that use of the registers is variable and inconsistent and is suggesting a more standard approach across agencies to its use.

## Conclusion

This chapter has described the political and moral climate in which The Children Act 1989 was written and has explored the philosophy of welfare consumerism and user involvement underpinning a range of social legislation. The legislation and practice imperatives are seen as reflecting international concerns about civil liberties which find expression in, for example, the United Nations Convention on the Rights of the Child (1989). The principles of partnership, parental responsibility and no order underpinning The Children Act 1989 are set within this context and seen as proactively promoting positive change. However, the principles are also seen more negatively, as a reaction to the public scandals and moral panics of the 1980s, when social workers were castigated for riding roughshod over parents' rights, on the one hand, and failing to protect the child on the other - too much too soon, or too little too late. I suggest that the ambiguities inherent in the system are a product of this history and are acted out on the playing field of the conference. This book aims to provide evidence for this view from a study undertaken in a Northern city between 1991 and 1993.

Involving parents in decisions that are made about their children by the health and welfare agencies was, thus, seen as simultaneously meeting the demands of natural justice while at the same time opening up the workings of the child protection system to public scrutiny. Professionals - particularly social workers - also believed that involving parents and family members in the child protection plan would result in more effective practice based on partnership principles. In discussing the literature on partnership, I observed that social workers are committed to the principle but find it difficult to operate in practice. The research studies presented suggest that parents often have a different view, both of what partnership consists in and of what would best meet their needs. There does, however, seem to be general agreement that best practice results where there is congruence between the views of professionals and clients on what the problem is and how to tackle it.

Finally, an exploration of the background to Working Together 1991 suggests that a number of the opportunities and dilemmas of working in partnership with parents who may have abused their children became, at that time, entombed in the system. Working Together 1991 lays out the guidance for enacting the principles of The Children Act 1989. It provided policy makers and Area Child Protection Committees with the framework to be used in setting up procedures for involving parents and families in the child protection investigation. Most importantly, family members should be involved in the initial child protection conference. The conference holds a central place within the system for detecting and reporting child abuse and establishing an inter-agency plan for the protection of the child. Local procedures and practices for involving parents and family members in the conference were developed cautiously at first. While many practitioners were genuinely committed to the principles of working in partnership and parental participation, in practice there were concerns and there were some difficulties.

Today some of those difficulties have evaporated or been addressed, while others have not. Different ways of meeting with parents are being tried out (Atherton and Ryburn, 1996) although it is not within the scope of this book to explore these in detail. Gibbon et al. (1995) suggested that the registers are being used effectively for the purposes for which they were devised and that children are being protected by the system, although the government now believes the operation of the registers should be improved. At the same time, all the research studies cited have found that too many children are being drawn into the child protection system. While their need for protection is generally met, their welfare needs are not. Further, the experiences of the families of their involvement in the process are not happy ones and so, it is argued, other means should be found for managing child abuse investigations.

Having presented the context in which my research was carried out, in the next chapter I will explore the main underlying themes in more detail. The methodology and design of the research study will then be explained, prior to the presentation of the findings.

# 2 The Issues: relativity, ambiguity and power

The previous chapter outlined the reasons why the initial child protection conference developed a pivotal role in the child protection system and the context within which this took place. This chapter discusses the issues raised with regard to the nature of moral judgments, conflicts of rights and the related issue of power and justice. It is suggested that the complexity and nature of these issues create contradictory demands and ambiguous tasks for practitioners.

## Relativism: cognitive and moral

Working Together 1991 defines the purpose of the conference as being:

> a forum for sharing information and concerns, analysing risk and recommending responsibility for action,...not for a formal decision that a person has abused the child 6.1.

In the guidance a distinction is drawn between information and concerns. The implication is that information is about the representation of fact, whereas concerns are about their interpretation as being abusive *and that the two are different.* (My italics.) The issues raised here relate to concepts of relativity - how 'facts' are defined, and about the validity of what philosophers call "first-order moral judgment" (see Blackstone, 1968). The

21

recent postmodernist debate (see Thorpe, 1995, Parton, 1994, Wattam, 1992) has focused attention on the moral nature of the discourse in child protection work. These writers have suggested that definitions of abuse are relative and derive more from the professionals' moral judgments than from an objective or absolute standard. Turning to the child protection investigation, clearly the perspectives of all the participants on the way parenting behaviours are presented will critically determine the decisions and recommendations made, and the willingness of the families to cooperate.

While to do justice to the debate on absolute and relative concepts of child abuse is not within the scope of this book, the arguments essential to the debate were most helpfully drawn together by Messages from the Research (1995). The overview begins:

> Any discussion of child abuse and child protection services will benefit from agreement about definition. Unfortunately, there is no absolute definition of abuse. If, from a list of behaviours, ticks could be put against those which are abusive and crosses against those which are not, the task of practitioners and researchers would be made easier. In this list, hitting children might be ticked, indicating that such behaviour is abusive. But some might argue that in certain contexts it is good for children to be hit and, as at least 90% of children have this experience at some time, the behaviour could be said to be 'normal'. The tick might be replaced by a cross or, at best, by a question mark.
>
> (Messages from the Research, p.11)

While most of us would agree that neglect, sickness and death among children are undesirable, as the above quotation illustrates, we would also all agree that child abuse is not an absolute concept. Hitting children provides a good example of how parenting styles and societies perspectives on what is good and bad change and what is considered normal and abnormal change over time and between class and culture. Newsom (1989) found that 95% of the parents in their survey hit their children in 1960 and 80% thought that was all right; in the 1990s, when they repeated the survey, 81% hit and half thought they should not. Another example is provided by Smith and Grocke (1995) who looked at patterns of sexual behaviour within English homes. Their findings expose a gap between what is actually occurring - behaviours such as touching mothers' breasts and drawing genitalia which occur frequently but in moderation - and popular images of family life where they do not occur at all. Further, while some behaviours, such as watching a sexually explicit video might be undesirable, the effects are not necessarily harmful. In searching for a definition of abuse Smith found that charting patterns of punishment in families did not help either.  While some factors previously found to be associated with physical maltreatment, such as the mother's age, were mild predictors of frequent or severe punishment, other factors - specifically those arising from daily stressors - such as sibling fighting were stronger. Conversely, as Waterhouse (1993) discovered, some situations that are not perceived as abusive, such as marital breakdown, can have dire effects.

The latter point also highlights the influence of culpability and intent in defining abuse.  In situations of physical abuse the parents' culpability may be fairly clear cut.  By contrast, in situations of marital breakdown or domestic violence, the children may suffer serious emotional abuse which remains undefined because it is hidden and because it is not intended  (see Fantuzzo, 1989, Bell, 1997). Dingwall (1981) found that, in identifying and confirming child abuse, two types of evidence were used initially; the child's clinical condition and the nature of his social environment.  The third and concluding factor was whether the parents' behaviour was intentional. 'Evidence' in all of these three types is rarely clear cut and generally open to interpretation.

Turning in greater detail to the factors that contribute to differing perceptions of what constitutes abusive behaviour or good enough parenting I will consider class, race and gender.

## Class

Standards and patterns of child care practice vary across class dimensions as well as by race and culture. Children from working class households, for example, are more likely to experience health problems (Blackburn, 1991) or to be involved in road traffic accidents (Wynne, 1992). Their parents may well have experienced, learned, or assimilated as children models of parenting based on values and social structures very different from those enjoyed by the middle classes where employment, educational and health advantage and social mobility provided very different experiences of family life and parenting behaviours. Their perception of what constitutes good parenting and abusive behaviour is therefore very likely to be influenced by factors associated with class. Further, since working class families are more likely to be living in poverty, in substandard housing accommodation and to have a less healthy diet, stressors which are known to contribute to the conditions in which abuse is more likely to take place, they are also likely to contribute to an overall assessment of a situation as potentially abusive (Blackburn, 1991, Korbin, 1991).

**Culture and race**

There is some evidence that parents from different cultures also have different views on what constitutes abuse (Korbin, 1981, Newson and Newson, 1976). Again, differing racial and cultural family patterns may incline white professionals to perceive as abusive a situation which is accepted within the culture as the norm. British social work is essentially Eurocentric and white middle class norms or stereotypes may be used to judge the parenting behaviours of other cultures negatively (Ahmed, 1986). The perception that black families are more likely to be judged negatively is supported by studies that show the over representation of black children in public care (Barn,1990), although the situation is more complicated than Barn implies. For example, other studies have shown that Asian children are under represented in the care system (see Rowe et al, 1989). Other writers have suggested that practitioners, because of their non-judgmental value base, may put children at risk by taking an overly optimistic and essentially amoral stance to behaviour which they perceive as being 'normal' within another culture. As Dingwall (1983) has pointed out, this can have equally damaging consequences.

Further conflicts in judgments about behaviour arise where the values of the parent and the child have begun to diverge. Examples are where they hold different belief systems about acceptable sexual and marital partners, female circumcision or family rites of passage. From the professionals' point of view, as well as the child's, some firmly established cultural practices may seem oppressive and potentially abusive, whereas from the parents' point of view they are essential to the culture. Shared perceptions are particularly difficult to establish across the culture gaps of class, language and race, and misunderstandings and distorted communications are likely to permeate the ways in which the situations are defined by the different parties.

Dutt and Phillips (1996) point out that even where social work practice is culturally sensitive it can not address the impact of racism on the attitudes and responses from black families. Their response to a child protection investigation will be based on experiences they have had of hostility and marginalisation (Butt, 1994) and this will also colour their response to the investigating social worker's assessment. Culture and race therefore both play a part in the subjective interpretation of events as abusive.

# Gender

> It is indeed a burning shame that there should be one law for men and another law for women.
>
> (Wilde, 1895, The Ideal Husband)

Gender issues may also contribute in subtle and not so subtle ways to the definition of some situations as abusive. The gender stereotype of males as abusers and females as protectors of children is as pervasive in social work theory and practice as it is in society, resulting in unreasonable expectations being placed upon women. Farmer and Owen (1995) found in their study of investigations of child abuse that the focus on mothers pervaded all aspects of the child protection system. This seemed even more surprising in consideration of the fact that it is men who have been responsible for the majority of well publicised deaths. Where there is not, as is often the case, the resource provision to support mothers who are single or who are living with violent and abusive men, incidents happening in these families are more likely to be defined as abusive by the professionals. Race is an added factor, especially in Asian families, where many women do not speak English and where the daughter's role may be narrowly defined by her parents; or for women from the middle east, whose role may be subservient to their husbands.

# Childhood experiences

Finally, one of the most powerful influences on an individual's under-standing of what is acceptable behaviour in a family stems from their own experience of parenting. Much of the literature relating to work done with parents who were abused as children describes the work as enabling the victims to grasp, firstly, that their abusive family behaviour was not normal, secondly that it was wrong, and thirdly that it was not their fault. The long term effects on families of child abuse is well documented in the literature (Lieberman, 1979; Egeland, 1991).

To summarise this discussion, it seems it is the context that determines whether the behaviour is seen as abusive, or not ... where it takes place, who else is present, and the age of the child rather than simply the behaviour itself. The context may also determine the outcome. As Messages from the Research concludes, in a warm, supportive environment hits and short periods of neglect are unlikely to have harmful long term effects. It is in families "low on warmth and high on criticism" that negative incidents accumulate. The threshold for determining abuse therefore involves deciding the point at which, firstly, behaviour and/or parenting style is maltreatment, and, secondly, whether it is necessary for the state to intervene.

These judgments are not strictly determined by the facts. The post-modernist debate referred to earlier has, at its most radical, sometimes seemed to suggest that, in the manner of Dostoevsky where all things are possible, no act is abusive and no truth valid. However, as the philosophers Krautz and Meikland (1987) have pointed out, relativism is different from scepticism:

> Relativism, like scepticism, gives up the pursuit of a single truth which is the same for everyone - which is objective, absolute and knowable. But relativism, unlike scepticism, does not conclude that there is no such thing as truth or that truth is not knowable. Instead the relativist maintains that truth may be and often is different for each society or each methodological approach or even each individual (p.2).

Even if it is true that moral judgments are nothing but expressions of attitude, it does not follow that it is mistaken or fallacious to express the attitudes we have, or that there can be no agreement on the morality of the attitudes expressed. What is important to our understanding is that, as Cleaver and Freeman (1995) have suggested, these attitudes form an essential part of the perspectives that operate in the conference. An understanding of their etiology and influence will therefore facilitate our understanding of the complex dynamics that operate around the conference table.


## Rights

As described in the previous chapter, the involvement of parents in the conference resulted from a range of factors, one of which was the strongly held ideology that parents had a right to participate in the conference. It was observed, however, that in spite of the moral fervour for the right of parents to be involved, they have no right in law to attend. The guidance in Working Together 1991 made clear the intention that parents should be included, but was deliberately vague in defining participation. This has meant that Area Child Protection Committees have devised models of family participation which generally allow for parents to contribute information and respond to information that is presented, but vary widely in the degree to which parents have a say at the crucial decision making stage. In other words, there is an effective distinction in practice between a right to be present - which is generally upheld, and a right to influence decisions - the operation of which is left to local procedures. This raises questions not only about rights, but also about justice.

It seems clear that the confusion about parents' rights in this matter arises because people are talking about different rights. Becker (1982) argues that there is a difference between the specialised and unspecialised use of the term 'right'. In the unspecialised use, "I have a right to do it" may mean no more than "I am justified in doing it". In some respects this is the tone of the ideological arguments presented. In the specialised use of right, however, "I have a right to do it" carries with it a moral claim which entails a correspondent duty. Rights are generally regarded as belonging to individuals and if respect for persons is regarded as a moral principle, then it follows that individuals have certain rights which society has a duty to respect.

The most widely used distinction of different sorts of rights was made by Hohfield (1923), an American legal theorist, at the beginning of this century. He distinguished four sorts of rights, as follows:

*Claim rights* A claim right is a right which has a correlated duty. For example, if I have a right to be paid for my work my employer has a duty to pay me. Other philosophers later drew a further distinction between positive claim rights - rights against a person and negative claim rights - rights against the world at large. Positive rights are claims against someone else to do something, such as medical treatment. Negative claim rights relate to the freedom to do something without interference. Free speech would be an example.

*Liberties* Liberty rights are privileges in the sense that they do not have correlated duties. An example is that, in this country, women can have an abortion but no person has a duty to perform one.

*Powers* A power is a right conferred by law, carrying with it a corresponding liability. For example, in my will I can appoint an executor and give him the power to act in a particular way.

*Immunities* Immunities are barriers against powers, such as the right of silence.

Schematically, Hohfield's distinctions look like this:

| CLAIM RIGHTS | LIBERTIES | POWERS | IMMUNITIES |
|---|---|---|---|
| correlate with | correlate with | correlate with | correlate with |
| DUTIES | NO RIGHTS | LIABILITIES | DISABILITIES |

Turning to the parents' rights to attend the child protection conference, it seems that from a legal point of view parents do not have claim rights, powers or immunities. There have been cases where parents have tried to claim their right to attend. In 1988 Mr. Justice Lincoln did not agree with a mother's application that 'the case conference was vitiated by her absence and that there was a breach of natural justice in that she was not given the opportunity to persuade the participants of her innocence' (*Regina v Harrow L.B.C., 1988*). It was his view that Working Together 1988 and the Cleveland Report only expected that parents be kept informed. While this judgment is far more restrictive than current thinking or practice would advocate, the legal situation has not changed.

We are therefore left with the right to liberties. Essentially the debate here is about the extent to which the parents' rights vis à vis the conference are based on the moral claim of their absolute rights as citizens, rather than a legal right. Macdonald (1984) argues that doctrines of natural law have a long and impressive history from the Stoics and Roman jurists to the Atlantic Charter and Roosevelts Four Freedoms. However, the argument that people are entitled to make certain claims by virtue simply of their common humanity has been punctured by a number of other philosophers, such as Hume, Marx and, in particular Bentham. So, it seems, the right invested in civil liberties arguments is one that, however closely it touches our hearts and moral souls, is not generally agreed by philosophers and is difficult to uphold in law. The European Court did uphold the right of a parent to attend, but the injunction on British Law is moral, not legal.

A way forward has been suggested by Dingwall, Murray and Eekelar, (1983). They moved the debate away from parent's absolute rights as citizens by introducing the concept of 'duty rights' as parents. These authors assert that:

Parental rights must be exercised for the child's benefit. They are duty - rights which parents are not free to abandon, extinguish or waive as long as the child is in their care. If we accept such rights for children, we must accept corresponding restrictions on parents rights and on family autonomy. Most mistreated children are physically unable to initiate their own remedies. Other must be licensed to do it for them.

This scenario returns us to the field of relativity. If parents' rights are instrumental to the benefit of the children, they are not absolute and they are contingent. The suggestion is that they can be waived when parents do not exercise parental responsibility in a way which accords with the best interests of the child. However, as we have seen, judgements about the child's best interests are themselves relative. The logical conclusion of this position is that parents who (for whatever reason) are mistaken about what is in their child's best interests would be derelict in their duty and hence forfeit the right to attend the conference. This position seems untenable. It does not resolve the rights issue but pushes further consideration of it firmly into the domain of justice.

## Justice

> 'I'll be judge, I'll be jury,' said cunning old fury: 'I'll try the whole cause, and condemn you to death.'
>
> (Carroll, 1865, Alice's Adventures in Wonderland)

As with human rights and civil liberties, the principles of natural justice are also reflected in the arguments for family participation in conferences. The principles of natural justice in this arena were laid down as early as 1982, in the Barclay Report.

> Many agencies have legal and quasi-legal functions and important decisions about peoples lives are often made within the agency and outside the framework of the courts. It seems reasonable where such decisions are being taken that the rules of natural justice should apply in the agency as they would in the court room. That is, the person so affected should have the right to know the grounds upon which the decision has been taken and to present his own case personally or through a representative to question any disputed facts or to appeal against the decision.
>
> (Barclay, 1982)

Morrison et al. (1990) observe that four elements are contained in the natural justice argument; information, representation, fact disputation and appeal or complaint. Presumably, if these four elements can be identified in the conference process it could then be said that the process was just. I will examine each in turn.

As stated previously, information sharing is a primary task in the conference. The research studies have all found that there is agreement that families should hear and contribute to the information base; this is just and it achieves better outcomes. Representation is more tricky. Again, there is general agreement that the views of all the family members should be represented. At the same time, there are a number of difficulties in operationalising representation in the conference and these will be demonstrated by the research findings. Suffice to say, at this stage, that the difficulties are such that the quality of representation that actually takes place would not accord with the principle of natural justice. Fact disputation, again, presents problems for similar reasons. Technically, parents can dispute the facts that are presented if they are there. However, as will be seen, the power imbalance is such that they are disadvantaged to the degree that they could not claim to have been justly treated in this respect.

A further complication here has been suggested by the research studies which observe that, when parents are present, there is rarely disputation of the facts by any of the participants in the conference. For various reasons that will become apparent conflict is avoided and consensus prevails. Finally, in accordance with natural justice, parents have a right to complain. This is a claim right, but it is a negative right since it depends upon the authority providing the parents with the information and the support to make the complaint. Again, we shall see from the empirical data that the potential for injustice is ripe.

Returning to Mr Justice Lincoln's judgment in the case of *R. v Harrow L.B.*, he expressed doubt if the term natural justice was appropriate to the process of a conference, preferring to ask if the conduct of the conference was unfair or unreasonable. Clearly, issues relating to justice as fairness and the relationship between empowerment and whether people feel they have been fairly treated are raised by including families in the conference. Philosophers with such widely disparate views as Aristotle, Kant and Hume agree that the formal concept of justice rests on the idea of equality. Equality, treating like cases alike or giving each her due relative to rights or needs, is the cornerstone of distributive justice. However, philosophers ask, even if everyone is treated the same what is it justice is trying to achieve or equalise? Attempting to adjudicate on what it is best to achieve has taxed philosophers for centuries. Further, if justice depends upon producing the best consequences, best for whom?

One of the most influential political philosophers, Rawls (1971), argues that justice is about the way institutions address due process rather than about the distribution of deserts. The example he gives is from aristocratic and caste societies which are unjust because the basic structures of these societies incorporate "the arbitrariness found in nature" rather than because nature is arbitrary. Applying these principles to the way the conference is managed, it becomes clear that justice, for the parents, is more likely to be determined by their experience of the process, rather than outcome. Justice, in this sense, is not an end in itself but relates rather to the means of administering justice. As Lord Devlin said,

> If it can be shown in any particular class or case that observance of a principle of this sort does not serve the interests of justice, it must be dismissed, otherwise it could become the master instead of the servant of justice.

The issues to be explored here in relation to justice as fairness, then, relate to how the conference process is managed rather than simply to the outcome of, for instance, whether it is just that the child is registered or not. A focus for the data analysis will therefore be upon whether or not the users felt fairly treated, and upon aspects of the conference task and management which could be said to facilitate fairness. For example, were the parents encouraged to present their view; what methods existed for representing the views of other family members; or were the rights of parents and children to be kept informed supported? Since fact disputation and representation seem essential components of procedural justice, did they exist?

## Ambiguity

### i) For the conference
The preceding discussion has suggested that the rules of natural justice do not apply automatically to the conference because it is not acting judicially or functioning as a tribunal. The tone of Working Together 1991 and the way conferences are perceived and managed certainly reinforce the view that the conference is an inter-agency meeting "for sharing information and recommending responsibility for action ... not for a formal decision that a person has abused the child" (6.1). However, the guidance continues by saying "before a child is registered the conference must decide that there is, or is the likelihood of, significant harm ... there must be one or more identifiable incidents which can be described as having adversely affected the child ... Significant harm is expected on the basis of professional judgment" (6.39).

The research to be presented here, and the studies already cited, have suggested that information presented in the conference is treated as evidence, and it is then used to construe the parents' responsibility or culpability for the alleged abuse (see Farmer and Owen, 1995). There does seem to be a massive ambiguity in the conference task - on the one hand to share information and not to make a judgment - on the other, to identify harmful incidents and to decide that significant harm has happened, or is likely to. Only when that judgment has been made can the conference decide whether to register the child as being at risk of significant harm. This leaves open the possibility that the conference is effectively fulfilling a judicial function. Matters of fairness and rights to parents, then, have to be seen in the context of the ambiguous nature of the task. The question posed here, 'are parents fairly treated', can more easily be addressed with reference to the process - the way families are treated, rather than to outcome - whether a just decision has been made.

Turning away from discussions about justice and fairness, another ambiguity in the nature of the conference task is identified. This concerns the primary purpose of the conference. Everyone agrees that the primary purpose is to protect the child. The way this is done is by collecting information about the incident and about the family background, by analysing risk, by registering the child and by recommending protective action. However, the research studies suggest that the sharp focus on the assessment of risk has the consequence that the families needs are not addressed. Messages from the Research (1995) has illustrated powerfully the massive welfare needs of families drawn into the child protection system. Yet there is no reference in Working Together 1991 to how needs will be addressed in the child protection conference or any acknowledgement that the division between risk and need is in many respects artificial. Further, the time given to discussing the child protection plan is minimal - it has to be, because it can take between one and three hours to present the information. The ambiguity the child protection system is facing here is whether the structures in place for running the conference meet the families needs in such a way that they will be better helped to exercise parental responsibility, or not.

*ii) For the social worker*
Turning to the social workers involved I will argue that the ambiguity of the conference task is reflected in the ambiguities inherent in the social work role. I will, further, suggest that the parent's presence in the conference can serve to highlight these ambiguities and that the chairperson deals with these by avoiding conflict and promoting consensus. Again, there are various dimensions to this. One ambiguity for the social worker is the inherent conflict of role between being an investigator for the conference on the one hand, and being a therapeutic partner for the parent or child on the other. All of the research studies have found that families experience shock and bewilderment when the allegation of abuse is made

public (see also Dingwall, 1982). The social workers' attention, however, is not on helping the family with the emotional impact of the crisis that has hit them, but is on gathering information to present to the conference. Moreover, in pursuit of this, they closely follow the guidance relating to procedural regularity and inter agency collaboration. As pointed out in the last chapter, while bureaucratic procedures are important they do not, in themselves, protect the child or facilitate direct work with the family (Geach, 1983). At the end of the day it is the family who protects the child, not the social worker.

Another ambiguity inherent in the social work task concerns the conflict between their role as an employee of the authority - meeting the demands of the state, and their role as advocate or mediator for the parents or child. The conflict here is more intense than that faced within the traditional care/control dilemma (see Satyamurti, 1979; Day, 1981), because of the additional duty of advocacy placed on the social worker in the conference. In various respects these roles may conflict. For example, the social worker may have a different perspective on the alleged abuse than the parent or, as sometimes happens, the social worker holds a different view to the authority. Equally, parents may disagree with each other or with the child both about what has happened and about what to do to put it right. There are no rules for the social worker to follow in these conflictual situations. As Allsopp (1994) has observed, "the chronic dilemmas endemic to social work practice seem to be encapsulated in the concept of partnership rather than solved or made easier by it".

Finally, there is a long-standing and basic ambiguity concerning the nature of the social work task, and what it is possible to achieve which is highlighted by the role of the social workers in the conference. Although social workers know that there is a relationship between poverty and discrimination and child abuse, they have neither the means nor skills to meet the social needs of a number of their clients. This research will suggest that these ambiguities make for quite specific difficulties in cases that are, themselves full of ambiguity and uncertainty.

## Power

> 'When I use a word,' Humpty Dumpty said in rather a scornful tone, 'it means just what I chose it to mean - neither more nor less.'
>
> (Carroll, 1871, Through The Looking Glass)

Bullock et al. (1995) have suggested that the participation of parents in conferences is "the best place to monitor the balance of power between the key players". As previously suggested the conference is a critical meeting where the balance of power between professionals as well as between families and professionals operates and can be examined.

The danger of the conference taking the shape of a pyramid with a pecking order of different professional groups and parents at the bottom was raised in 1992 by Moore. Within a process that aims to prevent the abuse of power it is important not to mirror the abuse of power within the system. On the other hand it is equally important to use the powers the conference and the professionals do have to attempt to redistribute the power dynamics in the family system that have led to the abuse. Frequently this will mean empowering the mother and the child and disempowering the abuser. A number of the difficulties here have already been suggested.

The centrality of power in professional work in general has been recognised for some time by a number of writers (Etzioni, 1962; Wilding, 1982; Cousins, 1987). More recently, Hugman (1991) has analysed the interconnection of power and caring in health and welfare provision, while writers such as Stevenson and Hallett (1992) and Murphy (1995), have analysed the dimensions of power in inter-agency work in child protection. The literature suggests that power is exercised in several ways. By members of a profession in relation to each other; by different professional groups; by those who control resources; by those who use the services; or by wider institutions, including the state.

Power issues between different professional groups in child protection were discussed in 1980 by Hallett and Stevenson. They pointed out the ways in which different organisational structures and differing professional training and traditions created and maintained differing professional perspectives which contributed to issues of inter-professional power. In relation to the conference Hallett's more recent research (1995) has shown that difficulties arise when there is 'an outer circle' of conference attenders who encounter abuse less often, but who are expected to participate fully. This creates confusion because while these attenders, such as teachers, feel they lack the knowledge and experience necessary, their contribution is perceived by others as very important.

The discomfort and confusion caused by power issues in the conference is, further, reflected in the role of the chairperson. Lewis (1994) has suggested that the power invested in the chair has three dimensions. Power is focused in their personal authority, in their role as the social services spokesman, and is effected by the style with which they manage conflict and anxiety in the conference. Some of the research studies suggest that by appointing their senior managers as chairmen, social services is stood at the top of the pyramid. The effect of this is to make the other professionals feel less powerful. Hallett (1995) has argued that this has had the effect of contributing to the high degree of inter agency consensus in relation to conference decisions. She suggests 'the outer circle', or the less experienced defer to the experts because they are anxious about 'getting it wrong', and because "working within any system or organisation limits fundamental questioning of its dominant paradigm" (p.281). In other words, the system is disempowering for some while supporting the position of those who hold and distribute power.

An alternative approach to issues of power in the conference is provided by the philosopher, Habermas (1977). Habermas also perceives power as being invested predominantly in social relationships. However, in his analysis power is exercised through the manipulation and/or distortion of communication. He sees communication as being directed towards the achievement of ends and not towards reaching agreement. For example, where a parent is asked to agree to family therapy the request is directed to accomplishing professional goals, not to reaching an agreement with the parent. This would certainly fit with the understanding of process and power in the conference that has so far been suggested. By this view, power is exercised in the structuring of the social framework within which ideas, interests and issues are formed and known. The power of the professionals is, then, based in the control of language and the discourse.

Applied to the conference, this analysis would suggest that, because the content of the meeting is controlled by the professionals, the professionals are in control of what issues get pursued. Fairclough (1989) shows that this can be done by body language, clothes and the use of particular words, as well as by 'scripting' the dimensions of the communication. The uncooperative parent, then, is defined by the professional as being the one who does not follow the professional rules of the discourse. Discourse is about the interplay between language and social relationships, in which some groups are able to achieve dominance for their interests in the way in which the world is defined and acted upon. This analysis also sits comfortably with the earlier discussion on the relativity of definitions of child abuse. This discussion, it will be recalled, addressed issues of class, race and gender in the construction of definitions of abuse. Such issues are also fundamental to considerations of power. In the conference the dominant groups are likely to be white and middle class and the chairpersons are more likely to be male. In Lewis' study, there were ten men and four women, thirteen of whom were white Europeans.

To summarise, power is not an isolated element of social life, but one which interweaves occupational and organisational structures with the actions of professionals. The professionals enter the conference with differing personal and professional values and backgrounds, and with varying degrees of power - situational power, and dispositional power. Many of the social negotiations that go in the conference highlight differences in power. The clothes, the rooms, the language used are all vehicles for these messages to be communicated. The research studies have generally suggested that the balance of power is heavily weighted against parents in the early stages of the investigation, including in the conference. They have no control over the agenda and are dependent on the chairperson to manage the process. However, taking into account parental perspectives to some degree involves surrendering a degree of control to the powerless, although professionals cannot surrender this if the child is put at risk. So the parents who are empowered are those whose views are congruent with those who hold the power. The degree to which this happens, and how, is a theme to be explored throughout this book.

## Conclusion

In this chapter I have identified the themes which will form the basis of the analysis of this policy initiative. A number of the themes arise from moral issues which are central to  the way judgments are made and are focal to concerns about rights and justice. Different approaches to justice and the relationship between power and justice were also discussed as a means of understanding both what the conference is trying to do and how it sets about its task. Finally, an attempt is made to explore and identify the conflicts the conference faces in addressing the dual tasks of classifying risk and addressing need and the ambiguities this raises for social workers with regard to conflicting roles and meeting different interests.

The next chapter will describe how the research was designed to allow these themes to be explored.  Much of the debate on this initiative had been polemical,  based on a simplistic view of rights, claims and liberties. The design was intended to enable an evaluation of the benefits of the initiative from the perspectives of all the participants and a more focused and detailed understanding of the difficulties within the framework discussed above. The main points at issue concern process and outcome. Regarding process, how were the issues perceived by the participants, and how did this appear to influence their behaviour? Regarding outcome: did the process contribute to the assessment of risk, for example through the provision of information, or by allowing the views of the parents to prevail? Did involving parents make them feel they had been more fairly dealt with? Thirdly, were outcomes affected in the sense that parents were more likely to collaborate with the future plans?

# 3 Research methods and design

**Background to the study**

This research was conceived and carried out in 1991-1993, at a time when there was great interest nationally in how family involvement in child protection would work in practice. Local authorities were experimenting with different procedures and the organisational framework of child protection conferences, and were anxious to share their experiences. Bradford, for example, initially operated a policy which excluded all cases of sexual abuse (Fisher, 1990). North Tyneside required all written reports to be formally submitted and discussed with parents forty eight hours in advance of the conference (Taylor and Godfrey, 1991). More commonly, in many areas parents were asked to leave the meeting toward the end when decisions were taken about registration.

From the research perspective, the initial child protection conference provided researchers with an arena in which a number of the critical issues could be explored. The research undertaken on the involvement of parents and family members in the conference falls into two blocks; that published before Working Together 1991, and that completed after. These studies are relevant in that they provide comparative data and were influential in identifying the main issues to be pursued.

**An overview of the other research**

*1   Research published before 1991*

The first published research of parental attendance at conferences was undertaken by Housiaux, in Coventry (1984). Debates in the ensuing years were carried on in the literature, the most notable of which were the proceedings of the conference of the British Association for the Study of the Prevention of Child Abuse and Neglect (BASPCAN), written up by Brown and Waters and published in 1986. In the same year McGloin and Turnbull (1986) published the results of their study in Greenwich, analysing seventeen review conferences to which parents had been invited. They found that professionals felt inhibited and were concerned about the effect on parents, about confidentiality, and that the conference could become a pseudo court of law. Phillips and Evans (1986) furthered the debate. Corby's (1987) study of fifty five conferences was the most wide ranging. He looked at the decision making processes and social work practice, as well as the views of some parents. He found evidence to suggest that conferences were not achieving the tasks they were intended to achieve, and described a scene of some confusion and conflict, particularly over the issue of parents' rights and the protection of the child.

Other related research provided similar results. McDonnel and Aldgate (1984) studied review meetings in seventy five social service departments, and emphasised the lack of opportunities for social workers assertions to be challenged and alternative views put forward. Other work (Sinclair and Webb, 1983) recommended that client participation in important meetings be increased in order to act as a check on the quality of the decisions taken. Evidence was provided by Vernon and Fruin (1986) that where adolescents in care or their parents had attended review meetings expecting active participation, professionals regarded them as being there to provide information rather than to participate in the decision making process. While there was excitement about the way that policy and practice was developing, in 1990 Morrison and his colleagues produced a monograph for the NSPCC which urged caution.

Also in 1990 Thoburn and Shemmings (1990) evaluated a pilot project in Hackney, identifying an "extremely favourable" response by the parents and the professionals to attendance. A number of other small scale studies, many of them in-house, were producing similar findings, concluding positively for the involvement of families in conferences, despite the difficulties (see Burns, 1991; Smith, 1990; Merchant and Luckham, 1991;

Taylor and Godfrey, 1991; Lonsdale, 1991). Atherton (1984), for the Family Rights Group, surveyed a number of social services departments, but found it difficult to be clear what was happening because different areas meant different things by participation in conferences. She suggested that parents were uniformly positive about being invited to conferences and negative about being asked to withdraw.

To summarise, these studies evaluated the growing practice of inviting parents to decision making meetings. The main findings were that family members generally find the experience difficult, but nevertheless want to be present. Partial attendance was not welcomed by the parents, but professional opinion was divided on this. The majority of the professionals believed that parents have a right to be present, and that the intervention is more likely to be effective if they have been involved in the proceedings. The role of the chair in managing the conference and preparing the parents for it was seen as being crucial to a favourable outcome.

## 2 Research published after 1991

Following the publication of The Children Act 1989 and Working Together 1991, the Department of Health funded a number of major studies of the child protection investigation, including the initial conference. These studies take a wide perspective although they all analyse in detail what happens in the conference as it is seen as being seminal to the investigation process.

*Thoburn, Lewis and Shemmings (1995)* looked at a total cohort of two hundred and twenty children from seven local authorities who might be in need of protection. They identified some cases where full partnership was possible, some where a lesser model of participation was more practicable and a small number where the objective of partnership was unattainable. The likelihood of involvement bore a direct relation to the sort and severity of problems that existed in the family. Where a high degree of participation was achieved the contributory factors were the attitudes, skills and efforts of the social workers. They were more likely to succeed in working in partnership where they had agency backing. A number of recommendations are made for the chairing and management of the investigation and the conference on the basis of factors critical to the parents' experience.

*Gibbons, Conroy and Bell's (1995)* study was designed to identify variations in the numbers of children on registers in similar authorities and to determine the extent to which these resulted from discrepancies in professional practice. They found wide variations between areas in the amount and type of services provided and in deregistration rates. In every case, those registered received more services. Gibbons and colleagues observed that many families struggling with child rearing in difficult socio-economic circumstances were prematurely defined as potential child protection cases, rather than as families with children in need. Inter-agency collaboration during the investigation was generally good, but dropped off after the conference when it was needed just as much.

*Hallett and Birchall (1995):* This study is of a large empirical investigation into inter-agency collaboration. Profession was identified as the factor most affecting individual perception of cases. Inter-agency co-ordination was found to exist in the early phase of the investigation, comprising mainly information exchange, but fell away after the conference.

*Cleaver and Freeman's (1995)* study surveyed five hundred and eighty three child protection cases in one authority, and thirty families over two years in two authorities.   Many allegations were not substantiated and fewer than one third of the children conferenced were registered. Parents felt invaded and humiliated and a mood of recrimination sometimes beset the home. Social workers were swept along and lost sight of the emotional impact on the family in their desire to follow procedures. Ultimately, these researchers felt there was a fine balance to be drawn between the benefits and drawbacks of intervention.

*Farmer and Owen (1995):* One hundred and twenty conferences in two authorities were observed, and interviews held with parents, children and social workers. Distinctive patterns in the process of the risk assessment were identified.   Methods of assessment did not provide a basis for long term care planning, parents felt unhappy about the treatment they had received and social workers faced an uphill battle in engaging their co-operation afterwards.   Where the child protection plan was thought to be adequate, the child was more likely to be safe. Twenty months after the registration, 70% of the children were considered to be protected, and in 68% of cases the child's welfare needs were adequately addressed. In only one third of the cases were the needs of the primary carer met. The researchers concluded that the priority given to child protection often obscured the children's broader therapeutic and developmental needs and the severity of their parents' disadvantage.

In summary, these studies draw similar conclusions about the direction interventions in child protection have taken and that attitudes and experiences acquired early in the process have long standing effects. The early investigation is stressful for all the participants, reaching a zenith in the conference. The professionals are obliged to work in partnership with each other as well as with the families. It seems the demands of one partnership system may obscure the other. The needs of many of these families for welfare services are not met initially, or in the longer term because of the exhaustive concentration on risk assessment. Perspectives fashion how behaviour is defined, and these are influenced by profession as well as by psychological and sociological factors. The conference is seen as having a central place in the system, but positive opportunities for intervention are missed because of the preoccupation with procedures. Children are generally protected by the system, but too many are unnecessarily drawn into the net.

## The research project

### *The design*

This study was undertaken in response to a request by the Area Child Protection Committee in a large, industrial northern city to evaluate their pilot project. The project was to include parents in conferences in four teams in the city for a six month trial period before the policy was implemented city wide. The design involved a comparison of all conferences held in six area teams between May 1991 and June 1992. The experiences of parents and other family members in the four pilot teams were to be compared with the experiences of parents from two teams who were not, then, invited to the conference. Additionally, the design included a comparison of the attitudes of the professionals attending all the conferences held in the research teams in the six months before, and the six months after the implementation of the policy. The research is unique in having a control group and in gathering information on professionals' attitudes at two points in time. In including a comparative component an analysis of the effects of parental involvement in the conference per se is possible. The design thus builds upon and adds to other contemporary studies of parental involvement.

*The teams*

The four pilot teams were similar in that they all served inner city areas. One included a high proportion of Asian and African-Caribbean families, thus providing the opportunity to include an assessment of issues raised in the conference that may be attributable to race and culture. The two control teams were selected to resemble the pilot teams in as many respects as possible. Both were inner city areas and similar in respect of their demography, size, and housing stock. Additionally, the chairmen were common to both pilot and control teams, so ensuring some standardisation in relation to the management of the conferences, as well as the completion of the research instruments. To ensure that any differences between the pilot and control areas did not arise from idiosyncratic characteristics a number of objective indicators were identified, such as the numbers of conferences held in the teams before the study began and the rates and categories of registration. Such indicators also made it possible to judge whether differences between the two sets of areas changed in character or became more pronounced.

*The conferences*

The format of the conference was the same for the pilot and the control teams, excepting for the involvement of parents. Based on a chronological approach to the investigation the conference started with information sharing about the alleged abuse, moved on to a discussion of the family background, and ended with the decision making about registration and the child protection plan. In the pilot areas, parents could be present up to the decision making stage, returning after the meeting to be told the registration decision and the skeletal child protection plan. Arrangements in the pilot areas were made for separate reception facilities, some child care support, translation of letters into different languages, and interpreters. The chairperson took responsibility for managing issues regarding confidential information, for deciding who should be invited and for meeting the parents first and last.

The chairmen of the conferences comprised six male child protection workers, senior managers, employed by the social services department. Three were key to the project because they chaired conferences in the teams both with and without parents. They were also members of the steering group, and so involved in the questionnaire design and in contacting families and engaging their co-operation. While the procedures that the chairs followed for all the conferences were the same there were some differences in process resulting from different styles of chairing and the nature of the area in which the conferences were held. The majority of the staff in the pilot areas had received in-house multi-agency training and were familiar with the procedures.

*Negotiating research access to the child protection agencies*

> Negotiations to set up a child abuse project are of little interest in themselves. But in a context where there is a mandatory requirement for inter-agency work and where uncertainties about good practice abound, the difficulties of mounting such investigations have wider implications. They illuminate the contrasting ideologies of the professionals involved, highlight the problems of achieving co-operation and further elaborate the context in which investigations are undertaken.                                    (Cleaver and Freeman, 1995, p.21)

The difficulties encountered in gaining the co-operation of agencies in this sensitive area of research have been well described by Cleaver and Freeman (1995). The Area Child Protection Committee's initiation of this research was key in gaining the co-operation of the professionals, in the design of the research instruments and in gaining access to the families and the authority's information base. Additionally, the researcher took part in a number of inter-agency training events, thus facilitating the dual objective of collecting valuable illustrative data and ensuring the co-operation of the professionals in the research.

This model of research, including involvement in training, feeding back findings as they emerged and contributing to ongoing policy discussions fits the model of participant action research described by Whittaker et al. (1989) and was a factor contributing to the success of the data collection. Everitt et al. (1992) likewise support the view that the more successful research is practitioner and not just researcher led. The contact with professionals from all agencies and at all levels was invaluable in providing opportunities to check out ideas as they developed and in pointing up the more contentious issues as they emerged from the policy initiative. For example, after some weeks it became clear that the role of the local authority solicitor in the conference was problematic because of the potential conflicts of role. On the one hand, the solicitor was present to advise the conference on the legal options available to the authority to protect the child. On the other, where court proceedings were possible, the solicitor was also responsible for collecting the evidence to support the authority's case. This he did by asking the parents detailed questions in the conference. The potential for injustice, unfairness and disempowerment is obvious - especially since parents at this stage were not allowed legal representation for themselves. For a number of the professionals and the parents this practice was antithetical to the spirit of the enterprise and raised concerns about injustice. Such concerns were being played out in other local authorities. Lewis (1994) interviewed chairpersons from fourteen different authorities, and describes the following statement as expressing a common view regarding the potential for injustice in the conference: "a kangaroo court with a touch of the Old Vic".

This example illustrates the value from the research point of view of being a party to ongoing discussions which informed developing policy and practice. It facilitated the development of the hypothesis - that issues around power and justice were key to an understanding of the subject. More importantly, this debate raised the possibility, which became a key question, that the contradictions which were emerging in relation to the functions of the conference were endemic to the nature of the task. The issue provided a clear example of how the interaction of the professionals and the content and process of the conference had to change to accommodate the new objective of the conference - viz. achieving partnership with parents. It also called into question the assumption on which partnership is based - that the dual goals of working in partnership with parents and protecting the child are complementary. Perhaps there were some cases in which they were, and others in which they were not? Consequently at an early stage of the research some key research questions and possible hypotheses were formulated and were able to be incorporated into the questionnaires and interview schedules.

## The research objectives

The overall aim of the research was, therefore, to evaluate a pilot scheme involving parents in the initial child protection conference by exploring the effect on the decisions taken and the attitudes and views of the parents and professionals involved. Comparisons would be drawn between conferences with and without parents present to determine the degree to which it was involvement in the conference per se which determined outcomes, such as the attitudes of the parents to the intervention. The hypothesis was that it was the skill with which the policy was implemented in the conference proceedings, rather than simply its existence, which would determine the quality and experience of the enterprise. The overall aim was, therefore, to identify procedures which facilitated the genuine participation of parents in the process and to assess whether practice was more oriented to partnership principles when parents were involved. More detailed objectives were to explore the attitudes of the professionals toward parental involvement before and after the implementation of the policy and to see if conferences with parents present presented particular difficulties or opportunities to them.

Within this broad framework the research objectives of the research were to appraise parental involvement in the initial child protection conferences in relation to:

* the conference process
* the decisions and recommendations made
* the views of the parents and professionals involved.

## 1 The conference process

Although Stevenson (1995) has suggested that the available research "tells us less about the dynamics of the conference than it does about the attitudes of the participants and the steps taken in reaching decisions and recommendations", an analysis of inter-professional interactions and attitudes is fundamental to understanding process. A focal area of scrutiny here, is therefore on inter-agency process, particularly in relation to the management of anxiety and uncertainty by the chairman and to the implementation of the procedures devised for involving parents. Other aspects of the conference process to be monitored related to the contentious area of exactly how the involvement of parents, as opposed to their attendance, was managed. As Atherton (1984) had already suggested, participation took many forms and meant different things to different people. The research design therefore took into account such details as the way parents were welcomed into the meeting and the means by which their contributions were encouraged. Additionally, other concrete indicators, such as size and length, were to be measured for comparison across the pilot and control areas. Other research (Vernon and Fruin, 1986) on meetings with parents present, such as review meetings, has suggested that size is a deterrent to their and their child's attendance and adversely affects the quality of the participation. Length may present difficulties to professionals who have other calls on their time, especially groups such as general practitioners whose primary task is health care and not the management of child abuse (Hallett, 1995). If conferences with parents present lasted longer and were bigger, this would have resource implications, as well as some quite specific effects, and this would be demonstrated by comparing the findings from the pilot and control areas.

## 2   *The decisions and recommendations made*

The second main objective of the research was to evaluate whether the involvement of parents affected the decisions and recommendations made by the conference by comparing the findings from conferences with and without parents present, and before and after the policy was implemented. The conference has two decisions to make - whether or not to place the child's name on the child protection register as being at risk of future harm and under which category. One of the major concerns about involving parents was that fewer children would be registered because of the fear that professionals would be inhibited (Phillips and Evans, 1986). Additionally, it was thought that the category under which children were registered might reflect the parents' presence. Some professionals (see Fisher, 1990) believed that cases of sexual abuse - especially where parents were denying their culpability - would present particular difficulties where parents were present.

The conference can make a number of recommendations in relation to the child protection plan. In later chapters, the place of the child protection plan is discussed. It is a contentious issue, touching again on the functions and purposes of the conference in relation to childrens' and families welfare, and the legitimacy of the decisions and recommendations made in the meeting. An aim of the research, then, was to collect information about the child protection plan and the views of the participants on it, in particular, whether registration is used to gatekeep scarce resources (see Gibbons, 1995). A further objective was to assess the degree to which parents and professionals views on the help offered were congruent. Research dating back to that undertaken by Mayer and Timms (1970) has illustrated that effective practice is built upon the client's definition of the problem and its resolution, not the workers.   Finally, the research was designed to evaluate the degree of relationship between what the conference decided and recommended and the attitudes of parents to the ongoing work. Information about the conference recommendations in relation to the keyworker, whether statutory action was recommended how this was understood by parents was therefore also collected.

## 3 *The views of the parents and professionals involved*

In looking at how partnerships are established at a time when parents are angry, bitter and shocked and the professionals primary concern is the safety of the child, two approaches were indicated. Firstly, to establish what went on during the enquiry into the allegation it seemed important to explore any differences between the two groups of parents in, for example, the amount of information they had been given and their feelings about being invited to the conference or not. How sensitive issues were managed in the conference, levels of agreement about the need for a conference and the parents' views regarding the relevance, validity and presentation of information were other determinants of attitude and experience to be explored.

The second approach was to explore the experiences and actions of the professionals. A key area was assessment. Research questions included: was there time to make one, what information did social workers rely upon, which family members they had seen, what professional consultations had taken place? Other writers (Hallett, 1995; Lyth-Menzies, 1988) have drawn attention to the connection between agency policy and structures and the quality of the workers experience and practice. An additional area for exploration was, therefore, the training, preparation and support structures, such as supervision, provided by the agency. The documentation produced to support the initiative, both for parents and for the professionals, needed to be reviewed from the perspectives of all the participants in relation to whether it had been received, as well as how it was rated.

## Methodology

The research design and methodology was constructed to reflect these objectives requiring data to be collected from different sources and in different ways.

Table 3.1 sets out the methodology, and the sources of data collection.

### * *Monitoring study*

A questionnaire was completed at the end of each conference by the six chairmen involved. This recorded details and characteristics of the child and the family and information about the alleged abuse and the pattern of the investigation. It also collected information about the conference, such as the timing, the location, attendance rates, the decisions and recommendations made as well as specific issues such as whether it had started late.

*\* Attitude survey*
A brief postal questionnaire was sent to all the professionals in attendance at conferences in the research teams in the six months prior to the implementation of the policy of parental involvement. It collected information about the views of the professionals on the perceived advantages and disadvantages of involving parents and about the training and preparation received. Six months after parents had been involved, the process was repeated by sending the same questionnaire to all the professionals who had attended conferences in the teams involving parents.

*\*Professionals opinion survey*
To collect data on the professionals' opinion of the involvement of parents in the particular conference, rather than their overall attitudes to policy and practice, a brief questionnaire was given to each professional to complete at the end of every conference where parents had attended. The questionnaire asked the professionals whether they felt the parents' presence had been helpful in assessing risk to the child, the degree to which it had affected their participation and whether the decision to register or the recommendations were influenced by the parents' presence.

*The interviews*

Two sets of interviews were carried out by means of semi-structured interview schedules:

*Interviews with social workers*
During the last six months of the project, interviews with the investigating social workers were carried out to capture the detail of their work and experience of involving parents. A semi-structured interview schedule was used to gather data about the work they did with parents and children and other professionals before, during and after the conference and about the support they had from their agency in carrying out the work.

*Interviews with parents and family members*
To compare the views of the parents and other family members who had and who had not attended conferences, all the parents whose children were conferenced in the research teams during the year of the research were

invited to be interviewed. A semi-structured interview schedule was used, collecting information on the experiences of the family members from first hearing about the allegation, through the investigation and conference proceedings and the following weeks. The interviews took place in the family home between one and four weeks after the conference.

**Table 3.1   Sources of data collection**

---

**Monitoring study**

All cases in 6 teams held between 1.5.91 and 30.6.92
83 cases:         50 pilot         33 control

**Observation**

Randomly selected in pilot area    22 conferences

---

**Attitude survey**

All professionals who attended a conference in the research teams

6 months before implementation    141 respondents (62% response rate)
6 months after implementation    119 respondents (60% response rate)

**Professionals opinion survey**

All professionals attending 36 conferences with parents present
        261 respondents (88% response rate)

**Interviews with social workers**

All cases in pilot teams, January - June 1992:    22 interviews

---

**Interviews with parents (and other family members)**

All families of children conferenced in the research teams

51 families responded (61% response rate)
33 from pilot teams   (65% response rate)
18 from control teams (59% response rate)
71 interviews in all

*\* Observation study*
In order to get a complete picture of the conferences with parents present twenty two conferences with parents present were observed. An instrument for recording was designed which enabled the material to be recorded in themes. Other information was process recorded, such as what happened when parents were upset.

**Analysis**

The research study combined an in depth qualitative analysis with a design which allowed for statistical analysis. Additionally, the observations of the conferences and the researchers involvement in the sub-committee and training events informed the analysis. Such a pluralistic approach is advocated by Smith and Cantley (1985) as being a key requirement for research into the complex area of child protection work. Cheetham et al. (1992) have also emphasised the importance of taking into account the concerns and interests of all parties in conducting research into social work effectiveness.

The statistical analysis allows for an overall evaluation of the effect of the new policy, as well as providing detailed information about the process and the experiences of all the participants. All the questionnaires were coded and the computer analysis was undertaken with the use of the statistical package for the social sciences, SPSS. The data was analysed using a mixture of statistical techniques, such as chi square and analysis of variance. Where the numbers were small, the Mann-U Whitney test was applied, thus enabling a procedure to be devised for summing up and scoring parent's attitudes. Cross tabulations of the data from all the research instruments was carried out, allowing for other connections to be drawn.

The qualitative analysis allows a detailed consideration of issues which concern practitioners, parents and policy makers but do not easily yield to a statistical approach. By tapping the experience and views of the participants, and by drawing upon the qualitative material from the observations, impacts which are not picked up statistically are nevertheless recorded. For example, the statistical analysis of the most difficult conferences revealed that professionals found situations of uncertainty and ambiguity particularly difficult to handle, and the observations suggested some reasons for this. The combination of quantitative and qualitative analysis makes it possible to assess a wide range of possible effects, such as the degree to which the involvement of parents is associated with a sharp change in the pattern of decisions.

## Conclusion

This research study was set up in response to a request from an Area Child Protection Committee to evaluate a small scale pilot project to involve parents in four area teams in their city. The research was designed so that basic information about individual conferences in the four pilot and two control areas would be routinely gathered and the experience of all the participants would be tapped at different points in time. A number of different instruments were designed to allow comparisons of the routine monitoring of the decisions taken and parental involvement, a repeated attitude survey of professionals before the policy was implemented and after, and a study of the professionals views on conferences with parents present. In addition, the design included interviews with parents and other family members - including children where possible, interviews with the investigating social workers and observation at conferences with parents present. Data was collected in the first year of the research by means of questionnaires and semi-structured interview schedules, and the data was analysed by a combination of in depth qualitative and statistical quantitative methods.

A limitation of this study is that it evaluated only one model of parental involvement in one authority at a time when practice and policy was evolving. However, although different authorities do vary the detail of arrangement in some respects, policy and practice remain largely unchanged. The most significant change that has taken place since the research was carried out - in this and in other authorities - is that family members now generally remain present for the duration and they now can take a friend/advocate. In the event, in some of the conferences researched the parents did stay for the duration and some took friends. The conferences studied were themselves part of an evolving process and the research attempts to capture and explore developments while also undertaking a time limited study.

The research design is unique in having a control group and in gathering data at two points in time. Additionally, the statistical analysis is sophisticated and enables important conclusions to be drawn about conference attendance *per se*. It builds upon and fills gaps in the existing research. The aforementioned studies range widely, exploring aspects of the investigation and follow up work for up to two years after the conference. While this is equally important in contributing to the knowledge base in child protection work, these other studies do not yield definitive evaluative conclusions on the policy of parental involvement at conferences per se. These studies, such as Thoburn's (1995), deliberately contrast areas which have adopted different approaches to involving parents, thus making it difficult to be sure whether any differences found reflect the characteristics of the area, the effects of different approaches to involving parents or the skill with which different workers carry out their tasks. They are, therefore, complementary to mine.

# 4 The conferences and the participants

The previous chapters have explained why the initial child protection conference - the 'crucible of the system' (Blom-Cooper, Kimberley Carlile Report, 1987), plays such an important part in the investigation and management of children at risk of abuse. This chapter presents the basic information on the children and families and on the conference procedures collected from the eighty three conferences that make up the study. This information provides context by monitoring the effects on the conference of involving parents. It yields information about the children and families, the sources and types of referral, the decisions and recommendations made and a number of features of the conference process. In itself, this information provides a useful and detailed picture of child protection work. For the particular purposes of this study the data also provides the opportunity to explore the issues previously identified, such as professional concerns that the involvement of parents might result in a drop in the number of conferences held or change the characteristics of the children conferenced. The information also lends itself to some direct comparisons with the other research studies cited and generates discussion about the particular and the wider issues raised by the present child protection system.

## Method

A monitoring study was set up in the four pilot and two control areas to collect information on every conference held during the research period. A questionnaire was designed in conjunction with two of the principal chairmen and the implementation sub-group of the Area Child Protection Committee to be completed by the chairmen at the end of each conference. The questionnaire required the chairmen to record basic facts, such as the age of the child, as well as to make more complicated judgments, such as whether the allegation was proved and why they thought parents who were invited did not attend. Specific questions about incidents that might happen with parents present were also asked. For example, did they leave early, was their behaviour disruptive or was confidential information withheld? Separate questionnaires were completed for each child in the family, but for research purposes the analysis was undertaken on the questionnaire completed on the child nominated by the chairman as the first child. At the same time some comparative data was collected from the authority's records on all conferences held in the research areas in the previous year. This provided information about the numbers of conferences held, the numbers of children registered and the categories of registration used.

Over the thirteen months of the project, fifty questionnaires were completed on conferences in the four area teams in the pilot area involving parents, at thirty six of which parents were in attendance. In the two teams in the control area where parents were not yet included thirty three were completed. This represented a response rate of 100%. The completed questionnaires were analysed quantitatively by means of SPSS, and the analysis was informed by the written comments of the chairmen and the researchers observation study.

## Results

*Numbers*

Once a referral has been received, an investigation is carried out under Section 47 of The Children Act 1989. All of the cases included in this research concerned referrals that reached the conference. Gibbons and colleagues (1995) suggest that 160,000 Section 47 enquiries take place annually, of which 40,000 are conferenced, resulting in 25,000 additions to the child protection register. It is without the scope of this study to speculate about the referrals in this authority that did not result in a conference. The focus of enquiry in the research described here is whether the policy of parental involvement resulted in a reduction in the numbers of conferences held.

Table 4.1 illustrates the numbers of conferences held in the research teams during the year of the study.

**Table 4.1  Numbers of Conferences held by Pilot and Control
(May 1991 - June 1992)**

| Teams | No. | % |
|---|---|---|
| Pilot area (with parents) | 50 | 60 |
| Control area (without parents) | 33 | 40 |
| Total conferences | 83 | 100 |

Table 4.2 demonstrates that the *number of conferences* held in both the pilot and control areas dropped in the year following the introduction of the policy. This drop was also experienced in other areas of the city and so was part of a trend city wide. This was thought to be due partly to the introduction in the city of new criteria for calling conferences. A further influence was the introduction of the Children Act 1989. The 'no-order' principle, which was intended to result in a reduction of the number of cases brought before the court, and the principle of parental responsibility required agencies to develop new ways of working in partnership with parents. The immediate impact was of a down fall in court activity. It seems likely that the same reasons influenced the reduction in the numbers of conferences held nationally, from 45,300 in 1991, to 38,600 in 1992 (Children Act Report, 1992). In this study, the reduction in numbers was more pronounced in the control than in the pilot areas (see Table 4.2). There was therefore no evidence that the introduction of the policy had lowered the number of conferences held.

*Referrals*

A report of child abuse becomes a child protection case when a referral is made.  As discussed in Chapter 2, the process by which this happens is complex and depends upon a range of factors, such as whether the child is believed, how the person hearing the report interprets what they hear, and whether they fear the consequences of telling (see Wattam, 1992; Gibbons et al., 1995). One way of furthering the debate about the way abuse is constructed would be to explore in detail the sources of the referral, and the perspectives of the referents. Information about referral behaviours can also be used to further our understanding of particular aspects of the child protection framework.   Wattam (1992), for example, argues that  the way in which reporting comes about is a crucial variable when scrutinising the testimony of children for validity in court testimony.  The presence of parents in the conference could also influence referral behaviours and that is the primary focus in this analysis.

**Table 4.2  Numbers of Conferences held before and after parental participation**

| Numbers Held | Teams | | |
|---|---|---|---|
| | Pilot | Control | Total |
| Year | No. | No. | No. |
| Year 1 (April'90-March'91) | 66 | 48 | 114 |
| Year 2 (April'91-March'92) | 43 | 22 | 65 |
| Total during year 1 to year 2 | 109 | 70 | 179 |

$$109 \times 70 \times 65 \times 114 > 3.84$$

Two stages in the referral process were identified to determine the effect of involving parents on referral patterns; the point when the first concern was raised, and when the referral for investigation was made to social services. Clearly the referrer at those stages might differ. For example, a child may raise the first concern by disclosing abuse to the teacher, whereas the teacher may act as the formal referral agent to social services.  Wattam (1989) provides us with a number of reasons why teachers do not refer cases of abuse to social services. It is possible, and suggested by recent research (Gibbons et al., 1995) that, because the threshold for determining maltreatment moves over time, much abuse is undetected and unreported.   While this study did not allow for the uncovering of unreported cases, the methodology was informed by the belief that the dynamics suggested by the above studies also operate at different stages of the referral process. One hypothesis was that referrals to social services could drop, or the patterns change, where the referrer believed the parents could be party to this information at the conference. Neighbours, for example, or partners intimidated within a violent relationship, may not want a parent to know of their report.

As can be seen from Table 4.3, leaving aside those cases already known to social workers and referred by them (21%), the largest group initiating the first concern was self (13%) and family (12%). Although the numbers are lower, the finding that the largest source of referrals was a parent, followed by the child, compares with findings from the other research studies described in the previous chapter. Thoburn et al. (1995), Farmer and Owen (1995) and Corby (1987), all found that the family were the most likely to initiate the referral. Cleaver and Freeman (1995) also found abuse came to official attention through the disclosure of the child or family (51%) by professionals already working with the family (39%), or by unrelated incidents such as a home visit (10%).

Returning to my study, and the influence of parental involvement on the people initiating concern, there were no major differences in the profile of those judged to have *raised the first concern* in the control and pilot areas. The numbers are small making analysis difficult and the differences revealed are slight. For example, in the pilot area, no health professionals are shown as raising the first concern. The study did not allow for these trends to be tested further. They could, for example, have arisen by chance or been already established patterns in the areas. The strong suggestion is, however, that parental involvement did not deter people from expressing their concerns. The second stage, *who referred to social services*, is regarded as the most important step in a child protection investigation for it is then that it becomes public property (Dingwall et al., 1983). In the other research cited, initial concerns were generally passed through intermediaries to social workers. Teachers and day-care workers played the major part in Thoburns' (1995) study, followed by health professionals. Gibbons et al (1995) group the sources of referral into those closest to the child - teachers, school nurses and education welfare (23%) - health visitors, General Practitioners and hospital staff (17%), household members and other lay people (17%), social services (13%), police (12%), other (18%). The groupings in Gibbons' study are slightly different to the groupings in mine so comparisons are tentative. However, her findings are similar to those laid out in Table 4.3 when the pilot and control areas are taken together, and the categories assimilated.

**Table 4.3   Profile of Referral to the Conferences**
**83 cases; 50 pilot 33 control, 1.5.91-30.6.92**

### First Stage: Who Raised First Concern:

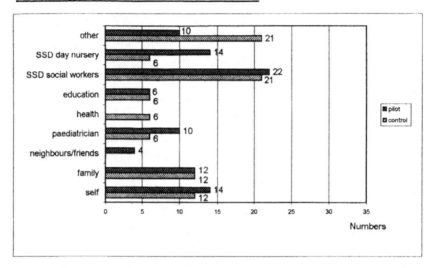

### Second Stage: Who Referred to Social Services:

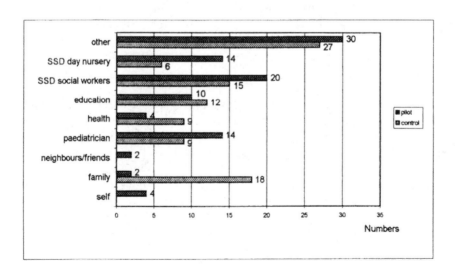

The most notable difference between the first and second stages in my study is, as would be expected, in relation to children. Only four refer themselves at the second stage - all from the pilot area. Of particular interest is the reduction in the number of families in the pilot area who refer on to social services. Here there is a difference between pilot and control areas that could be explained by parental attendance. However, there is no means of testing this further. Another trend worthy of comment is the large number of referrers (28% and 30%) within the 'other' category. This includes police and voluntary agencies, such as the NSPCC, who might be expected to be more confident in taking on this more formally responsible role. As the catch-all category it also includes a smattering of the more unusual referrals that make up the welfare net, such as one made by the owner of a riding school who noticed severe bruising on a child's arms. Interestingly, the percentages in the pilot and control areas under 'other' are similar.

In summary, the patterns of referral identified in this research compare with other research studies. It is possible that one effect of involving parents was to reduce the number of referrals from parents to social services, but this could not be established definitively by this methodology.

*Attendance*

*1 Attendance of professionals*

As suggested in the previous chapter, research findings (McGloin and Turnbull, 1986; Bedford, 1986) and events in other areas had demonstrated that some professionals stayed away from conferences with parents present. Police and paediatricians in some areas had concerns about disclosing confidential information or believed the child's safety could be jeopardised. Teachers and nurses feared that speaking openly in front of parents might jeopardise their relationship with the family. Attendance was, therefore, thought to be an area of the conference activity which could be profoundly effected by the presence of parents (see also Farmer and Owen, 1995).

Other aspects of interest emerging from studying the attendance of professionals concerned the rates of attendance and roles of senior and managerial staff. Additionally, it was thought the attendance of professionals who are routinely invited but only occasionally attended could be effected. Such groups included Probation Officers and General Practitioners, teachers who may only attend one conference in their career and community leaders in the case of families whose ethnic origin was non-European. As Hallett and Birchall (1992) pointed out, the conference is a meeting comprising a core group of professionals whose key task is child protection, such as social workers, and others who are more or less closely tied in to the child protection framework, such as teachers and hospital staff. The issues of power and control that are raised by this mix of professional groupings have been a subject of considerable debate (Stevenson, 1980; Hallett, 1995) and will be a theme to be further explored. The research was therefore set up to allow for a careful inspection of who was invited and who attended.

**Table 4.4 Professionals invited to and in attendance at 83 conferences, 1.5.91-30.6.92**

| Professionals | Invited | | Attended | |
| --- | --- | --- | --- | --- |
| | Pilot | Control | Pilot | Control |
| | (Percentages) | | | |
| Principal social worker | 100 | 100 | 90 | 84 |
| Principal case worker | 100 | 100 | 59 | 55 |
| Social worker | 100 | 100 | 94 | 94 |
| Residential social worker | 21 | 23 | 24 | 25 |
| Nursing officer | 100 | 100 | 67 | 91 |
| Health visitor | 86 | 71 | 74 | 62 |
| School nurse | 51 | 69 | 47 | 54 |
| Midwife | 17 | 37 | 15 | 23 |
| Police | 100 | 100 | 92 | 88 |
| Probation | 98 | 88 | 26 | 21 |
| Teacher | 62 | 73 | 54 | 48 |
| Education welfare officer | 90 | 94 | 22 | 46 |
| Educational psychologist | 56 | 23 | 0 | 0 |
| Community medical officer | 88 | 67 | 2 | 11 |
| General practitioner | 96 | 100 | 19 | 14 |
| Paediatrician | 62 | 65 | 15 | 18 |
| Family Service Unit | 4 | 3 | 7 | 4 |
| NSPCC | 92 | 93 | 11 | 11 |
| Other voluntary agency | 15 | 8 | 18 | 0 |
| Local authority solicitor | 92 | 97 | 50 | 48 |
| Other professional | 31 | 29 | 27 | 63 |

Data was collected on the attendance of professionals in relation to who had been invited, and is laid out in Table 4.4.

As can be seen the range of professionals involved is wide. Certain professional groups, such as the police, probation and nursing officers, are routinely invited; others are invited where they are known to be involved in the case - such as the community midwife, the teacher, and Family Service Unit staff. Social Services are clearly the key agents. They generally have present the principal social worker, who works in a managerial capacity across Divisions, the principal case worker, who is the senior in the team, acting with and responsible for supervising the investigating social worker. In addition any residential or day care staff who know the family may also be employed by social services. Apart from the social work representatives, nurses (including Health Visitors) and the police occupy key roles, attending most of the conferences they are invited to, as do teachers. The rates of attendance for the Doctors - General Practitioners, consultant paediatricians and community medical officers - are surprisingly low given the essential nature of much of their evidence or, as in the case of General Practitioners, the likelihood of their involvement with the family. This finding is in common with that of Farmer and Owen (1995), Stevenson (1980) and Hallett (1995). Hallett suggested that, although General Practitioners commonly reported time pressures as a reason for not attending, other reasons could be their lack of familiarity with the work, the pace, and divided loyalties. Lastly, the local authorities' solicitors attended any conference where it was thought legal advice might be necessary, which was in half the cases.

One aspect of attendance that is not pursued in this study but was raised by Farmer and Owen (1995), is that professionals varied in the extent of their influence over the proceedings. They found that, although Probation Officers did not attend most of the conferences to which they were invited, their attendance at the few they did attend was associated with a high registration rate of 82%. This compared with a registration rate of 50% when General Practitioners attended. They conclude "either the Probation Officers brought with them more damaging information than the General Practitioners, or else they were successful in selecting conferences which really justified their attendance" (p.103). Another possibility is that they communicated their concerns more successfully, being used to the quasi-legal nature of the proceedings.

In summary, there was no difference between the pilot and control areas in the percentage of *professionals who were invited to attend*, and who did so (55% in each).

*2 Attendance of parents*

Turning to *the parents* two questions were important to determine. Who had been selected for invitation to the conference, and who had come? One critical factor in determining who gets invited is how the definition of 'the parent' is constructed. In this authority, the chairperson decided who to invite on the advice of the investigating social worker. As will be observed in Chapter 8 the family may be already known to the investigating social worker, or the referral may be new. Even where families were already known to the social services department - 60% were - information relevant to the child's key attachment figures may not be recorded, available or accurate (see Thoburn et al., 1995). The issue of how the 'effective parent' is defined is, therefore, extremely complicated. A feature both of modern society and, in particular, of families who abuse their children (Gough, 1993), is that family units and reconstituted family units often do not contain both parents. Different children in a family may have different parents. In some cases, the primary attachment figures for the child may not be the parents or the carers and may not be in the household at the time of the alleged abuse. Other factors also come into play, as will be revealed here.

The matter of which family members to invite is determined to a degree by the policy of the Area Child Protection Committee. The policy in this authority (see Appendix 1), in common with a number of others, was to exclude parents suffering from a defined serious mental illness, parents in the process of a criminal investigation or those known to be violent. During the time of the research study, ten 'effective' parents were excluded on this basis - four undergoing criminal investigations and six known to be violent. The chairmen did exercise discretion, so that in a few cases men who were known to be violent were invited. Cases where police were considering prosecution were particularly difficult where an investigation of a single parent carer was ongoing, as Thoburn et al. (1995) also found. In one conference observed by the researcher where the police were preparing criminal proceedings against the mother for neglect, the police felt obliged to caution the mother in the middle of the conference.

Further complicating factors effecting attendance were raised by other family characteristics. Where the parents' first language was not English (9%) an interpreter was required. For one Asian family an interpreter was necessary to translate for the mother but the father spoke English. An interpreter was present in 6% of the conferences. Community leaders of ethnic minority groups were able to be present in a supportive capacity and one or two African-Caribbean families brought them along. While it was not policy at the time of the research to allow parents to bring a friend, the particular needs and problems of parents with learning difficulties were recognised and they were encouraged to bring an advocate: most did. Lastly, while members of the extended family were not, as has been said, routinely invited, in one or two cases a grandmother and an Aunt were present. The inclusion of these individuals, in addition to the parents, increased the numbers present at the conferences, and had other effects which will be discussed later (see Bell, 1996).

Table 4.5 illustrates the attendance rates of the parents who were invited. A number of issues are revealed by these figures. Firstly, the attendance rate of 72% is low compared to the national figure of 80% (Messages from the Research, 1995). It was also low in Thoburn et al.'s (1995) study where 20% of those invited did not attend. In Farmer and Owens' study (1995) parents or other family members were present at only 59% of the conferences. These low rates of attendance can be partially explained by the newness of the policy at the time in the authority studied. In my study, analysis of data from the parents' interviews suggested that there were other reasons for non-attendance, such as fear and difficulties in making child care arrangements. In some cases, particularly in one team known for its poor administrative back up, the parents had not received the letter inviting them to the conference or the notification had been inaccurate. The issues arising from this will be pursued further in Chapter 7, describing the parents' experience.

**Table 4.5 Attendance rates of parents and others at 50 conferences, 1.5.91-30.6.92**

| Parent or Other | Invited | | Attended | |
| --- | --- | --- | --- | --- |
| | No. | % | No. | % |
| Mother | 47 | 94 | 35 | 70 |
| Father | 22 | 44 | 12 | 24 |
| Stepfather | 9 | 18 | 6 | 12 |
| Others | 2 | 4 | 2 | 4 |
| Friend | 0 | 0 | 3 | 6 |
| Interpreter | 0 | 0 | 3 | 6 |

Secondly, the data reveals who was selected for invitation. A striking, although not unexpected finding, is the prominence given to mothers. 94% of mothers were invited, as against 44% of the fathers. Possible explanations for this discrepancy are that the child lived alone with mother or had no meaningful contact with father. In fact, only 21% of the children lived with their mother alone, 34% of the children lived with both parents, and a further 32% lived with other parental or family combinations. Even where step-fathers are included the percentage invited reaches only 62%. A further factor in the absence of fathers was that separated fathers were not pursued even where contact between child and father had been maintained. Some fathers (20%) were excluded on a policy basis. However, in some cases, social services did make strenuous attempts to include fathers, such as timetabling the conference so that a father who was in prison could attend. Only a tiny percentage of the extended family - 2% - were invited even where the child had very close contact. In one conference observed by the researcher, for example, the mother read out a letter from grandparents who were clearly attached to their grandchildren, but had not been invited to be present. The reasons for this are explored with the social workers and reported in Chapter 8.

In this context, it is not surprising to find the focus on mothers reflected in the attendance. In only one of the parental attendance conferences was the mother formally excluded because of a serious depressive illness and in this case the father attended alone. In over one third of the conferences the mother attended alone. Farmer and Owen (1995) also found that the mother attended alone in 30% of their conferences and in only 18% were two parent figures present. Here is another example of the gendered nature of the subject.

*Size and length*

> 'If everyone minded their own business,' the duchess said in a hoarse growl, 'the world would go round a deal faster than it does.'
>
> (Carroll, 1865, Alice's Adventures in Wonderland)

Other studies on the numbers in attendance at conferences have reported rates of attendance as being between eight and twenty (Corby, 1987). Questions have been raised about whether all those present need to be there. Corby found that 10% of those in attendance at the fifty five conferences included in his research made no verbal contribution, and that many agencies sent more than one representative for support purposes. Size has also been found to be an important variable in higher registration rates (Farmer and Owen, 1995), and was associated in Corby's research (and, as will be later discussed, in mine) with more difficult conferences.

One effect of including parents in the conference is that the conference may be bigger and because there are more people to speak and manage it could take longer. Table 4.6 demonstrates these effects. As can be seen from Table 4.6, where parents were in attendance the average number present increased from eight to ten. There were fewer conferences in the pilot area with less than ten in attendance. 76% of conferences in the pilot area had over ten participants, compared to 63% in the control area. These figures in fact under represent the size of conferences with parents present because they include those conferences in the pilot area (28%) where parents did not actually attend.

Related to size was the *length* of the conference. Those held in the pilot area lasted, on average, twenty nine minutes longer than those in the control. Some lasted up to three hours. Again, these figures are under representative for the reasons outlined above. A few conferences were longer because parents were disruptive. For example, one conference was held up for fifteen minutes after the mother left the room in an upset state. The main reason associated with increased length is increased size - there are more people to speak and be heard. Stevenson (1980) suggested that another reason for conferences being longer was the means used by the chair for facilitating the process. The observations in this research lend support to this suggestion. Where parents were present, the chairperson took great care to ensure that parents were treated with sensitivity and dignity, and accorded every opportunity to speak. It is, therefore, not surprising that including parents makes some conferences longer.

Other features significantly associated with long conferences were the presence of a paediatrician, the consideration of neglect, the ethnic origin of the family and whether or not their first language was English. With the exception of language there was no evidence that these characteristics distinguished the pilot and control areas, and so (again with the exception of language) they could not have accounted for the greater length of conferences in the pilot areas. The numbers of parents who did not speak English was in fact very small and the difference between these two kinds of areas remained if the parents were omitted.

*Registration*

"Messages from the Research" (1995) makes it clear that the register is seen by professionals as an essential tool in the planning of child protection services. "It gives case conferences a focus and fosters inter-agency cooperation" (p.31). Outcome measures (see Farmer and

Owen, 1995, Cleaver and Freeman, 1995) show that, whatever the deficiencies of the system, most children are protected from reabuse. Studies of registration rates and the factors underlying them are important in themselves. They are also, clearly, an area where the presence of parents could effect the decisions made.

**Table 4.6    Attendance, size and length of conferences by Pilot and Control, 83 conferences, 1.5.91-30.6.92**

|  | Pilot | Control |
|---|---|---|
| Attendance by Area |  |  |
| Percentage professional attendance at conference | 55 | 55 |
| Average number of professionals attending | 8 | 8 |
| Percentage of parents attending | 72 | 0 |
| Average number of attenders (inc. parents, etc.) | 10 | 8 |
| Size by Area |  |  |
| Percentage size of conference:        under 10 | 24 | 36 |
| 11 - 14 | 62 | 48 |
| over 15 | 14 | 15 |
| Length by Area |  |  |
| Average length of conference (hours) | 2.25 | 1.96 |
| Percentage length of conference    under 1 hour | 10 | 12 |
| 1 - 2 hours | 53 | 79 |
| 2 - 3 hours | 35 | 9 |

Before presenting the data collected on registration in the conferences studied, however, the limitations of child protection registers require mention.

It should be emphasised that the Register is not a record of the extent of child abuse as some children are registered because of concern about future abuse and will not have been the victim of actual abuse, whilst other children who have been the victim of abuse will not have been placed on the Register because there was no need for a multi-agency protection plan under child protection procedures.

(Thoburn et al., 1952, p.2)

Research has demonstrated that a number of variables operate in levels of registration. Gibbons et al (1995) identified two sets of factors: socio-demographic, such as unemployment rates and poor service provision; and operational factors, such as no regular updating of the register. What is clear is that professionals are basing their decisions to register not only on what they interpret as abusive behaviour, but also on the environmental factors in a child's life and on the resources available (Dingwall, 1983, Thoburn et al., 1995). Some of these factors are revealed in my study, also.

Table 4.7 outlines the numbers of cases registered in the study and the categories of registration. The four main categories of registration suggested in Working Together 1991 are neglect, physical injury, sexual abuse and emotional abuse. In the authority studied, the combined category was also used. Grave concern was in the process of being withdrawn, so the effects are difficult to determine. As with the referral process, different stages in the process of registration were defined as a means of determining the impact of parental presence. The hypothesis was that certain cases might present particular problems which would affect the registration decision. For example, in cases where children had disclosed sexual abuse but this was denied by their parents, the conference might find it more comfortable to register the case in the category grave concern rather than sexual abuse. Wattam (1992) points out that cases of sexual abuse are materially different from other types of abuse because the evidence is usually so difficult to get at and because they raise painful and complex emotions. It might therefore be expected that they would be more difficult to address and determine in front of the parents.

As has been observed, there was also a general fear that information might be withheld in front of parents - either because it was too difficult for the professionals to say openly, or because it was feared the child or other family members might suffer as a result of hearing things not previously known. The monitoring questionnaire therefore asked the chairmen to describe the main concern at the point of referral, the indicators of abuse that were presented to the conference, as well as the numbers and category of registration.

## Table 4.7   Registration Rates

### Main focus of concern

**Before Registration**

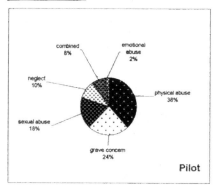

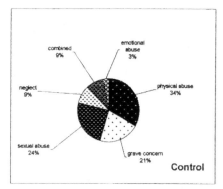

**Post Registration**

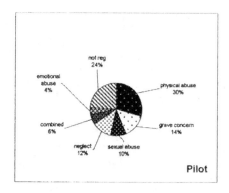

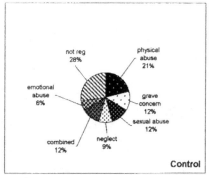

As can be seen from Table 4.7 there was no apparent difference between the areas either across time, or by area, in the initial foci of concern, the proportion of those registered or the categories of registration used. At referral the main focus of concern in both pilot and control areas is physical abuse, comprising over a third of all referrals. Grave concern accounts for the next chunk (23%), followed by sexual abuse, comprising just under a quarter of all referrals, and lastly neglect (10%). The remainder constitute emotional abuse, the 'combined' category (neglect and physical abuse, neglect and sexual abuse) and physical and sexual abuse. These findings are broadly comparable with Thoburn et al.'s (1995) with the exception of sexual abuse, which is more frequently categorised in the authorities she studied (27%). One possible explanation for this difference is that grave concern was more widely used in my study at this pre-conference stage - ie. before the allegation had been investigated. Although there was some evidence for this possibility in the data analysed in the early days of the research this pattern did not continue. In addition, some of the combined category included sexual abuse cases.

At the point of registration just over a quarter of cases in both the pilot and control areas are not registered. This rate is low compared with that determined by both Farmer and Owen (39%) and Thoburn (35%). However, the categories of registration recorded in my study do compare with the national averages for that year (Children Act Report, 1992) The registrations for neglect, emotional abuse and combined have increased slightly from the first stage, whereas in all other categories the rate has decreased. Physical abuse, sexual abuse and grave concern receive less registrations proportionate to the higher rate at the initial stage. The effect of the phasing out of grave concern as a category can not be determined. However, there was a clear trend for the professionals to be more likely to register cases of neglect and emotional abuse than physical and sexual abuse. Gibbons et al. (1995) offer an explanation for this which seems plausible. Her research demonstrates that, because the risk assessment of neglect is particularly difficult, the cases that reach the conference stage are severe and therefore more likely to be registered. In contrast, some physical injuries turn out to be a one off incident; and sexual abuse is notoriously difficult to prove.

Turning to the potential impact of the parents' presence, there is no difference between the registrations in the pilot and control areas and therefore no evidence that the presence of the parents has any impact on the decisions made. This is surprising in view of Farmer and Owen's (1995) suggestion that decisions not to register were heavily influenced by the way people responded to the investigation and what they looked like.

There was no evidence for this in my findings. Cross tabulations revealed that there were some differences between children who were registered and those who were not. Children were more likely to be registered if they were female, aged under five, in cases of neglect, and where the family were already known to the social services department and previous abuse had been confirmed. 60% of the families were known to social services in this authority at the time of the conference and some to other authorities. Farmer and Owen (1995) drew similar conclusions, but added severity, which was not a variable taken into account in my study. The pilot and control areas did not differ in the proportion of conferences with these kinds of children, so these variables are not relevant to the lack of differences between the areas.

*Recommendations*

In addition to making decisions about registration, the conference *makes recommendations* for the child protection plan for those children who are registered. These include whether further inter-agency meetings should be held, whether statutory action should be taken, who the keyworker will be and what resources should be made available. Table 4.8 lists the recommendations of the conference by area.

**Table 4.8    Recommendations of Conference by Pilot and Control, 83 conferences, 1.5.91-30.6.92**

| Recommendations | Pilot | | Control | | Total | |
|---|---|---|---|---|---|---|
| | No. | % | No. | % | No. | % |
| Strategy Meeting | 30 | 60 | 22 | 67 | 52 | 63 |
| Statutory Action | 13 | 26 | 14 | 42 | 27 | 32 |
| Keyworker | 39 | 78 | 24 | 73 | 63 | 75 |
| Resources | 18 | 36 | 11 | 33 | 29 | 35 |
| Other | 5 | 4 | 13 | 17 | 9 | 14 |

In this authority the recommendations of the conference in relation to the child protection plan were intended to be only skeletal. Other studies have also found that the average time spent on the child protection plan was minimal. In Farmer and Owen's (1995) study, it was nine minutes. In this authority the strategy meeting, comprising the key professionals involved in the ongoing work and the parents, was seen as being the appropriate place for the detailed child protection plan. Strategy meetings were set up in 62% of all cases. Not surprisingly the most frequent recommendation - in 75% of all conferences - was to nominate a keyworker, invariably a social worker. Farmer and Owen (1995) also found that the main intervention recommended in registered cases was social work contact, and that for a number of families no new resources were suggested.

These findings lend weight to the view that child protection procedures are preoccupied with protection, rather than welfare. This suggestion is further supported by the figure of 35% for resource allocation which seems remarkably low relative to the massive welfare needs of a number of these families, over half of whom were on income support. The low rate of resource allocation could be seen as reflecting a number of differing factors, such as the scarcity of available resources, the perceptions by the professionals of what the families need, as well as what the families are prepared to accept. In a few cases, for example, families refused ongoing social work involvement - even when the child had been registered. Different perceptions of need may be a factor affecting resource allocation. Although the evidence for this hypothesis is not forthcoming from this data, it was suggested by the interviews with the parents and will be discussed further in Chapter 7.

Statutory action was recommended in 32% of all the cases. Interestingly, this recommendation is the only one which throws up a difference between the pilot and control areas in the recommendations made. Statutory action was more likely to be recommended in the control area. Since, as is known from the parents' interviews, the possibility of statutory action was their greatest fear, it seems reasonable to speculate that the reduced rate in the pilot area may be influenced by the parents presence. Their presence could have had an inhibiting effect, making it more difficult for the professionals to recommend. Conversely, it could have had the positive effect of increasing the professionals' confidence following the parents' presentation in the conference. This suggestion is supported by the observations of Farmer and Owen (1995) on the reasons for not registering children.

*Children*

A detailed profile of the children conferenced was collected, containing basic information about age, sex, ethnic origin and family composition and characteristics, as well as who the child lived with at the time of the conference. Table 4.9 provides this profile.

**Table 4.9a   Profile of First Child: Age and Gender**

| Age and Sex | Pilot | | Control | | Total | |
|---|---|---|---|---|---|---|
| | No. | % | No. | % | No. | % |
| **Age** | | | | | | |
| unborn | 2 | 4 | 2 | 7 | 4 | 5 |
| 1 - 4 | 20 | 45 | 8 | 29 | 28 | 38 |
| 5 - 9 | 10 | 18 | 5 | 16 | 15 | 20 |
| 10-15 | 13 | 29 | 13 | 46 | 26 | 36 |
| not known | 5 | - | 5 | - | 10 | - |
| **Sex** | | | | | | |
| female | 26 | 52 | 22 | 67 | 48 | 58 |
| male | 20 | 40 | 7 | 21 | 27 | 32 |
| unborn | 4 | 8 | 4 | 12 | 8 | 10 |

**Table 4.9b   Profile of First Child: Number of Siblings (numbers and percentages)**

| Number of Siblings | Pilot | | Control | | Total | |
|---|---|---|---|---|---|---|
| | No. | % | No. | % | No. | % |
| 0 | 11 | 26 | 7 | 24 | 18 | 25 |
| 1 | 12 | 28 | 9 | 31 | 21 | 29 |
| 2 - 4 | 19 | 44 | 12 | 41 | 31 | 43 |
| 5+ | 1 | 2 | 1 | 3 | 2 | 3 |

## 1 Age and gender

Over half of all the children conferenced were female. Nearly half of the children (43%) were aged 4 and under. There were some differences between the pilot and control areas in relation to age, 45% of children in the pilot group were aged under 4, compared to only 29% in the control group. The reverse was the case for 10-15 year olds where there were 48% in the control group and 28% in the pilot area. However, these findings are not statistically significant and could be explained by chance. The percentages for age and gender are in line with other areas in the authority studied and the national average. The numbers of unborn children, children conferenced because of proven harm to other children, or because, for example, the mother was on hard drugs was small and the same for both areas.

## 2 Number of siblings

> There was an old woman who lived in a shoe,
> She had so many children she didn't know what to do,
> She gave them some broth without any bread,
> She whipped them all soundly and put them to bed.
> Gammar Gurton's Garland, 1784.

Families containing two or more siblings living in the household featured, proportionately, more highly in equivalent rates in both pilot and control groups. This finding is, again, in common with other studies of families subject to child protection procedures (Miller and Fisher, 1992), where rates of abuse are higher where there are two or more siblings in the family. The representation of children with one or no siblings was similar, at approximately 25% for both areas. Research has suggested that risks to siblings are known to be underplayed (Farmer and Owen, and Miller et al.), and it is of interest to note the high number of children in this study (one hundred) living in households subject to a child protection investigation. Further research on these children is called for.

## 3 Ethnic origin of families

The percentage of families whose ethnic origin was not European was small - fifteen (18%) - comprising three Pakistani families, one Chinese family, five African-Caribbean and six of mixed race. However, the proportion of children from ethnic groups is higher than the 9% for the population of children under aged eighteen in England and Wales. As in Thoburn et al.'s (1995) study, children of mixed race parentage seem to be particularly over represented (1% for the population as a whole.) Thirteen of these families were from the pilot area, a finding likely to reflect the fact that the areas served by these teams were part of a deprived inner-city area. There were, however, particular problems for the professionals in a number of the conferences involving these families and the reasons are analysed and discussed in Chapter 6 (see Bell, 1996).

**Table 4.9c  Profile of First Child: Ethnic Origin of Families**

| Ethnic Origin | Pilot | | Control | | Total | |
|---|---|---|---|---|---|---|
| | No. | % | No. | % | No. | % |
| Pakistani | 2 | 4 | 1 | 3 | 3 | 4 |
| Chinese | 1 | 2 | - | - | 1 | 1 |
| Caribbean | 4 | 8 | 1 | 3 | 5 | 6 |
| Mixed Race | 6 | 12 | - | - | 6 | 7 |

*4  Family characteristics*

"Messages from the Research" pulls together the research findings on the characteristics of families where children are maltreated;

> Gibbons and colleagues found that over a third were headed by a lone parent and in only 30% of cases were both natural parents resident. Nearly three fifths lacked a wage earner and over one half were dependent on income support. Domestic violence and mental illness within the family also featured prominently and, in Thoburn's study, nearly a quarter had suffered an accident or serious ill health during the previous year. One in seven parents under suspicion were known to have been abused themselves as children. Most (65%) children had previously been known to social services and a previous investigation had been undertaken in almost half of the cases (p.25).

In my study the most frequently recurring associated features were families containing adults with a history of violence (44%), with a criminal record (42%), including previous abuse of others (47%), families on Income Support (58%), and families where a parent was mentally ill (17%).

Farmer and Owen (1995) found evidence of mental illness in the mother increased the chances of children entering care or being accommodated as it was viewed as substantially increasing the risks to the child The presence of a Schedule 1 Offender in the household - 21% of cases - requires the removal of the child. However, in some of the cases in my study (10%) the offender had left, but was visiting; or the mother was a prostitute whom sex offenders may well have been visiting.

**Table 4.9d   Profile of First Child: Family Composition and Characteristics (numbers and percentages)**

| Family Composition: Who child lives with | Pilot No. | % | Control No. | % | Total No. | % |
|---|---|---|---|---|---|---|
| Mother only | 8 | 16 | 10 | 30 | 18 | 22 |
| Father only | 2 | 4 | 0 | 0 | 2 | 2 |
| Stepfather/cohab'ee | 2 | 4 | 1 | 3 | 3 | 4 |
| Mother and father | 16 | 32 | 11 | 33 | 27 | 32 |
| Other family combination | 17 | 34 | 7 | 21 | 24 | 29 |
| Foster/residential | - | - | 1 | 3 | 1 | 1 |
| Other | 5 | 10 | 3 | 9 | 8 | 10 |

| Family Characteristics | | | | | | |
|---|---|---|---|---|---|---|
| Psychiatric illness | 7 | 15 | 7 | 22 | 14 | 17 |
| Learning difficulty | 8 | 17 | 10 | 31 | 18 | 23 |
| History of violence | 26 | 55 | 9 | 8 | 35 | 44 |
| Criminal record | 23 | 51 | 9 | 28 | 32 | 42 |
| Drug abuse | 7 | 15 | 4 | 13 | 11 | 14 |
| Schedule 1 Officer | 12 | 25 | 5 | 16 | 17 | 21 |
| Previous abuse of others | 20 | 43 | 17 | 53 | 37 | 47 |
| On IS | 32 | 70 | 13 | 41 | 45 | 48 |
| Number of cases | 50 | 100 | 33 | 100 | 83 | 100 |

The family composition of the children conferenced has already been discussed, particularly noting the high percentage of children living with mother alone. The family composition of the children in Thoburn et al.'s (1995) study was similar. There were notable differences between the pilot and control areas in the family characteristics of these two groups of children. This is likely to be a reflection of the social demographic factors of the areas served. More families with a history of violence and a criminal record and on Income Support featured in the pilot than the control areas.

To recap, there were few significant differences in the *kinds of children and families* involved in conferences in the pilot and control areas. There was little difference in the gender or family composition of the children conferenced in the pilot and control areas, and the percentages for age and gender were in line with other areas in the city and the national average. There were, however, some differences in the family characteristics of the children from the pilot areas; there was more likely to be a history of violence, a higher proportion of the families were non-european in ethnic origin and a slightly higher proportion were on income support. These differences probably reflected differences in the social composition of the areas rather than resulting from the new policy.

## Summary of main findings

*The conferences*

*Numbers, size and length*
There was no evidence that parental involvement in itself reduced the numbers of conferences held. The involvement of parents increased the average number of attenders from eight to ten. Conferences with parents in attendance were therefore bigger, sometimes involving up to fourteen people. Also, they lasted, on average, twenty nine minutes longer than those without, sometimes lasting between two and three hours.

*Attendance*
There were no differences in the average number or the overall percentages of professionals attending in the pilot and control areas, or in the overall percentage of those invited who chose to attend. Notably, the Doctors were the least likely to attend. Parents attended 72% of the conferences to which they were invited. Mothers were more likely to be invited and to attend than fathers. In over one third of the conferences the mother attended alone. Members of the extended family were rarely invited.

*The children*
There was little difference in the age, gender or family composition of the children conferenced in the pilot and control areas. There were some differences in the family characteristics of the children from the pilot teams, reflecting the inner-city area served by two of the teams. A higher proportion of the children in the pilot areas came from families whose ethnic origin was non-European; and a slightly higher proportion of the families in the pilot area were on Income Support. These differences were not, however, statistically significant.

*Referrals*
There were no significant differences between the pilot and control groups in the sources of referral either at the initial stage when the allegation was first received, or at the later stage when a conference was formally requested. The largest group initiating the first concern were the children and their families, whereas formal referrals to social services were most frequently made by the professionals involved.

*Registration outcomes*
There was no difference between the pilot and control groups in the numbers of children registered, and little difference between the pilot and control groups as to the type of abuse identified, either at the initial stage of expressed concern or in the categories of registration. 26% of the children conferenced were not registered. Physical abuse was the category most frequently used, followed by grave concern, sexual abuse and neglect. The involvement of parents therefore did not effect registration rates or categories.

In summary the professional concerns about the impact on referral, attendance and registration were not justified but there were resource implications.

**Discussion**

On the evidence of the monitoring study initial fears over the policy of inviting parents to case conferences proved largely unjustified. Some conferences were particularly difficult (Bell, 1996) and the reasons for this are analysed in detail in Chapter 6. The number of conferences did indeed drop but this apparently had nothing to do with the policy itself. Evidence that the source of referrals and the kinds of referrals were unaffected was slightly less convincing since it was possible that the research design did not allow for demographic differences between the pilot and control areas. Nevertheless the evidence did not suggest that the introduction of the policy led to different sources of referral, types of case or rates of professional attendance at the conference - consequences which would have suggested that some professionals were hanging back from involvement in the conferences because of the possibility of awkward confrontations with their clients.

Although parental participation did not apparently effect professional behaviour in the way that had been feared, there were other consequences. An effect of the length of the conferences was that professionals sometimes had to leave before the registration decision. Others, such as General Practitioners (see Stevenson, 1995), may have avoided the conference altogether because of the time implications. Another undesirable consequence is the difficulty for all the participants in concentrating for long periods of time, with the risk that important information gets lost. The more radical protagonists of parents rights, such as the Family Rights Group (Atherton, 1992) have campaigned for the conferences to be held at times to suit parents, for example in the evenings. It is likely that this would increase the number of professionals who do not attend.

The monitoring study demonstrated the range of professionals in attendance. Other parts of the study suggested that, where parents are present, the purpose of their attendance needs to be explicit and clear. Observations suggested that it was not always clear why some professionals were present and raised the question whether some were occasionally there more to cover the backs of their departments than to contribute to the discussion. Parents also questioned the numbers present, and the relevance of some of them whom they did not know, such as nurse managers. Further issues were raised with regard to the roles of interpreters, advocates, friends and community leaders. Interpreters and community leaders, for example, must share the professional ethics - especially in respect of confidentiality - yet it was not clear how this could be ensured, or what their lines of management and accountability were. Farmer and Owen (1995) found that a difficulty in their study was that no-one could be quite sure that complex meanings were being accurately relayed. They point out that  "In some Asian languages the words necessary for the description of sexual abuse do not exist, or are so rarely used that a balance has to be maintained between politeness and clarity" (p.114). Observation demonstrated that friends and advocates did indeed provide support but it was unclear who carried responsibility for putting boundaries round the advocacy role. In one conference, for example, of a girl who had been sexually abused, the friend's son had been a regular babysitter and one of the few males known to have access to the girl.

A major difficulty highlighted by this part of the study had to do with resources. Conferences which parents attended were on average longer and required costly back up services. The other research referred to has also demonstrated the importance of providing back up services for the conference. For example, since it is not appropriate for parents and professionals to share the same waiting facilities separate reception areas have to be provided. When this research was conducted parents were asked to leave the conference at the decision making stage and asked to return at the end to hear the decision. Sound proofed facilities were needed for them to go to, with the minimum of disruption to the conference. Other resources were needed for child care, for printing information and letters in languages other than English, and for training administrative staff to take minutes.

Discussion of resources goes beyond what is necessary for effectively managing conferences to the provision available to meet the welfare needs of the children and families identified in the conference. The monitoring study has illustrated that some vulnerable children are filtered into the child protection system who are found to be not at risk and that the focus of concern in this 'crucible of the system' is not on the identification of need, but on the assessment of risk. Many of the research studies cited question the appropriateness of the relentless concentration on risk which has been shown to have two effects. Firstly, the concentration on risk demonstrated here meant that little effort was devoted to considering in detail the recommendations for future interventions. The effects are circular; information is presented in terms of risk, rather than need, and intervention is therefore focused on risk, rather than need. The high rate of recommendation for a keyworker, a primary function of which is to monitor, compared to the low rate for services, can be seen as a reflection of the preoccupation with risk assessment over provision for the child's welfare needs.

In addition to the low rate of recommendations for service provision, another aspect of the preoccupation with risk over need is the lack of time and attention accorded to the child protection plan in the conference. Given the complexity of the conference task and process, and the length of time taken for decisions to be made, it seems understandable and sensible on the face of it for the more detailed child protection plan to be made at a future meeting. However, the parents' presence does create a golden opportunity for this plan to be discussed at a critical time, as the interviews with the parents reported upon later will show. Crisis theory suggests strongly that interventions are most effective at critical turning points in a families career (Caplan, 1964, O'Hagan, 1986), and here is one of them. Support for this theoretical position comes from Farmer and Owen's (1995) finding that there was a close relationship between the adequacy of the plan made in the conference and the child's subsequent protection - especially in cases not already known to social services departments.

The second effect of the relentless concentration on risk that emerged from this and the other research studies cited is to refocus attention on the purposes, roles and powers of the conference. As discussed in the previous chapter, the findings reported here lend weight to the observation that the conference is presented with an ambiguous task. The research has shown that the conference time is spent on sharing information with a view to making a judgment about what has happened in order to make a sensible decision about registration. Leaving aside the moral dimensions of risk assessment (Thorpe, 1994; Wattam, 1992; Parton, 1996), it seems that the conference is, effectively, exercising a judicial function. The presence of the local authority solicitors and the absence of the parents' legal representatives reinforces this possibility.

As previously suggested, the attendance of the local authority solicitor in the majority of conferences focuses concern on issues of justice and equality. The local authority's solicitor (and the police) had the right to ask questions in the conference, and to use the information gleaned there to prepare their case - and they did. Parents also had the right to ask questions, or to refuse to answer - and they did. However, following the debacle of The Cleveland Enquiry they could not have their solicitors present. Being there to prove their capacity as parents, and to make a good impression they were doubly disadvantaged - hardly an equal relationship, or basis for justice.

This discussion raises an issue which will be further pursued concerning the difficulty of combining a procedure designed to empower parents with a procedure designed to protect the child. The evidence of the monitoring study suggested that the introduction of parents did not change the likelihood that children were registered as at risk. It is possible, of course, that different kinds of child were registered under the new procedures but this seems a more complicated hypothesis and no evidence was suggested here for it. So there arises the question of whether the parents were truly empowered by a process on whose outcome their attendance appears to have had little impact.

Another crucial issue regarding the empowerment of parents that is raised by the monitoring study arises from the data concerning which family members get invited and who attends. The Government has recognised the need to give further guidance on this matter by their publication "The Challenge of Partnership", 1995. This guidance attempts to address the problems of the definition of a parent, as well as reinforcing the requirement to include all family members. The section 2.16, "Who do we mean by Families" lists family members who should be included. This includes people who do not have 'parental responsibility', such as grandparents, previous partners of parents, close friends, to be decided in consultation with parents and children.

What is not addressed by guidance is that in many conferences the mother attends alone. Theoretically, this raises issues around gender which are culturally and socially based. Evidence for the unequal burdens on mothers was also uncovered by Farmer and Owen's study. They found that where mothers were regarded as responsible for the abuse, the child's name was more likely to be placed on the register than when the male carer was blamed. But the problems are also practical. What can be done to relieve mothers of this burden; and how can the fathers' views be represented if he is not present? Social workers struggle with this dilemma as evidence drawn from other parts of the study will show. Again, there are resource implications for social work practice. To do the necessary work with mothers, fathers and grandparents before the conference, social workers need training, protected time, quality supervision and administrative back up. To provide the appropriate welfare help afterwards they need a massive injection of resources - from housing and health services to skilful family and child centred therapy.

So the final question raised by this part of the study is whether this policy is not something of a halfway house. Useful in itself it requires to be implemented in a way which does not greedily consume professional resources. Of itself it does not - and perhaps should not - make a readily apparent difference to the pattern of decisions. And so questions arise over whether the policy should be either applied in a more radical way - perhaps on the New Zealand model - or whether at the least it requires a greater injection of resources designed to assist rather than assess.

# 5 The Professionals: their attitudes and training

I am a part of all that I have met
... that which we are, we are.
                    Ulysses, Tennyson.

In his book 'Working Together in Child Protection' (1995), Murphy refers to the work of Peace (1991) who compares multi-disciplinary work to a long filament of plaited string. Where the agencies work well the strands will be closely woven and strong; where they are not the strands will be loosely connected and the filament weak. The importance of effective inter-agency work has been the subject of a number of the child abuse enquiries (Colwell, 1974; Beckford, 1985; Carlile, 1987; Cleveland, 1988), which formed a major plank of The Children Act 1989, and takes up the main part of the two Working Togethers (1988 and 1991). The attitude of professionals to working together in the child protection arena is thus a critical area for scrutiny.

As previously stated, government guidance on the centrality of inter-agency work in the initial conference has been unequivocal.

The conference symbolises the interagency nature of assessment, treatment and the management of child protection.

(Working Together, 1991, 6.1)

Reference has also been made to the literature and research inter-agency work. Hallett and Birchall (1992) have described in detail how professionals bring different priorities to each case and it was suggested that this gives rise to confusion about roles and issues of power and status. Cleaver and Freeman (1995) observed the confusion caused to parents by the health visitors' preoccupation with the health of the children, the policeman's concern with law enforcement, and the social workers' less straightforward role of balancing the child's protection with the need to support the family. Dingwall's earlier work (1981) yielded helpful insights into the role of professionals in identifying and confirming child abuse. He found workers in purely health settings drew upon evidence from the child's clinical condition, and this was found to lead to under-identification of abuse. Social workers, in contrast, looked to the family's "moral environment", and drew upon judgments of normality. On this basis, Dingwall suggested, health visitors were likely to identify more cases than social workers confirmed.

Professionals, then, bring to the conferences preformed attitudes and dispositions that influence their judgments about the diagnosis and management of the case, as well as their relationship with their colleagues. In their search to understand the forces determining the perspectives that parents and professionals bring to the child protection arena, Cleaver and Freeman (1995) draw upon the ideas of social psychologists, such as Harre. Harre (1985) suggests that much behaviour is predictable. In choosing a course of action, he says, we are more likely to chose what worked before. Social interactions are thus, to a degree, routine and explicable within their historical and cultural context. So if a parent's experience of social workers was previously negative, they are likely to approach and frame new interactions with social workers in a negative way. Similarly, the way in which a social worker defines a parent/child interaction will be determined by a complex set of personal social constructs derived from culture and past experiences.

The idea that the meaning of events is varied by the way different versions are produced clearly also draws upon concepts derived from social construct theory (Foucault, 1977), and discourse analysis. Discourse analysts, such as Potter and Wetherell (1987), suggest that a description of an event serves two functions. It discredits other accounts while simultaneously justifying one's own. In considering attitudes this framework provides some beginning concepts for understanding what Cleaver and Freeman term an "operational perspective":

that collection of socially oriented perceptions which people hold, use and have the power to modify in order to make sense of their daily lives and help them cope with an abuse accusation (p. 68).

Attitudes, then, are organised, enduring, socially and emotionally constructed perspectives. The previous chapter identified some of the influences professional attitudes had on behaviour in the conference. It was suggested that the initial conference is a set piece - a critical point in the intervention, when operational perspectives are modified by different experiences and new information. Reference was made to crisis theory in relation to the parents' openness to change. This part of the research seeks to establish whether professional attitudes to the involvement of parents changed as a result of their experience at this critical time.

The first function of this part of the research was, therefore, to establish the attitudes of the professionals to parental involvement before it happened, and to determine the levels and quality of training and preparation accorded to the different professional groups. Secondly, the intention was to assess the ways in which attitudes changed as a result of experience, and to explore the factors affecting attitude change. Two dimensions were identified; attitudes across time, and by agency. It was also intended to chart the differences between the areas involving parents (pilot) and those not (control), although in the event this was not fruitful because the respondents attended conferences in both areas.

## Method

The attitude survey aimed to establish the attitudes of all the professionals present at all the conferences held in the six neighbourhood research teams at two different points in time, before parents were involved and after, by means of a postal questionnaire. The names of all the professionals who had attended were obtained from the minutes of the conferences. The questionnaire was then sent to all who had attended the thirty four child protection conferences in the six teams (four pilot and two control) in the six months before parents were invited (November-April, 1991). One year later the same questionnaire was sent to those who had attended at least one of the forty conferences in the same areas (December-May, 1992). By this time the four pilot teams had involved parents and training had taken place across the city. Differences between the pilot and control groups consequently became blurred and did not play an important part in the analysis.

The questionnaire was designed to enable attitudes to be determined in two ways. Firstly, respondents were asked to rate their agreement with a series of statements which reflected the most commonly debated arguments for and against parental involvement (see Brown and Water's, 1986). These were outlined in Chapter 3. Negative statements suggested that, for example, in the presence of parents the worker/client relationship would be damaged, the interests of the child become less central and the collection of evidence would be more difficult. Positive statements centred around the greater likelihood that parents would cooperate and that their presence would improve the quality of information shared.

The respondents were then asked a number of open ended questions designed to check consistency, and to provide opportunity for more detailed comments from personal experience. For example, they were asked their views on the advantages and disadvantages of parental participation, on the local procedures, and whether any parents should be excluded.   To enable other determinants of attitude to be taken into account, questions were also asked about experience of other meetings with parents present, involvement in policy planning, training and seniority.   The open ended questions were coded, and a quantitative analysis of the completed questionnaires was undertaken using SPSS. The quantitative analysis was informed by the qualitative material obtained from the open ended questions, by the researcher's systematic observation of 22 conferences with parents present, and participant observation of the authority's planning and training before and during implementation of the policy.

## Results

### The sample

#### Respondents by agency
Table 5.1 illustrates the respondents to both questionnaires by agency. The greatest number was from social services (37%), followed by health (24%), education (10%) and police (9%). The range of different workers from each agency making up the sample has been described in the previous chapter, when professional attendance at the conference was considered. It can be seen that the size of the different professional groups corresponds to the four layers identified by Hallett (1995) commensurate with their involvement with the primary task. The largest group, social services, includes the managers, the field workers and their team leaders, as well as residential and day care staff. Health respondents represent the second

largest group, including nine Doctors and fifty three nurses. The nurses comprise twenty four health visitors, fourteen school nurses, two community midwives and thirteen nursing managers or officers. Education (25) included primary, junior and secondary school class teachers, sometimes the year tutor or head teacher and Education Welfare Officers. The police respondents were mainly specialist child protection officers. 'Other' includes voluntary agencies, such as NSPCC, Probation, Guardians ad Litem and solicitors.

**Table 5.1  Number of respondents by agency**

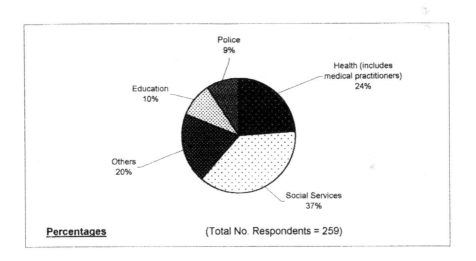

In total, two hundred and fifty nine replies were received from the range of statutory and voluntary agencies involved in seventy four conferences, representing a response rate of 61% overall. The response rate from the pilot areas was slightly higher, possibly reflecting the respondents' familiarity with the researcher from the training events.  Approximately two thirds of the social service employees and health professionals who were sent questionnaires responded. Teachers were the least likely to respond, their reason being lack of time. Other reasons given for not responding included that the worker had left or was sick. Police, although small in number, had a high rate of response.

*Respondents by time*

Table 5.2 demonstrates that three samples were produced:

**Table 5.2   Samples by agency and time**

| Respondents | Pre | | Post | | Matched | |
|---|---|---|---|---|---|---|
| | No. | % | No. | % | No. | % |
| Social Services | 49 | 34 | 48 | 40 | 10 | 40 |
| Health | 31 | 22 | 32 | 27 | 4 | 16 |
| Police | 12 | 9 | 12 | 10 | 3 | 12 |
| Education | 14 | 10 | 10 | 9 | 3 | 12 |
| Other | 35 | 25 | 16 | 14 | 5 | 20 |
| Total | 141 | 100 | 118 | 100 | 25 | 100 |

Pre\Post implementation of the policy

The three samples comprised: one of one hundred and forty one professionals who attended thirty-four conferences during the six months before parental involvement was implemented (pre- implementation); one of one hundred and eighteen who attended forty conferences after parental involvement had been implemented, including twenty eight with parents present (post- implementation); and a third, comprising the twenty five respondents who had been to conferences both before and after parental involvement (matched). The matched sample comprises workers mainly in senior or managerial positions with the most experience of conferences. The post sample differs from the pre sample in that the professionals by then had more experience of conferences generally, more had been involved in other meetings with parents and a higher percentage were trained.

*Training*

> 'Tis Education forms the common mind,
> Just as the twig is bent, the tree's inclined.
> Pope 1743, Moral Essays.

Education and training are not luxuries; it is essential that all members of staff working in child protection are properly trained for the jobs they are expected to do. Inter-agency training is essential if inter-agency procedures are to function satisfactorily.

(Working Together, 1991, 7.7)

Training in preparation for parental involvement was undertaken for the Area Child Protection Committee by the training section of the authority's social services department and provided on a multi-disciplinary basis. There were differences by agency and over time in the amount of training relevant to parental involvement received (see Table 3). Before implementation 41% of all the respondents were trained. As would be expected, more were trained in the pilot group at this stage than in the control group. Health professionals were the most likely to be trained (80%), and teachers the least (23%) At the post-implementation stage 62% of all professionals had been trained, the increase being mainly in social services. No difference was found with regard to training between the professionals who had and had not attended conferences with parents present, largely because by the time the second questionnaire was received training and preparation had been carried out on a city wide basis.

Respondents rated the training they had received as good, especially valuing the opportunity to share differing professional perceptions in an inter-agency forum. Training was regarded as providing an opportunity to relieve anxiety and to acquire the necessary knowledge about the legislative framework and local procedures. A principal social worker expressed this succinctly;

Training should include the rules of procedure, preparation of reports, what is and is not admissible at conferences, and how to protect a child who is making an allegation against parents who are attending a conference.

(Principal Social Worker)

Pre-implementation of the policy, only 39% of all the respondents had seen the authorities documentation, and only 26% been given an opportunity to discuss the issues. Post-implementation half of all the respondents had seen the documentation and a third discussed it. This emphasis in training on procedures is, therefore, not surprising.

Discussion of the role of the chair was also considered an important aspect of the training. In her research on chairing conferences, Lewis (1994) found that the chairperson was seen as critical in containing the anxiety of participants. This study also suggests that the participants expect the chairperson to manage difficult situations carefully and to contain the high level of anxiety generated. The fear of provoking violence, either during the conference or afterwards on home visits, was tangible and strategies for managing and defusing violence were high on the training agenda. Skills training was appreciated, particularly the opportunity to role play a difficult situation involving parents, such as "how to say nasties nicely". Role play as a method of learning was valued, providing opportunities to test out, for example, ways of presenting sensitive information about the abuse. From a senior nurse:

> Perhaps not all the full facts will emerge if workers have not had preparation on being used to sharing information with their client, and have tried this out.

**Table 5.3    Percentage trained by agency pre/post implementation of policy**

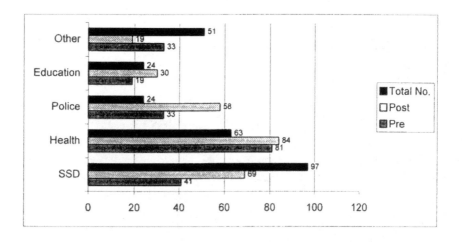

Table 5.4 illustrates the respondents' views on what the content and method of training should include. There were differences over time in what was

**Table 5.4 Respondents' views on what training should include**

| Training Content | Training Method |
| --- | --- |
| An information base:<br>    of the legal situation<br>    of Leeds procedure<br>    of the role of the chair | Formal input |
| Skills training - especially:<br>    assertiveness<br>    being open<br>    help in report writing<br>    presentation of self and material | Role play |
| Sensitivity awareness:<br>    awareness of how participants<br>    are feeling<br>    awareness of racial/religious issues<br>    awareness of use of language, jargon, etc. | Role play and<br>interagency<br>discussion |

highlighted, suggesting that levels of anxiety had been reduced following positive experiences. The sharp focus on skills training at the first stage was on the management of self: how to be assertive, how to be sensitive to cultural issues, how to use language and avoid jargon. By the second stage respondents were more interested in the management of particular issues, such as what to say when one parent had a secret from the other. An example was where a pregnancy had been terminated. There was a greater preoccupation with the special needs of participants who rarely attended conferences, such as teachers. Such respondents found it useful to share good practice guidelines with staff who had already been to conferences with parents present. The view of what was needed therefore changed over time, from wanting input on procedural issues and skills training, to a preoccupation at the second stage with the management of particular issues. There were also differences by agency in what was wanted and valued, reflecting the differing value and knowledge bases of the differing professional groups (see Hallett and Birchall, 1992). As was suggested at the beginning of this chapter with reference to Dingwall's work, social workers more commonly focused on the parents' feelings:

> thinking about how parents will feel at conferences, and preparing them before the meeting.
>
> (Social Worker)

The nurse respondents were more specific in their identification of training needs, citing help with report writing and training in presentation and communication skills, especially on how to be assertive and how to challenge parents in the conference without upsetting them. Nurses feared that parents would deny access to the child if they knew what the nurses really thought of them, particularly in matters of cleanliness (see Smart, 1992). Training was seen by the nurses as an opportunity to share experiences and to explore the emotional impact of the experience on themselves. Sometimes this was considerable. School nurses, in particular, and some health visitors raised in training events their feelings of isolation following a conference when no support was available to them in their agencies. The debriefing available to the small specialised group of police officers and to social workers through their supervision arrangements was not available to a number of the nurses, especially those working in non-social work agencies such as schools. The same was true for teachers, but generally Head teachers were involved or other support systems were provided within their service by designated staff. The main anxiety expressed by the teacher respondents was that their relationship with the child and the family would be damaged as a result of their involvement in the child protection work (see Webster, 1992). This belief could help to explain their poor response rate to the questionnaires and level of attendance at the training events. The reasons given by teachers in other studies are mainly logistic, for example lack of time and the difficulty in reorganising the timetable (see Hallett and Birchall, 1992). More sophisticated explanations for this behaviour were suggested in the previous chapter (see Wattam, 1992).

The police saw training as an opportunity to think together about how to manage sensitive information:

> How to be upfront with all the information throughout the investigation. And how to eliminate fear at the conference.
>
> (Detective Sergeant)

Their preoccupation with managing information is not surprising because of the primacy of their investigative role. The Police and Criminal

Evidence Act 1984 requires that a person committing a criminal offence should be warned that any statements they make about the offence may subsequently be used in evidence if trial ensues. However, information is invalidated as evidence if a caution has not been issued (see Kenward, 1992). Training events were used by the police to consider how these issues could be managed in an inter-agency forum and to consider the importance of planning and preparation beforehand, for example, in sharing confidential information with the chairperson.

In summary, the training needs of the respondents differed by agency, reflecting professional backgrounds and priorities. Training was valued, and was seen as an opportunity to share and modify perspectives. While inter-agency training does engender a more collaborative approach to working together in the conference, it seems likely that it also reduces inter-agency conflict and promotes consensus.

*Preparation*

In common with other areas, the Area Child Protection Committee in this authority produced a policy document outlining the policies and procedures to be used for involving parents in the conference (see Appendix 1). The consultation and planning process was ongoing throughout the year of the research, and a research objective was to ascertain the agencies' levels of involvement in the process. This information would reveal details about management and communication patterns within agencies which could further understanding of the professionals' attitudes to parental involvement (see Hallet and Birchall, 1992 and Thoburn et al., 1995).

Information about preparation covered four areas of activity. The questionnaire asked respondents if they had:

* *seen the relevant documents*, such as the policy and practice statement, the leaflets and letters for parents;
* *been given the opportunity to discuss them* in their own agency;
* *been consulted* about them;
* *been involved in planning* the implementation.

Again, there were differences over time, and by agency. The numbers involved on all four aspects increased over time. For example, by the time of the second questionnaire more of the respondents had seen the documentation (56%, over 39%), the biggest increase being in social services personnel. This finding compares with Thoburn et al.'s (1995). In her study 57% of the social workers were fully aware of agency policy, and team leaders had a key role in communicating it. It is of some concern to note from this study, however, that even at the second stage the numbers involved in planning (14%) and consultation (22%) remained very small, and only 34% had discussed it in their teams. This finding implies a remarkably bureaucratic approach to a sensitive issue closely affecting fieldworkers daily lives, and will be discussed later.

As with training, nurses were more likely than other professionals to have seen the documentation (62%), compared to the police (40%), and the social workers (38%), and they were more likely to have been consulted and involved in the planning. The situation was reversed when respondents were asked if they had been given the opportunity in their agency to discuss it: 50% of the social workers had discussed it at a meeting compared to 33% of the nurses, and 10% of the teachers. Clearly, there were particular problems for workers in the voluntary sector in accessing information. Since they make up a sizable proportion of the sample and make a particular contribution to the preventative aspects of child protection work (see Sanders and Thomas, 1997) this needs to be addressed. As the officer in charge of a mother and baby home put it:

> It would have been helpful to have received the policies behind the decisions and been a party to some discussions before the event.
>
> (Officer in Charge)

In summary, these findings suggest that agencies differ in the ways in which they disperse information. Social services appear to rely as much upon informal as formal means of communication, and over time information is communicated. Within the nursing profession, there was a pattern whereby nurse managers were commonly involved in planning and consultation, while their fieldworkers were less likely than social workers to have been given an opportunity to discuss the documents. There were particular problems for teachers who may only attend one conference in a career, and their preparation and training attempted to take account of that by providing designated staff within the school who would be available for consultation.

*Attitudes*

Overall, the findings on the attitudes of professionals to the involvement of parents confirm the largely positive findings from other studies mentioned (Thoburn, 1991, Thoburn et al., 1995). In this study the views expressed by an officer in charge nicely represent the common attitude to the strengths of the policy, as well as some reservations:

> Involving parents opens up professional relationships. The parents role as
> primary carers is acknowledged. It ensures information given is recorded and
> given objectively, and should lessen value judgments. However, it could be
> threatening for parents, and sometimes for staff - especially if violence has been
> threatened.
>
> (Officer in Charge, Children's Home)

Before implementation of the policy more than two thirds of all the respondents believed that parents would be more likely to cooperate (82%), that working relationships would improve (70%), that the quality of information shared would be improved (68%), and that parents would be encouraged to maintain contact with their children (68%). There was, nevertheless, a strong concern (72%) that discussion would be inhibited, and lesser concerns that conferences would become pseudo courts of law (46%) and that evidence would be more difficult to collect. There was also a shared view that parents should be excluded from some conferences, and that they should leave at the decision making stage. The issue of parents leaving at the decision making stage is controversial, and will be discussed in the chapter reporting the parents' interviews. Agencies differed in their attitudes at this stage, social services being the most positive of the four main agencies, and police and teachers the least.

By the time the second questionnaire was returned (post-implementation), there were differences over time and between agencies. Table 5.5 demonstrates that, overall, attitudes became more positive over time and by the end of the project 92% of all the respondents were in favour compared with 79% at the beginning.

> This is the first time I have been at a case conference with parents in attendance.
> I can only applaud the policy.
>
> (Midwife)

Social workers are the most positive on the first survey and there was less room for attitudes to change. Since they readily identify with the caring elements of the protective function, and form the 'core group' (Hallett, 1995), this generally positive attitude is to be expected. Health professionals are nearer in attitude to social workers on a number of points. The biggest attitude shift is demonstrated by the police. Writers have suggested that the professions of social work and police have moved closer together as a result of such initiatives as the recent joint interviewing procedures (Thomas, 1986; Parton, 1995). The evidence here of the way different professional groups have aligned in their attitudes supports this view.

**Table 5.5  Percentage in favour, overall, of parental involvement**

| In favour | | SSD | Health* | Police | Education | Other |
|---|---|---|---|---|---|---|
| Pre-implementation | | 93 | 80 | 66 | 78 | 62 |
| Post-implementation | | 92 | 93 | 92 | 100 | 87 |
| Total Replies | No.= | 95 | 62 | 24 | 24 | 47 |
| * includes Doctors | | | | | | |

Turning to the other professional groups, particularly those whose primary focus is not child protection, views generally became more positive.  An exception is the 'other' group, comprising solicitors, community workers and probation officers, who declared the impact on working relationships to be negative:

> Both parents and agencies may be intimidated from expressing opinions. Parents may say things that are prejudicial. Impossible to discuss future options openly.
>
> (Solicitor)

This data suggests that there is a relationship between the four layers identified by Hallett (1995) and attitude. Those professional groups closest to the core - to the task of child protection - are the most positive, at least in principle, to the involvement of parents. At the same time the analysis suggests that attitudes move closer together with experience. Social workers modify their principles in response to the difficulties of practice and the other professional groupings become more positive toward the principle.

Attitude shifts also vary by agency and over time on the specific issues. For example, the fear that conferences involving parents will become like pseudo courts of law is dramatically diminished, whereas the concern that discussion will be inhibited by the parents' presence continues to be held by 60% of the second sample.

> I feel other information may have been presented and considered regarding the child's home situation, especially mother's lack of protective skills, if parent wasn't there... Many views were muted.
>
> (Health Visitor)

Related to the fear that "people present may not 'dare' say something", was the conviction that in some conferences parents should leave for part of the discussion, and in others be excluded altogether. Categories mentioned included cases of sexual abuse where both partners were perpetrators, where the child had made allegations unknown to the parents and where parents may be disruptive. A sizable number of the health professionals (39%), teachers (40%) and the police (50%) continue to think some parents should leave at the decision-making stage.

> I feel members of such a mixed group need the opportunity to discuss sensitive areas together before the parents are involved, particularly where the situation is not clear cut.
>
> (General Practitioner)

The view that parents should be excluded from some conferences also continues to be held, and in the case of social services increases significantly from 37% to 65%. By the end of the project 59% believe that some parents should be excluded altogether. The reasons for this seem to connect with quite specific difficulties. These will be explored in the next chapter, which looks at the professionals' response to each case, rather than to the policy in general. It seems possible that the positive arguments in favour of parental involvement are similar to those relating to partnership identified at the beginning of this book. Social workers are, in principle, strongly supportive of the ideology, but find problems arise with the implementation.

The preoccupation of certain professional groups with particular issues remained. One third of the health respondents and three-quarters of the police maintained their concern about the sharing of confidential information, although this concern was not shared by social workers (12%). Nurses were also more likely than other professionals to find conferences with parents more stressful, partly because they were bigger and longer.

> Parental attendance lengthens the time taken and increases stress to

professionals already under pressure.

(Health Visitor)

Nurses remained uncertain how to handle hearsay or opinion in their reports, especially where this could not be substantiated. Some felt obliged to dilute negative statements and overstress the positives, which could seriously hinder the assessment of risk. And they shared the concern of other professionals that attention could shift onto the parents and away from the child.

> Parental attention can fudge the focus of the case conference by concentrating on fairness to the parents rather than risk to the child.

(Solicitor)

Some professionals expressed concern that parents' distress in the conference was communicated, thus affecting their concentration by arousing unhelpful feelings of helplessness, fear or sympathy.

> I found it difficult to separate off feelings of sympathy for the mother from risk to J. We eventually decided not to register on the basis that the mother was accepting help voluntarily and admitted the incident.

(Social Worker)

At the same time there was consensus on the benefits of parental involvement, especially regarding improvements in the quality of information shared, and in working relationships. Parents' contributions were seen as adding to the information available as well as correcting false information. In most cases it was felt the professionals were more focused and precise when presenting material in front of parents; "less unsubstantiated opinion and more facts".

Professionals from all the agencies also felt it was valuable for the parents to see an inter-agency perspective, and this made them feel less isolated:

> It certainly makes parents more aware of just how many agencies are involved with decision making. I'm sure very few know the school nurse is in any way involved.

(School Nurse)

Professionals clearly felt they worked more closely as a group in front of parents. As previously observed, the role of the chair in managing the group dynamic has been explored by Lewis (1994), and has also been found to be critical in dispersing conflict (Hallett, 1995). While defusing anxiety was seen as helpful by spreading responsibility for the decisions made - Farmer and Owen (1995) describe this as "a form of insurance cover...which many experienced as protective" - such a process may also result in conflict being minimised. It will be remembered that the move toward consensus was also seen as a product of inter-agency training events. Issues arising from this observation will be developed as the book progresses.

While the questionnaires elicited information about attitude trends, as suggested above the attitudes described here are not directly connected with the characteristics of the particular conferences attended. A study of this was undertaken and forms part of the analysis in the next chapter (see also Bell, 1996). It is important to note here that there is a divergence between the general attitudes recorded and the views of the professionals on a particular conference. The following comments from workers on one case illustrate this point:

> This case conference was too difficult for the professionals to hold with the parents present. Information was not forthcoming and had to be prized out of the professionals at various stages.
>
> (Consultant Paediatrician)

At the same conference, however, the social worker and the Health Visitor had very different observations:

> I had nothing controversial to say at this case conference but may have felt different in a more difficult situation.
>
> (Health Visitor)

> This was the first case conference I have attended with parents present. It was extremely positive to have them there. I did not feel restricted, and was able to speak honestly and openly while they were there.
>
> (Social Worker)

## Summary of main findings

*Professional attitudes over time*

Overall, attitudes became more positive over time. Ninety two per cent of all respondents who had experienced conferences involving parents were, on balance, in favour after the policy was implemented, compared to 79% before. Attitudes shifted markedly with regard to believing the quality of information shared improved and that the working relationship with parents was facilitated. By contrast, there were concerns that were maintained over time, particularly that professional discussion was inhibited and that the interests of the child were less central when parents were present. Professionals expressing those concerns believed that some parents should be excluded from certain conferences, which they specified, or required to leave at the decision making stage.

## Professional attitudes by agency

There were differences by agency before and after the implementation of the policy. Attitudes beforehand appeared to reflect a world view derived from the agencies focus on the child protection task. Workers from Social Services had a beginning optimism which is maintained over time; health occupied the middle ground; whereas workers from education and the police were initially more negative. The more negative respondents were, however, more likely to become positive as a result of their experience.

Attitudes on some issues reflect an agency orientation. Health (32%) and police (75%) maintained their concern regarding the sharing of confidential information; but it was not shared by workers from social services (12%). There was an increase in the number of social workers who thought, by the end, that some parents should be excluded from certain conferences. This was against the trend of all other agencies.

## Excluding parents from some conferences

Respondents thought some parents should be excluded from some conferences. These were cases of sexual abuse where one or both partners were the perpetrators; where the child had made an allegation not known to the parents; where certain information had not been revealed to them, or one of them in the case of separated parents; where parents may be disruptive; and where there may be repercussions on the child.

In summary the findings are basically positive. Professionals approved of involving parents and attitudes improved over time. Nevertheless there were abiding concerns over the degree to which the interests of the child remained central and regarding the need to exclude some parents. Moreover there were large differences between agencies in attitude, emphasising perhaps the need for joint training.

*Training*

*Amount*
There were differences by agency and over time in the amount of training received relevant to parental involvement. Before implementation of the policy 41% were trained, including 81% of all health professionals. Education professionals were the least likely to be trained. By the end of the project 62% had received training, the proportion of social service department workers having increased to 69%. However, only 30% from education had received training.

*Rating*
Respondents valued inter-agency training and rated what they had received as good. There were differences by agency in what the professionals valued in training events. Police were preoccupied with managing information, nurses with report writing, and social workers with the feelings of the parents. Their view of what they needed changed over time, from wanting input on the legal status and procedures and sensitivity awareness, to a preoccupation with the management of particular issues, such as the role of Local Authority solicitors, or the particular needs of professionals, such as teachers, who attended only rarely.

*Preparation*
There were differences over time and by agency in the preparation of the professionals for parental involvement, suggesting that the agencies differed in their methods of dispersing information and their involvement of fieldworkers in planning and consultation. Social workers were more likely to have had the opportunity to discuss the issues in their teams, whereas more nurses had seen the relevant documentation. There were particular problems in both the preparation and support of professionals outside the 'core group', such as teachers and school nurses.

## Discussion

The initial child protection conference is a crucial element in the protection of children at risk. The way in which the involvement of parents in this meeting is prepared for, managed and experienced by the professionals is therefore critical if the dual objectives of protecting the child and building a partnership with parents are to be achieved. This study demonstrates that the four main agencies - social services, health, education and the police -

are generally in favour of parental involvement and they become more positive as a result of their experience. Health professionals, and nurses in particular, are closest in their attitudes to social workers, occupying the middle ground between them and the police and teachers. While health continue to share with the police a specific concern about confidentiality, their anxiety that discussion will be inhibited, and that the interests of the child will become less central are shared with all other groups. The professionals suggested, further, that there were particular cases and situations where consideration of the child's protection was made more difficult by the parents' presence and this is explored in a later chapter.

The interagency consensus on the *advantages and drawbacks of involving parents* is important. This part of the research has suggested that both experience and inter-agency training bring perceptions closer together. Agreement on the benefits is likely to engender a shared commitment to the task, a factor known to contribute to good inter-agency relationships. Hallett and Stevenson (1980) have drawn attention to the difficulties arising in work where professionals with no common background in training or agency structure have to find ways of communicating in a conference "in an hour or two, without the kind of shorthand that is used by those who share a knowledge base or frame of reference". A shared commitment to the ideology of working in partnership with parents does provide a common language and value base, as well as an objective that is agreed by all the agencies and supported by the legislative framework of the Children Act 1989. It is significant, therefore, that one of the benefits professionals mentioned was that they felt less isolated as a result of being seen by the parents as a member of a working group.

Of equal importance is an acceptance that there can be drawbacks. Pressure to underplay the professional anxieties revealed here comes from a number of sources - the polemical nature of some of the literature, the emphasis in the research studies on the positives, and the understandable need of the agencies to present a united front. As previously observed, the need for all the agencies to demonstrate a commitment to collaboration and coordination came not just from Working Together. It was a response to the high level of criticism in a number of child abuse enquiries on poor interagency coordination and a reflection of the increased importance that the initial child protection conference had taken in the system. Involving parents heightened anxieties about interagency conflict, as it was felt that risk to the child might increase if parents observed chinks in the armour. The attitude survey illustrated the anxiety of the professionals on this point.

Parents will see that decisions are joint.

(Social Worker)

The meeting could end up as a battle ground if the professionals don't agree.

(Education Welfare Officer)

The possibility of parents seeing hostilities of the agencies could increase risk to the child.

(Detective Sergeant)

One consequence of the strong emphasis on working together is the push toward consensus, a direction that has caused concern (Hallett and Birchall, 1992, Stevenson, 1995, Farmer and Owen, 1995). Hallett found a striking absence of dissent and conflict between professions (1993), as did Farmer and Owen (1995). They wrote; "One important aspect of the conference was that it helped to cement relationships between agencies. Little overt disagreement was expressed about risks or registration, and there was a strong prohibition against any criticism of professional performance. As a result, some important dissenting information was not utilised, and deficiencies in the current handling of ongoing cases were occasionally glossed over" (p.101). Support for this position is provided by this research.

A further concern in relation to the push for consensus is discussed by Hallett and Birchall (1992) in their consideration of the work of Weiss (1981) and Steele (1976). These writers warned of the danger that communication and clear information sharing could become an end in itself. The risk that the conference becomes preoccupied with process and neglects outcomes was discussed in the preceding chapter in relation to the lack of attention paid to the child protection plan. It will also be pursued in more detail in the chapter reporting the parents' interviews. Murphy (1995) has suggested that a focus on procedures masks interprofessional problems, and risks marginalising the needs of the child. The emphasis on procedures that emerged from the findings on training provides further evidence in this debate.

The attitude study provides an original contribution to knowledge about *the training needs* of the different agencies. In Thoburn et al.'s (1995) research social work managers were committed to the idea of further training and believed resources were available to do it, although no information is forthcoming on the content or value of the training received. In this study, the value of inter-agency training, and the role of the Area Child Protection Committee in supporting that, was emphasised by all the agencies. The study also illustrated that training needs change over time, with the need for cognitive information and the opportunity to share anxieties shifting to a preoccupation with particular issues.

In addition to the information on content, the views on methods of learning highlight the different training orientations that the agencies bring with them. Nurses, for example, valued experiential methods of learning and were less used to this technique than the social workers. Nurses also most valued the skills training, especially in being assertive. They needed help in owning their expertise and in presenting it confidently in front of parents who might be hostile, upset or in disagreement with their definition of the situation as abusive. Tattersall (1992) has drawn attention to the impact on communication of power relations between the professionals involved. Because Doctors and some other professionals round the table are perceived to have a higher professional status than nurses and health visitors it can be difficult for the latter to speak and be heard. Nurse training, in particular, should therefore include teaching on how to communicate assertively. The issue of power is raised in all parts of the research, and will be a theme to be pursued.

The attitude study also drew attention to the impact of the *different organisational and management structures* on the professionals' experience of attending conferences, especially when anxiety was high. There was a clear connection between training needs and departmental organisational structures, since what was wanted in training - information about local procedures and the opportunity to discuss them - was not routinely provided within the agencies. Of course, discussion in an inter-agency forum will be beneficial, but should build on top of and not substitute for basic communication within agencies. A particular issue for management that was raised related to supervision and support structures. The essential part played by supervision in child protection work is now widely acknowledged (Sheldon, 1987; Jervis, 1988; Gibson et al., 1989; Working Together, 1998). Respondents in this study, particularly those not in the main core group, such as teachers and school nurses, vividly communicated their need for debriefing and support after the emotional experience of the conference. Supervision goes much further than merely providing support, however; it is often the only place professionals can be enabled to become aware of the feelings and inhibitions around the table, and of their source.

Drawing on Mattinson's work on the reflection process (1975), and Mattinson and Sinclair (1979), in their action research project tracing dynamic links between clients, practitioners and agencies, Woodhouse and Pengelly (1991) focus attention on the power of these unconscious processes in professional encounters;    "A case discussion group for example, can also be a reflecting medium whereby psychological features in one relationship system - the client - are unconsciously conducted, via the 'bridging' worker, into another adjacent one - the group". Professionals catapulted into a situation fraught with risk and anxiety, and working with children who have been seriously abused, require time, space and quality supervision before the conference to manage these feelings so that they do not get turned into inter-agency issues in the conference, thus affecting the assessment and consideration of risk. This is particularly true in cases of sexual abuse, which respondents mentioned as being among the most difficult cases, and included in their list of which parents should be excluded. Furnis (1991) draws attention to the particular problems raised by cases of sexual abuse: "The disclosure of child sexual abuse often leads to a crisis in the professional network which can be greater and sometimes more complex and confusing than the family crisis" (p.16). The effect of the mirroring process on the professionals' judgments will be returned to in the discussion on difficult conferences (see Bell, 1996).

Agencies differ in the ways in which they provide *support and supervision* for their members. In their work on dangerous families, Dale et al. (1986) drew attention to the importance of team working; "Teams need to allocate time to look after themselves. The teams need to meet the individual emotional needs of its members is of crucial importance" (p.208). This research suggests that the relationship between supervision and management in the agencies represented is most comfortably held in the Social Services Department. This is not to say that all the fieldworkers were happy with the quality and amount of supervision they received, as the commentary on the interviews with the social workers will later show. But the recognition and structures were in place. The difficulties referred to by social workers were not structural. The monitoring study suggested they related more to lack of resources, such as administrative back up, adequate time and space for supervision, and facilities to offer to families. The police, also, worked closely as a specialist team and did not express lack of agency support.

The findings show that, in contrast, the nurses were less likely than workers from the other professional groups to have had these opportunities within their own agency structure. Lyth-Menzies (1960) has suggested that nurses have traditionally organised themselves so that feelings do not interfere with the successful completion of practical tasks. This research suggests that the management structure of the nursing profession served them well in the consultation and planning process in which their senior members were involved, but did not so adequately meet the emotional needs of the fieldworkers. Nurses said that they needed the opportunity to prepare themselves for parental involvement by discussing their apprehensions beforehand, and that they needed support and debriefing afterwards.

Moreover, evidence from the parents interviews suggests that the attendance at the conference of managers as supervisors has implications for all the conference attenders (see Bell, 1996). While some nurses may experience their managers' presence as supportive, others perceive it as a threat to their professional autonomy and feel constrained and deskilled by it. This finding supports the work of Parkinson (1992), who found in studying the supervision of community nurses in child protection in Tower Hamlets,

> that the managerial and professional elements of the supervision function can be contradictory in that staff will not necessarily want to reveal their innermost anxieties to their line manager who has a personnel function in respect of them. And yet they actually need to share and explore such concerns if they are able to develop both personally and professionally.

The other agencies also had line managers present, but their roles were different. In the case of social services, for example, the team leader may also have had contact with the family, and the principals were present to offer expert guidance on the case, not as supervisors.

## Conclusion and practice points

This part of the research has suggested that the professionals involved continued to have some reservations about the advantages of parental involvement in all cases and strong and often complex emotions about the families who are attending and the abuse being investigated (Baglow 1990; Dale, 1986; Finklehor, 1985). Woodhouse and Pengelly (1991) have suggested that these powerful feelings may be carried into the conference in ways that are destructive to good decision-making. The attitude study has identified the nature of the hopes and fears the professionals carried in to the conference. The location of these feelings needs to be properly understood to prevent their interference with the child protection task. Some arose from general attitudes to policy and procedures, others were located in professional and inter-agency dynamics and others were more specifically rooted in emotions aroused by the particular family. In the following chapter these findings will be pursued further in relation to individual cases.

A number of practical suggestions emerged from the attitude survey. The role of Area Child Protection Committee in supporting interagency training, in ensuring efficient circulation of documentation to the agencies, and in reviewing and refining policy and practice is underlined. Matters of balance with regard to agency representation and priority are also raised. In their study of Area Child Protection Committees in Wales, Sanders and Thomas (1997) note that only one of the eight committees had a non social services chair. This reinforced social services responsibility for child protection and encouraged the 'skewing' of inter agency work toward investigation and registration. They suggest that the critical role of health and education, and the need to attend more directly to preventative aspects of the work could be reinforced by their fuller ownership of Area Child Protection Committees by, for example, rotating responsibility for chairing the committee.

Senior Child Protection Coordinators, in their role as chairmen, need to attend to issues raised by professionals in this study. For example, ensuring there are separate waiting facilities for families and professionals, ensuring that issues arising from confidential information are resolved before the conference; or by making special provision for the situations identified here which cause particular difficulties, such as where the child has disclosed but the parents deny the abuse. This may require that parents are asked to leave for part of the conference, or that other ways are found for presenting their views. Such measures would be supported by inter-agency training events, employing experiential learning and skills training, and by managers taking responsibility for ensuring that all staff receive the necessary documentation, and are given opportunities for group discussion. Special attention should be given to the provision of support networks for staff in agencies whose primary function is not child protection, such as school nurses.

# 6 The Professionals: their experiences of the conferences

All the world's a stage,
And all the men and women merely players;
They have their exits and the entrances;
And one man in his life plays many parts.
                    Shakespeare, As You Like It.

The last chapter described the attitudes of the professionals involved in all conferences in the six neighbourhood research teams before and after the implementation of the policy. Professionals approved of parental involvement and attitudes became more positive over time as a result of experiencing parental involvement. There were abiding concerns over the degree to which discussion in the conference might be inhibited and the view that some parents should be excluded from some conferences prevailed. There were some differences in attitude between the four main agencies involved and the concept of the operational perspective was used to explain this.

The purpose in this chapter is to undertake a more focused exploration of what it was like for the professionals to 'share honey with the bear' (Blom-Cooper, 1987) in conferences where parents were present. Additionally, it will construct a more detailed analysis of cases where the presence of parents was thought to affect the participation of the professionals, the assessment of risk and the decision to register. The cases are then further analysed to reveal which conferences the professionals found the most straightforward and which the most difficult. The aim is to determine whether any characteristics in the management of the conference or in a particular family situation or location were associated with negative responses.

## Method

At the end of the thirty six conferences involving parents the professionals present were given a brief questionnaire to complete. The questionnaire was designed to be easy and straightforward to fill in and addressed the main concerns that had emerged from the first attitude survey. The professionals were asked whether the parents' presence had been helpful in assessing risk to the child, the degree to which it had affected their participation and whether the decision to register or the recommendations were influenced by the parents' presence. Additionally, it asked them to judge whether they thought the conference and the registration was necessary to protect the child, and for any other comments.

Two hundred and sixty one questionnaires were returned from a total attendance of 298 professionals, a response rate of 88%. The number of questionnaires received per case varied from one to fourteen, an average of seven per case. The comments were coded and the completed questionnaires were analysed quantitatively using SPSS. A more sophisticated statistical analysis was undertaken to assess the degree of difficulty by case by constructing an index scoring the negative responses of the professionals. The analysis of the data also draws upon the researcher's observations of twenty two of these conferences and the data collected from other parts of the research.

## The sample

The respondents represented a diverse group of professionals from all the agencies involved in a child protection investigation and with varying amounts of experience of conference attendance and training for it. As can be seen from Table 6.1 and as would be expected the professional groupings are in similar proportions to the attitude survey. Social services form the largest group of respondents (36%), containing social workers (16%), principal social workers (16%) and workers from day care and residential establishments (4%). The second group comprises health personnel (27%): health visitors (13%), school nurses, community nurses and midwives (7%), and their managers (7%). Paediatricians, community medical officers and General Practitioners also responded but only formed a small part of the sample (4%). The police attended nearly every conference but comprise a relatively small proportion of the sample because they attended alone (13%). The same was true for the local authority solicitors (4%). Education was represented by primary and secondary school class and head teachers, special needs specialists and Education Welfare (9%). Other (5%) comprised the same groups as have been described previously.

**Table 6.1   Number of respondents by agency**

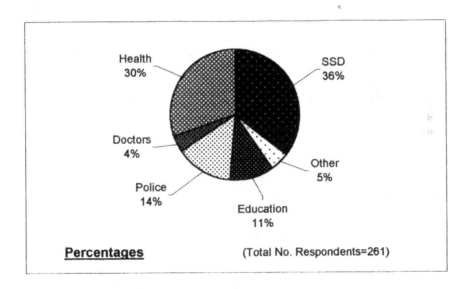

Health
30%

SSD
36%

Doctors
4%

Police
14%

Education
11%

Other
5%

**Percentages**                    (Total No. Respondents=261)

**Results**

*Overall opinions*

Table 6.2 shows that, overall, the respondents found the involvement of parents helpful in over three-quarters of the conferences researched (83%) and thought it provided a sound beginning platform for working in partnership. There was little difference between agencies, education being the least positive (73% said helpful) and the police the most (94%). Ninety per cent of the respondents believed it was correct to hold a conference.

> Parental attendance greatly enhanced the chances of the child and parent being helped effectively.
>
> (Principal Social Worker)

In some cases the professionals did not think that the parents' presence had any effect:

> I didn't think parental attendance made any difference whatsoever to the conference and was neither helpful or unhelpful.
>
> (Woman Police Constable)

However, 12% of the respondents considered the assessment of risk to have been hindered and 7% reported that the participation of some professionals was adversely affected.

> In all case conferences where parents have attended I feel it has worked against the interests of the child, except where some of the evidence has been given in camera. In other discussions I feel strongly that parents should attend, but not at case conference level.
>
> (Special Needs Coordinator, Education)

Generally the findings in this part of the study consolidated those already presented. The respondents believed that parents:

* had a right to attend;
* that involving parents resulted in more effective conference practice and decision making;
* and that interventions were more positive because parents had been included.

A number of the general comments in the questionnaires (often from social workers) reflected the prevailing value position that it was unjust to exclude parents and that the implementation of the policy was long overdue:

> Feels like taking parents with us, rather than doing things to them... makes us more precise... concentrates the mind.
>
> (Principal Case Worker)

**Table 6.2  Opinions of 261 professionals on the presence of parents at 36 conferences (percentages)**

Overall professionals' views

Parental attendance was:

| | |
|---|---|
| helpful | 81% |
| don't know | 10% |
| unhelpful | 9% |

Was consideration of risk:

| | |
|---|---|
| improved | 45% |
| unaffected | 42% |
| hindered | 12% |

Was participation of professionals affected:

| | |
|---|---|
| beneficially | 18% |
| not at all | 67% |
| adversely | 7% |

Was decision to register affected:

| | |
|---|---|
| yes | 11% |
| mixed | 6% |
| no | 74% |

Were recommendations influenced:

| | |
|---|---|
| yes | 20% |
| mixed | 9% |
| no | 67% |

> It is impossible to consider the child's future without full participation and involvement from the parents themselves.
>
> (Officer in Charge, Day Nursery)

The proportion of respondents who found parental participation helpful overall is higher than that found in similar studies in Lewisham (63%) and Hackney (53%). In both London boroughs a higher proportion of professionals said the parents presence neither helped nor hindered - it made no difference. As in this study, only 10% reported parents' presence as being positively unhelpful. Farmer and Owen (1995) reported that the social workers they interviewed believed that participation would be therapeutic for the parent. Thoburn et al. (1995) found that the social workers they interviewed strongly supported, in principle, the attendance of parents at conferences, the most frequently given reasons being rights and effectiveness arguments. Thoburn rates 49% of the social workers in her study as backing the effectiveness argument, 38% favoured the rights argument, and 9% the therapeutic argument. Since these views were also reflected in this study, Thoburn's comments are worth quoting:

> Over half the responses were that the presence of parents resulted in less gossip, and more accurate and clear information. Other positive responses were that the conference was a more honest meeting, more professional and more focused...and better organised...The negative replies contained views that the conference was more contentious, uncomfortable and longer; that it was daunting for parents; that some professionals colluded publicly with parents or browbeat them...The largest group suggested that the professionals were inhibited (p.113).

Taylor and Godfrey's (1991) survey of the views of professionals on Tyneside was also positive. "Professionals were asked about the contributions of parents. All those who replied felt that the parent had made a contribution, and that they humanised the conference" (p.21).

*The advantages of parental attendance*

The respondents were specific in describing the ways in which conferences improved as a result of parents' involvement. The following benefits were mentioned by all the agencies represented:

*a) The quality of the information shared*

The majority of the respondents reported that the quality of the information made available to the conference by both parents and workers was better. Information was provided by parents which:

* corrected wrong information, such as the age of the child;
* added information not previously known, for example about the criminal background of a possible perpetrator;
* and clarified by, for example, explaining the status of the parent's relationship.

Information contributed by workers was said to be more focused, objective and candid. A respect for privacy and the dignity of the parents combined with a strong sense of fair play resulted in the professionals paying special attention to their language, the authenticity of their judgments and the relevance of the material introduced. This led to a sharper focus on purpose.

> Case conferences involving parents are less woolly. There is less unsubstantiated opinion and more facts. The parents see the decision as fair, and as a multi-disciplinary one.
>
> (Principal Social Worker)

The social workers in Thoburn et al.'s (1995) study, and in Farmer and Owen's (1995) also found that the presence of parents resulted in less gossip, fewer value judgments and clearer information.

*b) Parents saw an inter-agency perspective*

A number of the respondents reported that the parents perceived the conference decision as reflecting a shared view on the abuse. This was thought to reduce the possibility of one agency being scapegoated:

> A very good conference in terms of multi-agency consideration of concerns which are directly shared with parents.
>
> (Social Worker)

It was also seen as removing from this arena inter-agency or interpersonal disagreements originating in other sources. Social work respondents commented, as did those in Thoburn et al.'s (1995) study, that they felt parents would see them as part of a team. As previously suggested, however, while the professionals perceived a united front as being beneficial there are potential dangers in subduing disagreement.

*c) Enhanced the assessment and child protection plan*
The respondents believed that assessments and plans for intervention were more realistic as a result of consultation with the parents in the conference. Observing parents' reactions and interactions enhanced the professionals' understanding of the dynamics of the relationship both in cases where they were able to see parents together and where one parent came and spoke about the other. Who came, as well as what they said or did not say, offered important diagnostic clues for assessment and intervention, as the following example illustrates:

> Mother's attendance was useful as an illustration of functioning, and nature of couple interaction similarly helpful.
>
> (Principal Social Worker)

Forty five per cent of the sample considered that the net effect of these factors was to enhance the consideration of risk. However, while case examples ater in this chapter illustrate the benefit to the assessment process of involving parents, it has been suggested that this is unfair because parents are disempowered by the power imbalance and the high emotional content of the conference. Parents who are frightened and feel under scrutiny may not put their best foot forward. The data presented here suggests it is unrealistic to expect professionals to ignore the parents' presentation and performance in making their judgments to return to the analogy with theatre, performance matters. Indeed, in terms of the risk assessment no diagnostic clues should be ignored. Juries, of course, are faced with the same dilemma; but in the court room the power imbalance is openly addressed. It is arguable that in this arena the difference in power between parents and professionals is reinforced by their presence in the conference. Clearly, the process and nature of empowerment and the related issue of partnership is far from straightforward.

*d) Improved chairing skills*
The importance of the role of the chairperson was discussed in the previous chapter. Farmer and Owen (1995) observed that the chairperson was most often mentioned by social workers as being influential in decision-making. He was seen as occupying a position of considerable power and as possessing a range of skills. In this study there was general consensus that the chairperson was a key actor in the conference and modelled the principles of good practice:

This is the second case conference I have attended with parents present... great improvement in chairing of meeting and professionals willingness to be honest.

(Health Visitor)

Lewis (1994) found that all of the fourteen chairpersons she interviewed were in principle in favour of parental involvement. Their responses ranged from being pro-active to paternalistic. The anxieties expressed were whether the parents would cope, whether social workers and other agencies would cope, and whether they as chairpersons could cope.

The way the chairperson conducts the meeting clearly is instrumental to the process of managing anxiety. The respondents in my study suggested that the presence of parents inclined the chairmen to be more business-like in order to keep the emotional content low. Lewis (1994) suggests that the chairperson is stage managing a meeting with a touch of the Old Vic (p.100). The idea that the conference contains elements of different public occasions - the theatre, the court room, the business meeting, an old boys' club - is fruitful because it conveys something of the complexity and nature of the arena into which parents are invited to enter and which the professionals have to manage.

*The disadvantages of parental attendance*

Only 9% of the respondents said they found the involvement of parents unhelpful in the conference being reported on. Twelve per cent thought the assessment of risk had been hindered in a particular conference and 7% reported that their participation had been adversely affected. There was no significant difference by agency, although education and health tended to be more negative, overall, than social services or the police. The disadvantages the professionals in this study mentioned are similar to those reported in the other studies referred to.

*a) Upsetting for parents*
The attitude survey reported in the previous chapter suggested that the professionals were concerned that the parents would be upset. A small minority in Thoburn's study also considered that the conference attendance would be upsetting for parents and could interfere with the development of trust between worker and parents. This part of the study provided more detailed information in demonstrating that there were some conferences where parents became distressed, withdrawn or angry. This had a number of implications for client-worker transactions. Firstly, there was concern that causing parents distress may hinder a parent's therapeutic progress:

The conference hindered greatly mother's progress and struggle to obtain qualifications after a lifetime in care. Because of this she gave up her course and Jean lost her place in the nursery.

(Social Worker)

Secondly, as suggested above a number of respondents reflected upon the uneven power balance between parents and professionals which they felt was unhelpfully reinforced:

I felt the meeting served to reinforce the power difference between the parent and the professionals... the important discussion took    place  after  she  had left... it didn't feel like a good experience for her.

(Social Worker)

Power and justice are clearly interlinked and this response again raises issues about the potential for disempowerment in the meeting. Cleaver and Freeman (1995) describe the fear that parents bring in to a meeting they see as being crudely judicial. This fear was echoed by the parents in this study, as the interviews with them will illustrate.

Thirdly, like Miranda in The Tempest, who "suffered with those I saw suffer", some respondents found their own emotions aroused by what they heard. The questionnaires and the observations suggested that the professionals' concentration was effected by the arousal of feelings of helplessness, fear or sympathy. Some were aware this distracted them from the main purpose:

I found this a difficult case conference... parents' presence hindered the (assessment of risk). I found it difficult to separate off feelings of sympathy for mother from risk to J... eventually recommended to register on basis that mother was accepting help voluntarily and  admitted the incident.

(Principal Case Worker)

Others were perhaps less aware of the subtle ways in which their judgment could be influenced by the emotional content of what they were hearing. Or they were aware but not able to control it. The impact on professionals of hearing the detail of exactly how, where and when a child has been abused has been well described in the literature (Morrison, 1992; Dale, 1989; Furnis, 1991). Having parents present did, in a number of situations, arouse conflicting and confusing emotions. The implications of this for the conference will be developed later in this chapter.

Fourthly, management issues became critical when, for example, parents walked out or became disruptive. The task of the chair in these cases was particularly difficult and highlighted the complexity of attending to process as well as to content.

> Mother walked out at point when deciding to register under sexual abuse. In this case mother had been operating under a number of aliases and been subject to concern, but no action had been taken over a long period. I feel her presence inhibited the primary consideration - Tracy.
>
> (Social Worker)

In this case there was concern that the chairman's attention would be diverted to attending to the parent's and the worker's distress at the expense of focusing on the information content. This was seen as being professionally dangerous. Eisenhardt (1989) identifies confidence and anxiety as key factors in decision making groups and describes the handling of emotional content as critical to the quality of the decisions made. Clearly, the management of anxiety, stress and upset is extremely important placing a heavy dependency on good chairing skills.

### b) Inclination to therapy

Another effect the respondents described was the inclination for professionals who felt uncomfortable to emphasise the parents' strengths and play down their weaknesses. This had the further effect of shifting the focus from the child to the parents. This was seen as being particularly dangerous in the context of child abuse, especially where the parents did not share the professionals concern.

> I did notice that following parents' departure from conference professionals were more negative re. prospects for the future. This hadn't been expressed so forcefully earlier.
>
> (Principal Social Worker)

> The focus seemed to be on the family not on the issue of child protection. After the conference two people said they were not going to be the ones to say the hard things that needed to be said. Very worrying.
>
> (Officer in Charge - Day Nursery)

The danger of some professionals colluding with parents was voiced by some managers in Thoburn et al.'s (1995) study. Farmer and Owen (1995) also found that there was some tendency for the chair to avoid raising contentious issues with the parent and to concentrate on subjects that were emotionally neutral. This finding adds support to the hypothesis that the chairperson is more likely to strive to avoid conflict when parents are present.

## c) Case conferences become longer, bigger and more complex
Evidence from the monitoring study was that conferences with parents lasted, on average, twenty-nine minutes longer than those without parents present and the average size increased from eight to ten. The increased time taken was said to cause stress and the size was daunting, especially for inexperienced workers. It also created particular problems. For example, Doctors were less likely to come to present their own case. In cases of sexual abuse this made the interpretation of medical findings difficult, even when a report was provided. In other cases doctors needed to leave early for prearranged clinics, thereby missing the important discussion on registration and the consideration of risk.

> Parental attendance lengthens the time taken and causes increased stress to professionals already under pressure.
>
> (Health Visitor)

> Drastically protracted...seriously extended... too many people.
>
> (Police)

More recent information suggests that while professionals will contribute information to the conference in front of parents they are less happy to express opinion on the registration. In consequence, the chair has to take a more active role and this is reflected in the process and the decisions made. Finally, it is also possible that one of the implications of increased time is that it can be used a reason for not attending. Although this hypothesis could not be tested here, the findings do lend weight to the suggestion that professionals who have negative views about parents attending may be less likely to come themselves.

## d) Adverse effect on professional participation
The most heartfelt comments received referred to the inhibiting effect of the parents' presence:

> I feel other information may have been presented and considered regarding child's home situation especially mother's lack of protective skills, if parent wasn't there.
>
> (Health Visitor)

Many of professionals were careful and hesitant about offering information.

(Social Worker, Voluntary Agency)

I felt many views were muted by parental attendance.

(Health Visitor)

There was less discussion between the professionals than usual - less testing of available information. Several professionals started to talk when parents left.

(Doctor)

There were a number of reasons why important information was not shared, as follows:

* that the worker did not know the agreed procedures.

For example, in two of the conferences observed the police did not know that information about a parent's criminal record should have been divulged to the chair beforehand. It was withheld from the conference until the parent left. The conference then debated whether it was fair and just for the information to be introduced. Hobson's choice for the chair; but the heated discussion about the potential for injustice took time and emotional energy and made people uneasy.

* a lack of confidence in saying harsh things in an acceptable way: "how to say nasties nicely" (see Bell, 1995).

As described in the attitude survey some respondents lacked confidence in backing up a professional opinion in the absence of clearly established fact. This meant some assessments were thin and some important diagnostic gut reactions failed to be expressed.

* anxieties about making public confidences and secrets shared in the privacy of the relationship.

These anxieties reflect the professional perspectives derived from their agencies primary task, as identified in the previous chapter. Teachers, for example, feared that they would lose the families' cooperation if they disclosed information in front of them. Health visitors were concerned that they would be denied access to the child. Social workers thought parents might withdraw their co-operation in the ongoing work, thus making their monitoring task more difficult. In some cases, especially where there was known to be a violent man in the household, the workers feared reprisal.

Many of the professionals who believed that certain things did not get said when parents were present were reassured by the existence of a safe zone when parents were asked to leave and there was scope for private discussion of the issues.   This finding was supported by data from the attitude survey. It has important implications for policy and practice. The departure of the parents at the decision making stage - the policy operating in this authority during this research - was generally favoured by the respondents. Some commented that it freed them to express  an opinion which they felt inhibited in expressing in front of the parents, important in the consideration of risk. Others, however, were made uneasy because the practice symbolised, for them, the acute tension being held between the rights of parents to hear everything and the need to adequately protect the child. For the chairmen it produced particular problems. In a number of cases he had to judge in the course of the meeting whether or not to allow new information to be introduced. In some cases, and in anticipation of changing policy, the parent was allowed to remain; in others, the information was not heard. Either way, the actions of the chair did not please all the participants. Respondents also commented, in the few cases where parents were present for the decision making, that workers were reluctant to engage in the discussion of risk and the need for registration. In those situations, the role of the chairman appeared to become more powerful in the decision making process and this, also, raised concern.

In conclusion, the professionals generally welcomed the involvement of parents but they shared common concerns about particular difficulties in particular cases. Asking parents to leave at the decision making stage was welcomed by some professionals but not by others and while it solved some problems it created others. This issue is controversial from a rights perspective and will be explored in the chapter reporting on the parents interviews. The next section describes how the difficulties identified by the respondents were analysed.

*Difficulty by case*

This case conference was too difficult for professionals to hold with the parents present.   Information was not forthcoming and had to be prised out of professionals at various stages.

(Consultant Paediatrician)

**Table 6.3   Cases by difficulty**

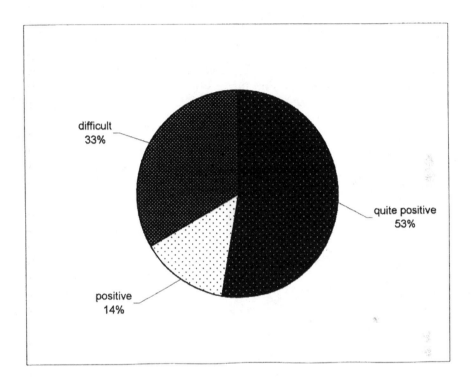

To determine whether any characteristics in the case could be associated with negative responses a summary variable of difficulty was created by adding together the negative comments on all the questions on the questionnaire. This produced a mean score for each case, and resulted in their division into three groups (see Table 6.3).

The three groupings that were defined were as follows:

*Group 1, the positive group*, contained five cases (17%) where the respondents were unanimously positive about the involvement of parents. The professionals in these cases found the inclusion of parents very helpful, the consideration of risk was said to have been improved and professional participation actively enhanced.

*Group 2, the quite positive group*, contained nineteen cases (50%), where the overall profile was positive but there were some negative responses in each case. In some cases the views of the professionals were strikingly at variance.

*Group 3, the difficult group*, comprised the remaining twelve cases (33%). In each of these cases a number of the respondents expressed concern about the negative impact of parental attendance on the consideration of risk, the professionals' participation and the decision-making process. The views were not confined to one agency.

In Thoburn et al.'s study (1995) the cases also fell into three groupings based on a rating of the extent the identified difficulties would create for working in partnership. The researchers judged 27% to be best scenario, 45% to be middle and 28% to be worst. These percentage groupings are similar to mine in size, and there are also similarities in the criteria used to construct the rating of difficulty.

Returning to my study, analysis of the data from this part of the study was combined with data from the parents' interviews. This showed that, in Groups 1 and 2 - the positive and quite positive groups - professionals and parents were more likely to be in agreement with the facts presented, in other words to share an operational perspective. It seems reasonable to propose that, since by definition these cases did not produce overwhelming difficulties for the professionals, a partnership approach to the intervention in these cases would be appropriate. This hypothesis will be pursued later.

The data were further analysed to see whether cases with particular characteristics scored 'on average' more heavily on an index of difficulty. The analysis used the Mann-Whitney U statistic to ensure that the statistical significance occurring did not occur by chance. This showed that eight characteristics were associated with 'difficulty' (see Table 6.4). Each of these characteristics was common in the twelve most difficult cases. They can be grouped broadly into those associated with family profile and those associated with particular features of the conference. Some 'difficult' families tended to come from an area where the conferences also had difficult features making it impossible to disentangle these effects by statistical analysis.

Table 6.4 lists the features which were of significance in the most difficult cases, as follows:

*1 Presence of violent man in household*

The presence of a violent and/or abusing man in the family or family network was a feature in eleven of the twelve cases. Violence had been directed against adults and/ or children on this or a previous occasion. The pattern varied including also a criminal record for indecency or grievous bodily harm. In two cases siblings had died. In three of these cases the violent parent had not been invited to the conference. However, even where the violent man did not attend, workers commented on the fear it induced in them.

**Table 6.4   The most difficult cases**

---

12 Cases containing at least one of the following characteristics:

---

1.  Presence of a violent man in the household (11 cases)
2.  Absence of (male) partner at conference (9 cases)
3.  Denial of abuse, especially when linked with disclosure by child (9 cases)
4.  Type of abuse (8 cases)
5.  Disruption of conference (7 cases)
6.  Area team (8 cases)
7.  Ethnic origin of family (5 cases)
8.  Size and length of conference (10 cases)

---

> Father's violent behaviour has meant that social services no longer visit the home and his threats inhibited workers from fully discussing the facts in mothers presence. People were clearly scared of father finding out what they had said so wouldn't speak in front of his wife.
>
> (Health Visitor)

As this quote makes clear, workers were frightened for their own safety and for that of the mother, as a consequence of information made public in the conference. This conference considered the alleged physical abuse and neglect of a child in the family.

The link between domestic violence and child abuse is well established by research (Mullender, 1996; Bell, 1997). Farmer and Owen (1995) found that men who physically abused their children were frequently also violent to their wives. They see this as one of the reasons why women become the focus of attention thus "allowing men's violence to their wives or partners to disappear from sight" (p.223). The next difficulty described strongly supports this view.

### 2  Absence of (male) partner at case conference

In nine of these cases (75%) the mothers attended the conference alone even though three quarters of the children lived with both parents or a parental combination. As was discussed in the monitoring study, research suggests that this pattern is common. Farmer and Owen (1995) found that 30% of their conferences were attended by mothers alone, and only 18% by two parent figures. While the presence of mothers alone is strongly associated with difficulty, conversely, the presence of fathers at the conference was correlated with positive responses. More commonly, fathers were present in the Group 1 cases.

Three concerns emerged regarding father's absence:

* concern that the mother was inevitably (and unfairly) targeted as the child's protector;
* anxious speculation as to why father was not present;
* frustration that his views could not inform the intervention plans.

> A lot of people attended the conference. A lot of personal relationships were discussed. This caused too much pressure on the mother on her own.
>
> (Health Visitor)

> I felt great sympathy for Mrs S who seemed to be bearing the brunt of the problem while not being involved in the possible non accidental injury.
>
> (School Nurse)

The anxiety induced in the workers by the attendance of the mother alone is created in part by uncertainty. The findings have suggested that, when both partners attend, uncertainties about the relationship and about the quality of concern for the child can be tested out by the workers, enabling them to be more confident in their risk assessment.

A further concern was identified in Farmer and Owen's (1995) research which links with the next area of difficulty. When a single mother denied responsibility for the abuse and there was no other person in the household to take the blame the worker could feel uncertain how to proceed. Uncertainty was a hidden component in the difficult cases.

### 3   *Unacknowledged abuse, plus disclosure by child*

The proportion of children disclosing abuse in this group of cases was, at 71%, proportionately much higher than in the other groups. In a number of the same cases the parents did not acknowledge that abuse had taken place. The inability of the parents to acknowledge abuse was connected to a number of factors, including disagreement on the facts as well as on their interpretation of them as abusive. Differing standards of child care, sometimes including cultural factors, played a part.

> It is really difficult when people say different things...issues get watered down... and there is a conflict between actual evidence and explanations of parents, particularly where there are cultural differences. In this case Liz wanted to be registered to protect herself [from physical abuse by her father], but her mother did not think the beating had been abusive. So there was no basis for cooperative work with the parents.
>
> (Social Worker)

There are many facets to unpack here. Obviously protection of the child is seriously compromised in cases where the parents do not acknowledge that abuse has taken place. These cases create raw anxiety in the workers because of their concern that no one would protect the child. Farmer and Owen (1995) also found that situations where parents denied culpability presented special dilemmas to the participants.

Another aspect is the sense of betrayal workers are left with when the child discloses but is not believed by the parents. Gibbons et al. (1995) found that the child's own confirmation was the most important factor in substantiating allegations of abuse. Yet where the child is not believed by the parents s/he is not protected and there is no basis for trust or for establishing an agreed child protection plan. As has already been suggested families that are dysfunctioning at this level can set up a mirroring process in individuals and in interagency groups. Dale (1986) has identified such a process as an important constituent of professional dangerousness.

The difference in operational perspectives complicates the situation. Class, gender, race all determine how the story will be told and 'the truth' defined; so even where there is agreement on what has happened there is disagreement when it is interpreted as abusive. For example, a mother who had herself experienced poor parenting as a child was unable to appreciate the concerns of the conference about the dangers to which her child was exposed as a result of her prostitution. In this case her 12 year old daughter had been seen having oral sex with a client waiting in the car outside the house. The child was registered as being at risk of sexual abuse, despite mother's insistence that she was safe.

Another example illustrates the effects of culture on judgements about parenting. In this case the fifteen year old daughter of a Chinese family had been severely beaten by her father with a kettle flex. Her mother did not dispute the fact that her daughter had been beaten by her husband. She explained to the conference - through an interpreter - that this was a normal way of dealing with difficult adolescent children in her community. Her daughter was difficult and needed to be punished. In the event, it was the expressed wish of the child for protection, verbalised by her teacher in the conference, which gave the conference the clear mandate to register this girl at risk of physical abuse.

Finally, as will be discussed at greater length in the conclusion, the inability of a child's mother to hear the child's disclosure of abuse or to accept its existence needs to be set in the context of the existence of a violent man in the household and the social deprivation in which families live.

*4   Type of abuse*
The data suggests that difficulty was connected with lack of specificity, so that cases of neglect and emotional abuse scored higher on an index of difficulty than those involving physical and sexual abuse. Physical abuse was experienced as the most straightforward, followed by sexual abuse. Six of these conferences considered an allegation of neglect and a further four considered non specific concerns arising from abuse to other children in the family or from mothers lifestyle, particularly prostitution.

> In this case [neglect] there was dispute between the agencies over the need to conference let alone register. I was worried about what the nursery staff would say - they sometimes make wrong assumptions and judgements and act on them where the issues are not clear cut.
>
> (Social Worker)

Two issues require discussion here. The first relates to the uncertainty caused by the lack of specific injuries, as is a feature of neglect cases. In cases of physical and sexual abuse, such as the ones described above, the medical and witness evidence may be unequivocal in so far as the injuries and incident are concerned. However, where the abuse is not so clearly defined and is more difficult to substantiate because it is more openly subject to matters of interpretation and definition, the workers become uneasy. Neglect happens over time - but the conference agenda is built around a snapshot of the present. Other research studies have also evidenced the particular difficulties professionals face in investigating and substantiating allegations of neglect. Gibbons et al. (1995) found that, of all referrals for suspected neglect in the eight local authorities she studied, only seven percent reached the child protection register. This demonstrates the unique difficulties of agreeing on the benchmark in neglect cases as well as substantiating the allegation.

A further difficulty in the management of neglect cases is the issues raised for professionals with regard to cause and effect. Professional interventions aimed at changing family interactions clearly have to be directed at the cause of the abuse which is generally attributed to poor parental skills or dysfunctional families. Corby's work (1987), however, demonstrated that external stress factors were rarely referred to in the conferences he observed, whereas "deprived childhood theories were used in a loose way to justify a belief that a parent had injured a child". This finding was replicated by Farmer and Owen (1995) and by Gibbons (1995), who also found little reference to material factors in the conferences they studied. This is odd, since the evidence of the massive welfare needs of the families in this and other studies and of the scarce resources available to meet them is overwhelming. Neglect cases confront workers in a very direct way with their helplessness in meeting these needs within the child protection system. One effect of the parents' presence was that these needs were verbalised and became a part of the interaction in the conference. The case examples illustrate well how discomforting this is for workers who, after all, are there because they want to help.

## 5 Disruption of case conference
Four of the five cases where parents left early fell in the most difficult group.

> Mrs T walked out at point when deciding to register Samantha. Her presence inhibited the primary consideration: the child.
>
> (Head Teacher)

Disruption involves more than physical departure. In some of the other difficult cases parents became distressed or made a strong statement pleading innocence or impossible circumstances, presenting workers with a daunting picture of social disadvantage as well as an often distressing account of a child's abuse.

This reinforces the hypothesis that one effect of involving parents in the conference is to present the professionals in a very direct way with the social deprivation that contributes to the families stress, yet which the professionals are not well equipped to redress. This may induce a strong sense of powerlessness and make the distancing strategies referred to earlier ineffective. This finding is important when set alongside the research included in Messages from the Research (1995) which demonstrates that when family support is offered, parents find questions about abuse less traumatic and are more likely to co-operate with professionals.

*6   Team*

A significant number of these cases (53%) came from one area team. The families, as reported in the monitoring study were characterised by a higher rate of violence and in this inner-city neighbourhood also subject to multiple disadvantage and discrimination. The team was served by the same office, noted in the research as having poor facilities, accommodation and administrative backup for case conferences.

> A horrible old reading room, not pleasant, crumbling plaster ... appalling facilities for the children.
>
> (Social Worker)

Firstly, the area. The two neighbourhood teams where these families lived served a deprived inner city area with poor housing, high unemployment and a high proportion of families from ethnic minority groups. The links between poverty and child abuse are well established (see Blackburn, 1990). Secondly, the accommodation. A number of the respondents commented on the lack of adequate reception areas and child care facilities in the building, as well as the poor quality furniture, ventilation and lighting of the conference room. The effect on participants of poor accommodation and facilities has also been described by Thoburn (1995) and by Cleaver and Freeman (1995). Anxious people like to be looked after and feel cared for when they are. Clearly the physical conditions in which the meetings are held are influential.

*7   Ethnic origin of family*

Five of the seven families whose ethnic origin was non-European were among the most difficult cases. This is a significant difference as against the families whose ethnic origin was UK European (see Table 6.5).   A number of factors contribute to explain this finding.   Four of the 5 ethnic minority families in this study lived in the inner city area also associated with difficulty. The problems they brought to the conference therefore have to be contextualised, so that the families' social circumstances receive attention alongside the family pathology. Another factor which has been already discussed and is further illustrated in the case examples is the difficulty for the conference of addressing differing cultural patterns of parenting. The way abuse is constructed and the referral made (Wattam, 1992) was explored in the monitoring study where it was established that ethnic minority families and families of mixed race children were over represented among referrals. Gibbons et al. (1995) found that black and Asian families were over represented among referrals for physical abuse but under represented among referrals for sexual abuse. However, it was the form the punishment took and not the nature of the injuries that initiated the referral. She believes this illustrates cultural differences in child rearing and the difficulty of determining acceptable physical punishment.

**Table 6.5   Non-European by degree of difficulty**

|  | Very difficult | Quite difficult | Not difficult |
|---|---|---|---|
| Non European | 5 (71%) | 2 (29%) | 0 (0) |
| UK European | 7 (25%) | 16 (57%) | 5 (18%) |
| Total | 12 (34%) | 18 (51%) | 5 (14%) |

The ten cases involving ethnic minority families in Farmer and Owen's (1995) research also produced difficulties, such as language problems, differences in the cultural value base and uncertainty. They draw attention to the work of writers, such as Phillips and Dutt, 1991, and Jones, 1993, who have pointed out the relationship between black people, material deprivation and low educational achievement and child abuse and neglect. For many black people educational success is difficult to achieve and low economic status and all that that implies is not unusual: "the main deficits in these cases...were attributable to the disadvantaged circumstances of many families and the services which were available to them" (p.321).

Clearly when concerns about the abuse of black children are raised the context of the parents' responses within a racist society must be taken into account. There was evidence from the observations that the mainly all-white workers did not always feel competent and confident when challenged by family norms different from their own. As Ahmed (1986) wrote:

> The important point for Asian clients... is not against an over reliance on cultural explanations ... the centrality of racism needs to be more explicitly acknowledged in the assessment process, and cultural explanations need to be considered in the context of racism.

*8   Size and length of conference*
In ten of the cases there were over fourteen people present at the conference and nine of them lasted over an hour and a half. As described this was experienced as stressful by a number of the participants and meant some people left early.

**Case examples**

The following case examples draw upon findings from the questionnaires, the keyworker interviews, the monitoring study and the observations. They have been selected from different teams and the conferences were held at different times in the research project. They demonstrate how the features associated with difficulty enmeshed to produce uncertainty, confusion and anxiety for the professionals.

*Case 1* was held in the inner city area office noted for its poor facilities. This was one of the first conferences involving parents. Reception and child care arrangements were poor and the conference began late and amid some confusion. Both parents arrived, accompanied by an interpreter for mother who spoke no English. Mother left at an early stage to attend to her two young children who could be heard crying in a nearby room. The interpreter was asked to present her point of view. The conference considered the neglect and suspected sexual abuse by her father of a four year old Pakistani girl. Bruises to the child had been noted at nursery school and the girl was reported as being unusually quiet. The nursery teacher felt the quietness could be explained by the girl's lack of confidence in speaking English. The medical evidence was that the child had been sexually abused and that she was neglected. This information was all that was available to the conference as the family had no previous contact with the agencies. Additionally, the social work investigation had been hampered by language problems and by the parent's lack of co-operation. As the social worker commented;

> I found working toward parental attendance particularly difficult with this family. The sexual abuse had to be denied because girls [in Asian families] have to be virgins when they are married, so mother sleeps with them. Therefore the barriers to disclosing and co-operating are huge.

Father actively disputed the medical diagnosis of sexual abuse, saying that the marks were caused by the child sliding down the bannisters. He made a strong statement declaring his innocence, expressing his concern that "all you lot are trying to see things in a suspicious way", and describing the negative impact of the investigation on the family, adding to their burdens of stigma and racism. The child was registered under the category, sexual abuse, but father made it clear he would not co-operate with any monitoring under registration procedures. The respondents reported that this father's involvement, combined with the mother's absence, made this a particularly difficult conference. It contained seven of the characteristics associated with difficulty.

*Case 2* has a number of similar features. It also illustrates how cultural factors can determine how facts are perceived and given significance and challenge the competence and confidence of all white workers when confronted by family norms which differ from their own. A seven year old Afro-Caribbean girl was found wandering in the middle of the night. There were concerns about the mother's lifestyle - she cohabited with men known to be violent, and appeared either unaware of or unconcerned about the potential risks to her child. A previous child had died of natural causes while unattended. This girl was conferenced as being at risk of neglect. In making their case, the white day nursery staff reported two additional concerns; they were unhappy about the quality of the mother/child interaction, which they described as containing too much "teasing", and they were concerned that an Aunt or Grandmother generally collected the child from nursery, not her mother. Their concerns were countered by the family's black social worker who suggested that the pattern of parental interaction described was commonplace within the culture, and that Aunt and Grandmother were attachment figures for the child, providing much of the caring. However, the fact that the child had been found wandering alone in the early hours was a matter for legitimate concern, and the child was registered.

These two cases have some similar characteristics; the area is the same, the families are non-European, and the parents do not agree with the professionals that the child is neglected. In both cases there was disruption in the conference - in Case 2, the Grandmother and Aunt became upset. There was also evidence that cultural factors, including different patterns of child rearing, made it particularly difficult for the professionals to assess and reach a decision about risk factors, especially with respect to neglect and emotional abuse. In both of these cases the presence of the family created particular problems, though of a different nature.

*Case 3* shares some features but is chosen to demonstrate how the communication of oppression, linked with strong affect, and where the definition of abuse is not shared by the parent, produces in the workers a sense of helplessness and powerlessness. In this example, a three-year old white boy was conferenced because of severe bruising and neglect. His mother said:

> I do smack my children, and I believe in smacking them...But I love them. I try to keep them clean, but it is impossible where we live. And how would you manage as a single parent with three boys under five, no money and a stinking, damp house? You've made me feel dirty.

She conveyed a powerful picture of her Amazonian efforts to raise her children in extreme poverty, in poor housing conditions, unsupported and under constant threat of violence. Observation suggested that this made the workers uneasy by arousing their sympathy for the parent. Further, their access to material resources was limited, thus restricting the help available for them to offer. The social worker described how, in her opinion, certain information was discounted:

> I felt mother's beliefs were not really considered, for example, she mentioned that the older child missed his father, which was ignored. Very obvious related facts, such as the mother's severe ill health, were also ignored.
>
> (Social Worker)

This little boy was not registered following a protracted discussion between those who felt registration would provide mother with a target - to work toward deregistration - and those who argued that 'voluntariness' would empower mother to be more adult and be more likely to promote her co-operation. Other factors discussed included the relationship between registration and priority social work help and its leverage on other agencies, such as housing; and the need to maintain the register at a manageable level. This suggests that there is a range of factors determining who gets registered, especially in cases of neglect where standards of child care are seen to reflect poverty and oppression rather than lack of parental love. It is argued that these factors contribute to the professionals discomfort in that they confront them with the difficulty of meeting the welfare of children within a child protection framework.

*Case 4* The last example has been selected to demonstrate the impact of class and communicative performance on risk assessment. The parents were articulate, middle class professionals. This case met the following criteria of difficulty; denial of abuse, alongside a coherent disclosure by the child, disruption during the conference, and length and size. Seventeen people were present. Two white girls, aged 8 and 10, were conferenced as being at risk of sexual abuse following their friend's disclosure of sexual abuse by the girls step-father during a holiday stay. No medical evidence was available because of the time lapse between the alleged incident and the disclosure, but the investigating social worker presented a detailed report in support of the allegation. Evidence of previous police and social services involvement in the family was offered by other professionals. Mother became extremely distressed and ran out: "That's it....its all lies", and stepfather delivered a speech pleading his innocence. From the professionals:

I felt somewhat confused as to what the outcome should be.

(Health Visitor)

The conference was polarised in terms of views of abuse. I felt that the professionals' view of the parents as 'nice' people affected their judgment about whether he was capable of sexually abusing children. Having taken the role of comforting mother, I felt more ambivalent about the decision making and had to push myself to suggest the children may be at risk.

(Principal Social Worker)

The decision regarding the child was, in my opinion, perhaps too heavily influenced by what the parent said and did i.e. burst into tears. I was not wholly convinced by her protests.

(Head Teacher)

These comments illustrate how class factors and verbal ability provide a frame in which workers find it difficult to locate abuse. In this case the parents presence meant this dynamic was acted out in the decision making arena. The stepdaughters were not registered.

## Conclusion

The inclusion of parents in the thirty six conferences studied was generally welcomed by the workers involved and in two thirds of the cases there were felt to be positive benefits. In a small number of cases (17%) the professionals believed it actively improved consideration of risk, in half it was regarded by most as helpful and in the remaining third there was concern that the involvement of parents was at best problematic and at worst seriously hindered the consideration of risk to the child. These conferences were found to contain clusters of particular characteristics and were rated as the most difficult by an index scoring the negative responses of the professionals. The nature of the responses can be linked to a degree with agency and the worker's concomitant experience of child protection work, social services and police being the most positive and health and education the least; but this is within a framework which welcomes the initiative and is confident, in the main, with its implementation. With regard to policy, the inclusion of parents at the decision-making stage was the most contentious issue and some respondents felt that a private discussion was essential in some cases.

However, in a third of the cases the involvement of parents raised professional concern. The features that are associated with these cases suggest that for a number of reasons they are particularly difficult from the assessment and the decision making points of view. Where certain features associated with the family and certain characteristics of the conference mesh the professionals experienced difficulty. In these conferences, the presence of parents introduced a dimension which some workers said made it even harder for them to participate freely, to attend fully to the consideration of risk and to focus on the needs of the child without distraction. Others, especially those with substantial experience in child protection work, such as principal social workers and the police, reported that these cases were among the most difficult anyway, irrespective of the parents' presence.   Some case examples served to illustrate how the presence of parents can heighten the difficulties in risk assessment but also suggest that these cases would always be difficult.

**Summary of main findings**

*Professional views on the conferences*

Over three quarters of all the professionals who responded reported that the involvement of parents was helpful to the conference in question. There was little difference between agencies, education being the least favourable (73%) and police the most (94%). Twelve per cent of the respondents considered the assessment of risk to have been hindered, and 7% reported that participation was adversely affected.

The main arguments for involving parents were that the parents had a right to attend and that their involvement meant the ongoing work would be more effective. The respondents reported that:

* the quality of the information both going in to and coming out of the conference generally was improved. Parents corrected wrong information, added information not previously known, and clarified uncertainties.
* parents saw an inter-agency perspective, and perceived the conference decision as reflecting a shared view.
* the assessment and intervention plans were enhanced because the parents had contributed to them.
* chairing skills improved.

Only 9% of the sample said they found the involvement of parents unhelpful in the conference being reported on. The respondents reported that:

* some parents got distressed, adversely affecting the professionals' concentration by arousing unhelpful feelings of helplessness, fear or sympathy.
* the power differential was unhelpfully reinforced.
* difficult management issues became critical, requiring the chair to attend to process at the expense of content.
* the professionals emphasised the parents' strengths and played down their weaknesses to make them feel better. This was regarded as potentially dangerous, especially where parents did not share the professionals' concern.
* professionals felt inhibited from speaking openly. This was caused by the following:
    a misunderstanding of agreed procedures,

a lack of confidence in saying harsh things in an acceptable way,
a fear of reprisal or withdrawal of co-operation,
an inability to back up a professional opinion with established fact,
and anxiety about making public confidences and secrets shared in
the privacy of the relationship.
* conferences became longer, bigger and more complex. This was
experienced as frustrating and stressful to a number of professionals.
Additionally, there were resource implications, and the question arises
whether the cost is justified. Many of the respondents were reassured by
the existence of a safe zone, when parents were asked to leave and there
was scope for private discussion of the issues.

## *Difficulty by case*

### *Three groups of cases were identified on a scale of difficulty*
The positive group contained five cases (17%) where the respondents were
unanimously positive. The quite positive group formed 50% of the cases
(nineteen), where the overall profile was positive but there were a few
negative responses. The difficult group comprised the remaining twelve
cases (33%) where a number of the respondents expressed concern about
the negative impact of involving parents on the consideration of risk, the
professional's participation and the decision-making process.

### *Characteristics of the most difficult conferences*

The characteristics of the twelve most difficult cases can be grouped
broadly into those associated with family profile, and those associated with
particular features of the conference. Unfortunately some 'difficult'
families tended to come from an area where the conferences also had
difficult features so that it is not possible to disentangle these effects by
statistical analysis.
The features which were of significance in the most difficult cases were:

* presence of violent man in household
* absence of (male) partner at conference
* unacknowledged abuse, plus disclosure by child
* type of abuse (emotional abuse and neglect)
* disruption of conference
* team
* ethnic origin of family.

The degree to which the difficulties reported on in these cases were directly attributable to parental involvement is open to debate. There was evidence that these conferences highlighted the ambiguity inherent in the conference task, and that the presence of parents was a contributory factor.

## Discussion

This part of the research has provided evidence that, in the majority of the cases studied, professionals and parents were in general agreement with the facts presented. This shared perspective provides an important base for the building of successful partnerships between parents and professionals - a factor identified as being critical to in positive outcomes, such as the future safety of the child. This research also found that the conferences that went well were those where the participants agreed on what had happened and with the professionals' judgment. In a number of the cases, Doctors were able to bring scientific evidence to support their medical opinion (Hobbs, 1994); the police provided evidence based on previous convictions; the social workers provided assessments based on an accurate family history, and so on. Also shared by professionals and parents across the chasms of class, culture and context were some moral judgments.

This is reassuring since it suggests that there are limits to the usefulness of the more radical postmodernist, deconstructionist perspective which sees no act as being abusive and no truth as valid outside the context of the event (Parton, 1994). However, this part of the research has also provided evidence that the conferences the professionals found most difficult were those where there was uncertainty and disagreement about what had happened and where there was uneasiness about the relevance of employing child protection procedures to meet the overwhelming welfare needs of some complex and stigmatised families. These difficulties were, in a number of the cases, compounded by the presence of the parents.

Gil and Parton (1991) have argued the need to contextualise reported child abuse, so that the social circumstances in which the families live receive as much attention as family/individual pathology. This part of the research has suggested that involving parents in the initial child protection conference has precisely this effect but that this is problematic because it confronts professionals with their own powerlessness. Case 3 provided a good example of the mother communicating her sense of hopelessness. Observation suggested that this communication of oppression, linked with strong effect, and where the definition of abuse was not shared by the parent, produced in the workers a sense of helplessness and powerlessness.

It seems that where there was disagreement and uncertainty about the abuse and where the multiple oppressions that the families experienced were contextualised, symbolised or communicated by the parents in the conference, the professionals were confronted with ambiguities which challenged their competence and professional integrity. These could, further, be said to mirror the parents powerlessness and sense of oppression. Jordan (1990) has suggested a dynamic explanation for this phenomena and this has been explored in the analysis.

Stevenson (1995) has argued that "the very concept of risk assessment at the heart of the conference process is distorting to sound welfare practice" because the assessments are of risk, not of need. This part of the research suggests that professionals operating the risk assessment system feel this mismatch acutely in some cases and this undermines their professional integrity and expertise. It seems likely that this would also contribute to the sense of helplessness that Morrison (1992) identified as being at the heart of the emotional stress experienced by staff working with abused children. The finding that cases of neglect were among the most difficult is relevant here. As we have seen, various factors are involved. The first relates to the differing operational perspectives that operate. Different standards of, for example, hygiene may be applied in constructing a diagnosis of neglect. Secondly, professionals from different agencies may be applying different indicators of vulnerability; so, to put it crudely, nurses look at hygiene, Doctors at bruises, teachers at learning problems and social workers at parenting skills. Is the allegation of suspected neglect a compound of these factors, or a measure of degree, or both? We have noted the particular problems in achieving an agreed standard because of class, gender and culture.

Thirdly, an allegation of neglect raises contentious issues over the cause. It makes sense to talk of physical and sexual abuse and sometimes emotional abuse as being 'deliberately' caused by acts of commission or omission (Dingwall, 1983). Neglect is different. If, as is now recognised (Blackburn, 1990), there is a close relationship between poverty and the problems associated with neglect, such as poor health, overcrowded housing and unemployment, then the cause is not necessarily poor parental skills or dysfunctional families but the social deprivation in which the majority of these families live. Thorpe's (1994) research supports this view by providing evidence that single parents and Aboriginal families - families known to be subject to extreme poverty and social stigma - are vastly over-represented in child protection investigations.

Fourthly, and related to this last point, the alternatives to parental care available to children within the child care system are imperfect. In making judgments about exposure to risk from neglect, social workers have somehow to balance what they know about systems abuse and what they know about the importance for mental health of secure attachments with knowledge about the quantity and quality of the resources that will be made available as a result of the child's registration on the at risk register. Impossible mental equations to which there are no right answers. It is hardly surprising, therefore, that only seven percent of all referrals for suspected neglect reach the register (Gibbons et al., 1995) and that cases of neglect feature in my 'most difficult' cases.

Parton (1994) frames the challenge to workers making risk assessments as being "to respond positively and with imagination to the prospect of living without securities, guarantees and order and with contingency and ambivalence". A feature these most difficult cases shared was that they required the professionals to manage layers of uncertainty, contingency and disagreement. The operational perspectives of the participants did not come closer together. Parents, children and professionals, especially in cases where parents denied that abuse had taken place, presented different versions of the truth. There was a high degree of uncertainty about what had happened, further compounded by disagreement at its interpretation as abusive. A number of factors were seen to operate. In cases where the evidence was unclear and where, as we have seen, class, culture and gender informed definitions of abuse the moral nature of the discourse was tangible. The professionals were then faced with the daunting task of avoiding 'cultural relativism' (Dingwall, 1983) and promoting 'cultural sensitivity' (Pardeck et al., 1995) while simultaneously maintaining a moral position which others did not share.

**Practice points**

While the use of specified risk factors for screening purposes may be limited because of the diverse nature of the variables involved (Browne, 1994) and could be stigmatising, it would be naive to ignore the commonality of the research findings on the causes of child abuse and, now, on what cases professionals find difficult. One implication is that Area Child Protection Committee conference procedures and local practice should reflect the fact that there may be a need in certain cases to a) ensure the case and conference management is discussed with the chair beforehand (for instance, who should attend), and, b) provide a safe zone where the professionals can share their concerns in private, if necessary. While parents do not like being excluded from part of the conference, recent work by Thoburn (1995) and Bell (1996) suggests that if partial exclusion is managed sensitively and within a genuine commitment to partnership the effect on parents is not as negative as was originally thought.   It is the professionals commitment to working in partnership throughout the investigation process - both with each other and with the parents and the child - that is the determinant of good practice and the critical factor in the parents experience.

The importance of effective agency systems for managing and supporting their workers through the emotional turmoil of child protection work was raised by the attitude survey and is further highlighted by this more detailed analysis. Agencies need to take seriously the impact of family factors and the workers' emotional response to them by providing adequate support, supervision and training.   Training should provide all the professional participants with an awareness that their emotional reactions can be unhelpfully brought into play by parents attendance at the conference, taking into account the impact of cultural and class factors on the assessment and definition of abuse and on the experience of the families conferenced. Professionals need to be sensitive to the dynamics influencing their decisions, they need to understand and  tolerate difference but they also have to hold on to  their wits and make  "professionally accountable decisions...which offer a means of filtering which is guided by more then hunches, organisational politics and situated moral reasoning...and which offer a means of detecting the right child" (Wattam, 1995).

This part of the research has demonstrated the power of professional operational perspectives and the ways in which perspectives can clash. Ways of enabling the clashes to be managed constructively have been suggested and it has been acknowledged that a number of the difficulties described are inherent in the ambiguous nature of the task. It is acknowledged that the way the child protection system is currently managed makes it difficult for the professionals to meet the families welfare needs. However, this chapter has also suggested that as far as the professionals are concerned, the majority of initial conferences achieve their aims with the help of the parents. What has been uncovered are the aspects of the conference that are disempowering for the professionals and it has been suggested that the factors contributing to the professionals disempowerment are the same for the parents. The next chapter will turn to the experiences of the parents to explore this hypothesis further.

# 7 The Parents: their experience of the child protection process

> I'm one of the undeserving poor, that's what I am. Think what that means to a man. It means he's up agen middle class morality all the time.
> Doolittle, Shaw (1913), Pygmalion.

The last chapter explored the professionals' experience of involving parents in the thirty six conferences researched. Although their experiences were largely positive concerns about particular situations were identified. On an index of difficulty it was judged the professionals found one third of the conferences more difficult as a result of the parents' presence. These difficulties arose from a compilation of characteristics of the family and location, the type and nature of the abuse and whether or not the parents acknowledged it. Discussion of the findings centred around the difficulties for professionals in defining abuse in situations of uncertainty and ambiguity and in managing the contradictions inherent in the conference task. The concept of the operational perspective provided a framework for understanding the ways in which the different participants constructed the diagnosis of abuse and acted upon it. Other central themes, such as justice, partnership and empowerment were also developed.

This chapter turns to the experiences of the parents and other family members. Other studies of parents' experience of conference attendance suggests that it is "the very opposite of the cosy encounter which simplistic talk of partnership may suggest" (Stevenson, 1994). Cleaver and Farmer (1995) interviewed thirty families about their experiences of a suspected child abuse investigation and found that most of the parents felt frightened,

145

ashamed, guilty and powerless. Farmer and Owen (1995) found that for many parents, hearing about the investigation came as a complete shock. The impact of the investigation on mothers whose children had alleged sexual abuse was particularly marked; "They experienced shock, bewilderment, anger and the onset of profound feelings of loss" (p.55). They compare the experience of parents in the conference to "castaways to a foreign shore". The purpose of this chapter, then, is to explore how parents can be empowered when they feel cast away and alienated paying particular attention to the impact of their feelings on partnership practice. A further purpose is to determine the degree to which the conference attendance per se affects the parents' overall attitude to intervention. This seems important to establish given Cleaver and Freeman's (1995) finding that the initial enquiry can have "profound and negative effects on families". The conference event was therefore explored within the context of the investigation, focussing on the parents' perceptions of the process from the first social work contact following the allegation, through the preparation for the conference, the conference experience and the ensuing weeks.


## Method

The study involved comparisons between the experiences of two groups of families, fifty who had been invited to the conference, and thirty three who had not. Data was collected by interviewing the family members by means of a semi-structured questionnaire. Previous studies of child abuse (Browne and Saqi, 1987) have concentrated on the child's mother, so the methodology here was designed to take into account the experiences of different members of the same family. The researchers therefore interviewed as many members of the family as were willing and that they could contact.

The interviews were held in the family home between one and four weeks after the conference. Their location and timing was organised to give parents space after the conference to formulate a more considered and reflective response, to see if feelings changed when the immediate trauma was behind and to net a wider range of family members. A further objective was to gather information about the process of the investigation in order to explore the relationship between conference attendance and attitudes to the longer term intervention. Other studies had suggested an association between the quality of the pre-conference preparation, the conference experience and the on-going work and the research was designed to incorporate these elements.

## The interviews

The ethics of conducting research interviews in this sensitive area of peoples lives while simultaneously engaging their cooperation is complex (see Smith and Cantley, 1985). It mirrors the dilemmas facing the practitioners and requires similar skills in balancing conflict between the value of client self-determination on the one hand and encouraging personal disclosure on the other. As Oscar Wilde suggested,

> The harm is done by...dragging before the eyes of the public some incident in private life...and inviting the public to discuss the incident, to exercise authority in the matter, to give their views, and not merely to give their views, but to carry them into action, and to dictate to the man on all other points...The private lives of men and women should not be told to the public.
>
> The Soul of Man

From the research perspective there was the need to balance the dependency on the social services department for access to confidential information with the requirements to assure anonymity, to distance the research from the authority and to offer real choice to parents who did not wish to participate. The families were therefore given the opportunity to withdraw from the research at the time of the formal notification of the conference. A letter outlining the aims and methods of the research project, offering a small remuneration and requesting an interview was then sent from the researcher. This payment underlined the value of the parents' contribution by acknowledging their time commitment and had the additional benefit of differentiating the research interviews from the social services department investigation. Families were very happy to receive it and many found the experience a positive one.

## Who was interviewed

The interviews were carried out by a trained team of three qualified social workers, two of whom were also experienced research interviewers. The investigating social workers were notified of the interviews and asked to advise on the appropriateness of interviewing the children. Access to the children proved difficult for a number of reasons - a not uncommon finding in empirical work of this nature. Although few parents formally withdrew a number chose to be unavailable when the interviewers arrived or had moved house and could not be traced. In all, thirty two of the eighty three families were not interviewed. There were particular difficulties (for us as

well as the social workers!) in finding separated and divorced fathers, some
of whom lived out of the area. This, also, illustrates a difficulty in working
with families in child protection and is reflected in the findings. Thoburn et
al. (1995) similarly found that very few of the parents and step parents
living away from home were involved in the social work task in any way.
There were also a small number of parents who were not interviewed,
either because they were known to be violent or because they were
mentally ill. Interpreters were used in the case of a Chinese family and a
deaf couple.

For the reasons given earlier the perceptions of all the family members
on the same situation were regarded as equally valid. Where the parents or
carers lived together, however, it was generally not possible to interview
them separately. Separate schedules were completed for each parent in an
attempt to acknowledge differences - and there were some - but it is
recognised that a drawback of this method is that some differences may not
have been expressed. The collusive nature of some adult partners in child
sexual abuse cases is well documented (Furniss, 1983; Bentovim et al.,
1988). In the last chapter there was evidence that mothers felt intimidated
within a violent relationship.  So there were situations where differences
between the different family members would not be accessed by this
method. Within those constraints, in most cases where both parents were
interviewed together their views generally coincided. Where they did not
this was picked up by the schedules. Farmer and Owen (1995) also found
that parents had a good many experiences in common, and they also treated
their cases as one.

**Format of the interviews**

The interviews lasted about an hour and were conducted by means of a
semi-structured questionnaire containing open-ended and closed questions.
The questionnaire was designed to elicit information about the degree and
accuracy of the knowledge held by the parents regarding the allegations
and the conference process and their feelings about what was happening to
them. The aim was to determine firstly, whether parents who attended
conferences had more or more accurate information than those who did not
and to judge whether this engendered a sense of empowerment. A further
and related aim was to measure the impact of the families' experiences on
their relationship with the professionals and their willingness to cooperate
with the consequent child protection plan. The themes of justice and
influence, seen as being core to the concept of partnership from the
families perspective, were pursued by asking the parents whether they felt

they had influenced the conference decisions and recommendations and whether they felt fairly treated. A key purpose was to determine the degree to which outcomes related to conference attendance and the parents' experience of the process.

## Reliability

Of the seventy one interview schedules completed, only 5% were deemed unreliable by the researchers. In twelve cases (16%) the interviewers judged that the parents had some limitations in their understanding. Reliability was addressed by cross-checking the schedules completed by the three interviewers and by regular meetings which helped to maintain standardisation in relation to the completion of the schedules and general approach to parents. Additionally, addressing the feelings provoked in the researchers by the families diminished their impact on the schedules and proved to be important in maintaining objectivity.

## Validity

Since the research design allowed for the collection of data from a range of sources the recordings of the family interviews were cross-checked against a number of other completed research instruments. In every case where parents were interviewed there was a monitoring study containing the information about, for example, the alleged abuse, the family profile, and whether they agreed with the professionals. In every case where parents had attended the conference, questionnaires were completed by the professionals and in twenty two of the cases also the investigating social worker was interviewed. Finally, validity was ensured by the continuing process of discussing the emerging themes with the expert practitioners, the steering group engaged in the project and with other researchers in the field.

## The sample

The sample consisted of all the families living in the six neighbourhood research teams whose children were conferenced during the year of the research. Fifty one of the eighty three families agreed to be interviewed, resulting in 71 interviews. Table 7.1 illustrates how the sample of the fifty one families who were interviewed was made up: forty six interviews from the thirty three families who had been invited to the conferences and twenty five from the eighteen families not.

**Table 7.1     Family interviews by area**

| Teams | Conferences | Interviews | Families | Response Rate |
|-------|-------------|------------|----------|---------------|
| Pilot | 50 | 46 | 33 | 65% |
| Control | 33 | 25 | 18 | 59% |
| Total | 83 | 71 | 51 | 62% |

The 71 family members interviewed comprised 40 mothers, 23 fathers and eight others, including adolescent children where the social workers thought this appropriate. At the time the allegation was received 34% of the children lived with both parents, 21% alone with mother and 32% with other family combinations such as grandparents. In only one family was the child not living with a family member. At the time of the conference 26% of the children had been moved from the abusive family situation. The composition of the families in this sample is similar to that in Thoburn et al.'s study (1995) where at the time of the allegation 60% of the children were living with both parents or a parent and step-parent.

As can be seen from Table 7.1, 32 familes declined to be interviewed. The higher response rate in the pilot area possibly reflects these families' familiarity with the research project as a result of their attendance at the conference. One striking finding was that parents were more likely to agree to be interviewed if they disagreed with the allegation of abuse (45% of the respondents, as against 19% of the non-respondents denied the alleged abuse) irrespective of any conference attendance. No explanation for this finding can be found in the methodology. A possible hypothesis is that these families were motivated by their anger and found it therapeutic to share their feelings and have them made public. This somewhat speculative suggestion is supported with reference to the similar behaviour displayed by the families who recounted their distress and anger to the pressure group, Parents Against Injustice (PAIN). Another slight trend was that mothers were more likely to agree to be interviewed if they had attended the conference.

In all, 72% of the parents who were invited attended the conference. This is slightly lower than the national average now of 80%, but higher than the 36% attendance rate quoted by Thoburn et al. (1995) and the 59% by Farmer and Owen (1995). Farmer and Owen raise the further issue as to whether what they witnessed could accurately be described as involvement. However, in their study the lower rate operating and the style of the participation is thought to reflect the newness of the policy at the time the research was conducted. The rate and model of participation in the authority researched here is nearer to common practice in 1996.

## Analysis of the interviews

The analysis of the interviews was undertaken on the two samples, the individual interview (71) and the key carer for the family (51). A judgment as to the key carer was made on the basis of the available data and 51 key carers were identified. Generally these judgments coincided with those made earlier by the chairperson regarding who should be invited to the conference. In nearly every case the key carer was the mother with whom the child lived or had lived with in the six months prior to the conference The distribution of replies between the two samples was very similar and for simplicity this presentation will concentrate on the data from the smaller sample in which each family is represented only once.

## Results

*The parents' views*

*Parent A; Invited and attended, positive:*
Now that I've been to the case conference I understand everything. I'm glad I heard what I heard. I'm a lot wiser today, and its helped Joanna that I know everything. Otherwise I would have known nothing.

*Parent B; Invited and attended, negative:*
I don't think parents should go because its too upsetting...loads of people going through the same problem...If they'd understood how awful it was they'd have supported us. It felt like a trial with the police there.

*Parent C; Invited, did not attend:*
We didn't want to go alone with so many people there - too overwhelming. I think my views were represented there by the social worker and the letter...

*Parent D; Not invited:*

> I wish I had been invited. I would have been able to talk to people myself which would be much better. I think they would not have gone for the care order if I had been there.

The discussion of the findings follows the natural chronological stages; the preliminary investigation following the allegation of abuse; the conference; and the four weeks immediately following.

*Parents' preparation for the conference*

The open sharing of information is fundamental to justice, feelings of fairness and empowerment. "Systems abuse" is defined by Parents Against Injustice in their recent study of thirty families who came to them for help (PAIN, 1992), largely in terms of information about the investigation process being denied. The parents in this authority were therefore asked what they knew about the social services department's concerns, what they had been told about the conference, how this information had been communicated and about the preparation received.

*i.  Knowledge of and agreement with the allegation*
Almost three quarters of the parents (72%) said they knew what social services was worried about. In most cases their perceptions were accurate regarding the nature of and the grounds for the allegation and the identity of the abuser.

> They had the case conference because I stayed out overnight. I was leaving her until she was hungry, and because my Dad's got a criminal record.

However, only a third (38%) shared the concerns and one quarter (25%) accepted that the allegations constituted sufficient grounds for action. For example, where the injury had been to another child, or the abuser lived outside the household, the parents thought they could protect the child without outside help. Cleaver and Freeman (1995) also found there was often disagreement between the professionals and, in particular, mothers about what had happened. They write "all the parents were unhappy about the power wielded by professionals and inclined to dispute the legitimacy of the abuse enquiry" (p.126). A mother in this study, who was not invited, expressed this view with great bitterness.

> We didn't need the case conference or social work help. Social services have gone over the top. They made us out to be right ogres. Jim is not at risk.

There were no differences between the pilot and control groups regarding their knowledge about the concerns or their views about calling a conference. In all, 44% thought it right to call a conference. In Thoburn et al.'s study (1995) the researchers rated 60% of the conferences as necessary lending support to the view that, in some cases, child protection systems are activated too readily. Some parents in this study equated the holding of the conference with removal of the child into care and could not assimilate what they were told about the conference process. From a mother who was not invited:

> I knew it could put a care order on the baby or make her a ward of court. I didn't know nowt about anything else. There was no help at all. All we got was blackmail...social services wanted the child in care.

## ii. Knowledge about what conferences could do

Moving on to knowledge of the conference, parents were asked what they understood about its powers and remit. Eighty-eight per cent of the sample, a higher proportion than the 66% in Thoburn's study (1995), felt they had a good understanding about what was happening, as expressed by this mother:

> Having a case conference was a cooperative plan agreed together in view of the past. The social worker explained what will happen and the new Children Act.

Table 7.2 illustrates that parents had a clear idea about the registration procedures and possible recommendations, such as statutory action. They knew registration would entail monitoring by social services in the form of a social worker but, like the parents in Farmer and Owen's (1995) study did not know what this would entail. Importantly, they saw it as a small price to pay for keeping the child at home and were prepared to 'play the game'.

A smaller number (47%) of the parents in my study were aware that the conference could recommend the allocation of resources, although many were seeking concrete help with, for example, housing and day care. Fewer still had any idea what happened to the list, how to deregister, or about the complaints procedure, although such information would be essential to any empowering process. Again, there were no discernible differences between the pilot and the control groups.

## iii. Feelings about the preparation for the conference

Questions about the preparation for the conference focussed on what information had been received and how it was delivered. The language letters were written in and their presentation was important. The Area Child Protection Committee had set aside funds to translate the written information into several languages and the leaflets were user friendly (see Appendix 2).

**Table 7.2   Parents' knowledge about registration and conference recommendations**

What parents knew about the case conference and registration

| About the conference | Knew No. | % | About registration | Knew No. | % |
|---|---|---|---|---|---|
| Could register | 39 | 78 | Name goes on list | 46 | 89 |
| Take stat. action | 42 | 82 | What happens to list | 14 | 27 |
| Name a keyworker | 37 | 74 | Monitoring implications | 39 | 75 |
| Allocate resources | 24 | 48 | How to deregister | 19 | 36 |
| | | | How to complain | 15 | 29 |
| Total No. = 51 | | | | | |

Seventy three percent of the parents we interviewed had received the letter and explanatory leaflets informing them of the conference and half of them found it helpful. 72% had been visited by the social worker who in some cases had gone through the procedures, suggesting to the parents ways of presenting their point of view.

> I felt I was well prepared for the conference. The social worker talked to me about what to expect and my solicitor helped me to write down a statement. I was anxious about going.

Although 76% of the parents said that they had felt able to put their point of view to the social worker before the conference, most felt that what they said had no effect. They did not believe that their views had influenced the social workers judgment or decision as to the management of the case. Cleaver and Freeman (1995) also report upon the parents' sense of impotence in the lead up to the conference.

> Parents often told us they felt trapped because everything they did or said was given a hostile interpretation. They felt guilty until proven innocent. To most

parents it is apparent that professionals not only hold all the cards but control the rules of the game (p.85).

Thirty per cent of the parents had turned to their own families for support. This percentage seems low and probably reflects both the families' social isolation and their anxiety not to have damaging information seep out to other members of the immediate family. Where parents had a good relationship with another worker, such as the nursery worker, they undertook the preparation. Only 27% of the parents reported that other sources of help, such as a solicitor, had been suggested. The reluctance of the investigating social workers to advise the families to seek legal help is possibly an expression of their anxieties following the Cleveland Enquiry, but again raises issues about the limitations on empowerment, the ambiguity of the social workers role and the function of the process in managing professional anxiety as well as creating partnerships.

Parents were rarely invited (20%) to put their views in writing, even when not attending. The same question arises; if social workers are genuinely seeking to empower parents by ensuring their views are put forward, why are so few of the parents who do not attend helped to find alternative ways of expressing their views? This finding is not unique to this study. It is also an issue in work with children, for example in preparing them for participation in a review cassette recordings, pictures, letters need to be used to take the place of the spoken word. One explanation is that the time schedule in the run up to the conference is too tight to allow for this degree of engagement with the family. In Thoburn et al.'s (1995) study many of the social workers and managers found it difficult to complete the necessary work in the time. Although eight days is recommended between the allegation and the conference, Gibbons et al. (1995) found the interval was thirty four days on average. Another possibility is that the social workers do not see preparing the parents as a priority because their concentration is on ensuring the correct procedures are followed. These discussions are clearly relevant to the issue of partnership and will be pursued in the next chapter which presents the data on the interviews with the social workers.

Parents in both the pilot and control groups were given detailed information about the conference process, for example who would be there and about registration. Specific information in relation to the participation of family members, including when they would be asked to leave, was given to the parents who would be attending. As has been said not all the information was assimilated at this stressful time and fears that the child would be removed surfaced throughout. However, there was no difference between the two groups in their understanding about who would be there and what concerns would be discussed, or the possible outcomes. This suggests that the invitation to attend the conference is not a strong determinant of parental attitudes to the intervention at this stage.

In response to a series of closed questions about the preparatory meetings, the parents expressed both positive and negative feelings; 64% said that they felt understood, and a similar proportion that they had felt involved and respected. At the same time, 49% felt they had been fobbed off and felt blamed.

**Table 7.3      Attitudes to professionals' intervention before the conference**

Effect of calling a conference on parents' attitudes to professionals at the preparation stage

| | Improved | | Unchanged | | Impaired | | No comment | |
|---|---|---|---|---|---|---|---|---|
| | No. | % | No. | % | No. | % | No. | % |
| Attitude to: | | | | | | | | |
| Social worker | 3 | 6 | 30 | 57 | 14 | 27 | 5 | 10 |
| SSD | 2 | 4 | 31 | 63 | 13 | 27 | 3 | 6 |
| Other professionals | 1 | 2 | 34 | 71 | 8 | 17 | 5 | 10 |

Total No. = 51

Table 7.3 illustrates the ways in which the parents' relationship with their social worker, the social services department and the other professionals changed at this pre-conference stage. Fifty seven percent of the parents said their relationship with their social worker was not changed by the calling of the conference, while 27% said it was made worse. Only 6% thought it improved, and the remainder could not comment. The profile was similar for attitudes to the social services department, suggesting that the parents do view them together. With regard to the other professionals there was some evidence that relationships were less likely to change. At this stage of the process there was no evidence of a generally more positive attitude to the professionals in the pilot than in the control areas, supporting the suggestion made above that attitudes at this stage are not determined by the conference attendance per se.

## Parents' experience of the conference

### i. Feelings about receiving an invitation to attend

Receiving an invitation to attend was extremely important to the families, a finding in common with all other studies. Over three-quarters of the parents invited (76%) said they were pleased to receive the invitation and most of them attended. Many said they felt it would have counted against them if they had not turned up. This finding supports the suggestion put forward in the previous chapter that all the participants on the stage are aware of the power of performance on the judgements made, as well as feeling strongly that they have a right to be present.

> We were really pleased to receive an invitation. It's not nice being stuck here not knowing what is being said. At least you know exactly what's being said.

Seven families who were invited chose not to go, claiming late or inaccurate notification, practical difficulties, including child care, and fear. With hindsight, most of them wished they had gone. They said they knew very little about what was going on, and felt negative.

> I didn't see her (social worker) before and wasn't told anything...They (SSD) are totally useless...I got a letter. It was just a note saying there was a case conference. It had my name on and where it was, nothing else...I was pleased that I was actually invited but my partner (common law husband) should have been...I don't think my views were represented...It wouldn't have made much difference (to the decisions) if I had attended.

Ninety one per cent of the parents in the control group wished they had received an invitation and felt angry at being excluded.

> If I had been invited I would have felt involved in what was happening. People can make a better judgment of you if you're there...the decisions were already made before the case conference. I would like to know how they decided what to do...who said what.

### ii. Feelings about attending

The questionnaire was structured so as to obtain information about the experiences of the different groups at this stage. The parents who attended the conference had both good and bad things to say about it. While finding the experience of being present extremely difficult and often painful, they, like the parents in Thoburn et al.'s study (1995), were almost all pleased they had gone, feeling it was better to hear what was said than not, even if they disagreed with it.

> I saw the case conference as a means to end the problem. Everyone helped as much as they could, introduced themselves and so on. We welcomed the invitation in order to say what we wanted to say. We found it difficult to reply on the spot...it was awesome for us; so many people there, some not known.

Justice requires both that information is shared and that it is accurate. Eighty percent of the parents in attendance believed that the information reported in the conference was largely accurate and well presented. It is notable that this level of agreement is much higher than that described at the beginning stages, replicating the trend toward convergence identified in Cleaver and Freeman's research (1995): "on all fronts over half the families were now in agreement with the professionals' views" (p. 130). This change of attitude on the part of the parents could be attributed to shifts within the family and the wish to be seen to be cooperative to achieve a desired outcome. However, previous chapters have suggested that all the participants agree that information both coming in and going out of the conference is more accurate and comprehensive because the parents have contributed to it. This finding does, therefore, underline the value of including them in the conference.

Only 22% of the parents in this study said important information had not been shared, in only one instance by themselves. Many parents felt able to add to, correct or challenge what was said. Evidence from the observation study is that they did and were supported in doing so by the chair.

> We sat next to him. He gave us every opportunity to make our own statements and invited us to correct anything we disagreed with.

However, while some parents agreed with the facts as presented, they disagreed with the professionals' interpretation of them as abusive. Cultural factors and different parenting standards seemed influential here, as the discussion in Chapter 2 and the case studies presented in the previous chapter illustrated. There was also a lack of congruence, as was also found in Cleaver and Freeman's study (1995) between the views of the parents and the professionals about the cause, and so the solution of their problems and this alienated some parents. The mother from Case 2 again.

> They should try looking after three little kids on no money and in a damp house full of rats.

For similar reasons, the parents' views about what information was relevant to the assessment of risk often differed from the professionals. They understood the necessity for a detailed presentation of the circumstances immediately surrounding the abuse, but questioned the ethics as well as the relevance of introducing information which related to their family background or lifestyle. A study by Fisher (1990) in Bradford describes how 'bombshells' can be presented in the conference - "information of critical importance given without warning" (p.3), creating problems not just for the parents but for the chairpersons in managing them. In Case 4 in my study, for example, the General Practitioner read from some transferred medical records that the mother had three children from a previous marriage, now in care in another authority. This was the first her present husband knew of their existence, and, not surprisingly, contributed to the disruption caused.

The picture is very similar, again, to that portrayed by Cleaver and Freeman (1995), where parents resented information being passed from one agency to another, feared information would be taken out of context, and believed that everything they said or did was viewed in the light of suspicion and given a negative interpretation. Farmer and Owen (1995) also found that the family members in their study were anxious to prevent damaging information spreading beyond the family, but felt they had had no power to prevent it. They point out the similarity of this description to Goffman's (1963) description of the stigmatised persons need to control information which has bearing on personal identity.

Parents interviewed here also felt bemused by the fact that the conference considered other children in the family, especially when they had not been informed this would happen:

> They were right to have a conference about Mark; but not about the other two children. I thought it was just about Mark - whether they could put him in care for his own safety. But up to this day they had never suggested the other two might be registered.

There were other aspects of the meeting the parents did not like. A number wished they could have been accompanied by a friend or solicitor which, at that time, was not possible. Farmer and Owen (1995) found that most parents who attended felt exceedingly lonely, a feeling that would be exacerbated by their often socially isolated lives. Many expressed concern about the composition of the meeting, both its size and membership. The police presence was not welcomed, especially by the small number of black families in the study, nor was that of professionals who appeared to have no direct connection with the incident, such as teachers who knew the family, but not the child in question.

> I don't think it made any difference to them whether I was there or not. Too many people there are not directly involved, health visitor, head teacher and school nurse were all new to us because N has only just gone to school...so they didn't know us. Other people had nothing to do with it at all.

At the time the research was undertaken most of the parents were required to leave the conference at the decision making stage. While 50% of the parents said they understood why they were asked to leave, 58% did not like it and thought 'secrets' would then be shared. Farmer and Owen (1995) thought partial exclusion had damaging effects, sometimes representing punishment. However, in this study parents' views on this issue were not sufficiently strong as to affect their attitude to the overall intervention, a finding which is similar to Thoburn et al.'s (1995):

> Contrary to our expectations...there was no statistically significant difference in the rates of participation between those who attended all the conference [just over a third] and those who attended most of it (p.205).

It is the way in which partial exclusion is handled that seems critical in determining attitude. Parents did not like being excluded but could see the situation from the professionals point of view and, to a degree, manage its emotional impact if they felt they were not being marginalised.

*iii. Management of the meeting*
There were aspects of the conference the parents liked. Half of them felt that the people sitting round the table understood them and were not prejudiced against them. Like the parents in Cleaver and Freeman's (1995) study they thought the professionals had already made up their minds about registration, but they also believed they were listened to.

> Q. Did they look like a group of people who could understand you.
>
> A. No. When I was talking they kept giving me funny looks as though they were thinking what are you on about and I didn't think they understood what I was saying...They listened, but they didn't understand.

Being cared about "as people" was important to the families in this and in Thoburn et al.'s study (1995). Farmer and Owen (1995) also found an important component of effective practice was whether the worker was able to convey an attitude of respect and liking for the parents. As the quote above suggests, this disposition seemed at least as important as whether the professionals had understood what they were trying to say.

The parents generally spoke very favourably about the management of the meeting which in most cases followed a clear and logical procedure which was explained before the meeting and again at the beginning. Being in the room first with the chairperson was considered the best arrangement and concrete things like seating arrangements mattered. The way in which the chair made them welcome and handled introductions received favourable comment from 82% of the parents. The chair's attitude was experienced as enabling, for example by his careful explanation of a point or of a procedure.

> The chairman was really nice. He spoke to me before. I sat next to him. He tried to put me at my ease.

The crucial role of the chair has been referred to in previous chapters. Another dimension is introduced here. Evidence from the observation study is that the three different chairs operated very different styles of chairing. For example, the chair in one division operated a pairing arrangement with the female principal social worker in which he took responsibility for process, she for content. There was no evidence from the parents' interviews to suggest that the different styles made them more or less positive to the chairperson or the decisions of the conference. This is particularly interesting when set against the research findings on the professionals' experience, which suggest that their assessment of what is difficult in the conference bears some relationship to the style of chairing. Parents were generally very positive about the way the chair managed the meeting.

Returning to the parents, respect was communicated by a polite attitude and a business-like approach. Attention to detail, such as providing paper and pencils, or a box of tissues mattered, as has also been highlighted in Thoburn's work (1993). Only 4% of these parents said the conference had been unhelpful to them or that it had adversely affected relationships within the family. The positive feelings arose from feeling supported, involved and being taken seriously. Parents were pleased to be a party to the reasons given for the registration decision and to respond to suggestions about the child protection plan, including whether they were prepared to cooperate with the key worker.

They talked about things in a civilised manner...not prejudiced by what I or husband said. It was very helpful for me and father to be there...It is better they should know now because they can help.

## iv. *Influence on decisions*

Returning to the issue of influence and the parents' impact upon the decisions, the parents were asked whether they felt they had been heard in the meeting and whether what they said made a difference. Although three-quarters of these parents felt fairly treated and that the professionals had listened to them, two-thirds did not think they had influenced the decisions about whether the abuse had taken place, whether the child should be registered or about ways of helping. These percentages are very similar to those found in Thoburn's study (1995):

> It was rare for any family member to be involved in decisions about risk and registration, but the main parents were more likely to be involved in decisions about the protection plan and the help offered (p.186).

Thoburn et al. (1995) found that only 50% of the parents in their study felt listened to, and 33% felt that their views were definitely not listened to. However, only 31% felt that their views had definitely carried weight about whether the child had been abused or neglected. The finding here was, similarly, that the majority of the parents felt that the professionals had already made up their minds. In the words of Cleaver and Freeman (1995), "they believed professionals held all the cards and controlled the rules of the game".

> They take notice of what the Doctors say but they didn't listen to us. I don't know if my being there made any difference.

> When I was talking they kept giving me funny looks as though they were thinking what are you on about and I didn't think they understood what I was saying...They listened, but they didn't understand.

The parents' belief that they did not affect the decisions received support from the monitoring study which demonstrated that there were no differences between the pilot and control areas in the numbers of children registered or in the categories of registration. This finding is also supported by Farmer and Owen (1995), who write:

> There seemed to be an expectation not that parents would influence the conference judgment but that they would be influenced by it (p.108).

An important finding for practitioners who are concerned about the trauma experienced by parents attending is that parents are often able to hold their anger and fear in balance with more positive feelings; parents could feel bad about what was happening to them, but still agree that the outcome was good.

> The police shouldn't have been there. It felt just like a court room...But we are happy about the decision to register, and review after three months. They even wrote to housing for me.

The experiences of parents in the pilot areas contrasted sharply with those in the control areas, nearly all of whom wished to have been invited. Over three-quarters of the parents who were not invited had no idea what had been said about themselves or their child or whether it was accurate.

> We would like to have been able to correct information and the way it was given-wrong conclusions were drawn.

While they share with the parents who attended a sense of impotence in the decision making process, parents in the control areas differ dramatically in feeling an overwhelming sense of injustice.

> Since the conference I can't talk to my social worker. It's unfair that I wasn't allowed to be there. I wanted to put my point of view. I don't feel any of the decisions made will be helpful to me or my children.

The experiences of this group of parents is more like those in Farmer and Owen's study (1995) who felt they had no influence over a process from which they felt excluded.

One of the most outstanding differences between the parents who attended and those who did not is in their sense of fair play; 47% of the parents in the pilot group felt they had been treated fairly, compared with 16% in the control group. As discussed in Chapter 2, fairness, as a concept, is linked to justice (see Rawls, 1971). The difficulties for conferences in being fair and just, given the ambiguous nature of their task, were also discussed in the chapter reporting on the monitoring study. It is therefore important to note that while these parents likened their experience to being in court, felt scrutinised, judged and blamed and had no legal representation or chance of redress, they felt fairly treated when allowed to be a part of the process. 'Messages from the Research' confirms this crucial finding:

A great deal of social work research shows that clients will cooperate even if it is against their obvious personal interests as long as they see the process as 'just' (p.47).

*Parents' experience after the conference*

*i. Information received about the decisions and recommendations*
Nearly all the parents in the sample knew what had been decided by the conference, although in this authority it was not the practice at the time for parents to receive the minutes. Generally, a letter with the main recommendations had been received. Only 6% of the parents had no idea what had been decided, the same proportion as in Thoburn et al.'s (1995) study. Clearly not sending the minutes to parents increases their sense of exclusion and conveys an important message to parents about how their participation is perceived. The small group of parents who had been invited provide a good example:

> I think it's a good idea to go, but I hadn't got the nerve because if I crossed them in any way they'd be awkward. Anyway it wouldn't have made any difference to the decisions made. I was refused a copy of the minutes. This is wrong.

Hallett (1995) draws attention to minutes as the key document in the inter-agency work. Working Together, 1991, is unambiguous in its recommendation: "a copy of the minutes should be sent to all who attended the conference" (p.47). At the time the research was undertaken practice varied widely nationally, partly because of the difficulties involved in training minute takers and in agreeing a format.

Surprisingly, nearly half of the families interviewed four weeks after the conference had not been visited by the social worker. Returning to the idea of crisis intervention, this seems to be a golden opportunity missed. It calls to mind the research findings on children admitted to care (see Rowe, 1973) who are forgotten when they are 'safe'. It seems likely that in this arena a number of dynamics are operating. Thoburn et al. (1995) suggest there may be an element of collusion. Her parents did not want to be visited. Even in cases where children were not registered she found parents felt obliged to accept a visit, but did not welcome one. Cleaver and Freeman (1995) also found that once the conference was over families were relieved that they still had their kids, wanted to get on with their lives and did not want to be bothered any more. Perhaps as 'Messages from the Research' suggests, "while professionals jealously guard the point of entry, less attention is *given* to the point of exit" (p.38).

Interestingly, in my study, a visit was more likely in the control areas than the pilot areas (82%/41%). This suggests that the social workers saw the visit as an opportunity to ensure that information had been understood rather than as one for consolidating a partnership arrangement. Thoburn et al. (1995) also found that there was a greater emphasis on explaining than on negotiating and that although family members used the words 'agreement' and 'contract' they did not always view them positively. This point will be looked at in the interviews with social workers in the proceeding chapter.

*ii. Were the decisions helpful?*
After the conference only 33% of the sample felt positive about the decision to register, although nearly one half were happy about the keyworker recommendation. Table 7.4 illustrates what parents did and did not find helpful. The high figure of 65% in the category 'not applicable', for allocation of resources reflects the fact both that initial conferences do not allocate resources and suggests that the parents in this authority have some understanding of the legal status of the conference and its limited remit. The 43% who declared registration to be unhelpful to themselves or their child were more likely to disagree that their child had been abused. They felt registration undermined their confidence in their own parenting skills;

I think they were quite out of order to register all three children. It's totally wrong. It makes us less sure how to treat our children.

Some felt that agreeing to continuing social work involvement was a high price to pay for the child's name remaining off the register;

The decision not to register seemed like blackmail to me. I was pleased none of the children were registered, but angry to see the social worker in order to achieve non registration.

For other parents, registration was regarded as a welcome alternative to the removal of their child, which was often what parents thought the conference was about.

We feared having the baby removed, so registration was fine.

One of the adolescent children interviewed expressed grave anxiety that the conference would break the family up, but then welcomed the registration decision as she felt it offered her protection;

I felt safer. If anything happened again I could go to my social worker. The conference has improved how I get on with my Dad.

**Table 7.4    Parents' views on conference decisions**

Which conference decisions did parents find helpful?

| | Helpful No.  % | | Unhelpful No.  % | | Not Applicable No.  % | | Total No. |
|---|---|---|---|---|---|---|---|
| Registration | 15 | 33 | 20 | 43 | 11 | 24 | 46 |
| Child protection plan | 10 | 24 | 11 | 26 | 21 | 50 | 41 |
| Allocation of resources | 11 | 26 | 4 | 9 | 28 | 65 | 43 |
| Allocation of key worker | 21 | 47 | 11 | 24 | 13 | 29 | 45 |

Total No. = 51

Farmer and Owen (1995) interviewed fifteen children in their study and also found that for some of them, uncovering the abuse led to feelings of relief. However, for children who had to leave home they had the double pain of telling and losing their place in the family as a consequence. Thoburn et al. (1995) interviewed fourteen children, and found that although most were pleased their parents had gone to the conference, they did not want to go themselves.

Moving on to the child protection plan the prevailing practice in this authority was to formulate this at a later strategy meeting to which the parents are also invited. It was, therefore, not surprising that over half of the parents could not describe what the future plans were at this stage. Opportunities were taken in the research to check out with parents what they would be prepared to cooperate with and what they would find immediately helpful.  When asked what other sorts of help would be welcome, parents mentioned "unifying the family", help with parenting skills and family therapy. Like those in Thoburn et al.'s study (1995), families wished to set their own agenda so they got the help they thought they needed and not what the social worker decided.

*Outcomes*

The important difference between parents from the two areas at the end of the conference process was not in their understanding of what was happening but their feelings about it.

**Table 7.5  Parents' views, outcomes on conference decisions**

| Parents' Views; Outcomes | Pilot | | Control | | Total | |
|---|---|---|---|---|---|---|
| | No. | % | No. | % | No. | % |
| Thought fairly treated by SSD | 12 | 45 | 3 | 17 | 15 | 34 |
| Thought relationship with social worker impaired | 5 | 20 | 9 | 53 | 14 | 33 |
| Felt involved in decisions | 12 | 39 | 4 | 22 | 16 | 33 |

No. refers to the basis on which percentages are calculated
xp = .06 after controlling for certainty

Table 7.5 illustrates that there were differences between parents in the pilot and control areas with regard to their feeling fairly treated and in their relationship with their social worker. The numbers are too small to demonstrate a statistical significance, but the consistency of the differences strongly suggests that they are real. In particular, parents in the control areas were more likely to feel unfairly treated and to report that their relationship with their social worker had deteriorated, a finding which was almost significant in the smaller sample and significant in the larger one.

As well as analysing the parents' attitudes towards the conference itself their attitudes towards the actions of the social services department throughout the investigative process were also explored. To measure parents' attitudes four scores were calculated: cooperativeness - which measured attitudes to plans (e.g. whether the child protection plan was helpful to them); attitude to the social services department before the conference (based on answers to closed questions such as "did they blame you" and "did they respect you"); attitudes after the conference (based on similar questions), and total attitude formed by summing attitudes before and after the conference. There were no significant differences between the pilot and control groups on any of these four scores. The factors most strongly associated with attitude were whether the child had been removed from the family either before or after the conference by statutory action and whether the parents agreed that abuse had taken place.

**Table 7.6   Attitudes to professional intervention after the conference**

Attitude to professional intervention by pilot and control status and statutory action

Average Attitude Scores*

|  | Pilot | Control | Total |
|---|---|---|---|
| Statutory action | 11.50 (N=18) | 10.23 (N=13) | N=31 |
| No action | 4.38 (N=8) | 7.50 (N=4) | N=12 |
| Total | N=26 | N=17 | N=43 |

Significant Effect Statutory Action; F= 8.27, df=1, P=.006
* A high score denotes a positive attitude
Statutory action is significant at .006

Table 7.6 gives results for attitudes towards the social services after the conference. In all cases where statutory action had been taken or was recommended, parents felt unfairly treated throughout the course of the investigation.

They were wrong to suggest a care order. They're like a set of Gestapo. Hitler's army.

The association between denial of the alleged abuse and various measures of attitude was similar. Parents who were denying the alleged abuse had a negative attitude to social services. Regression analysis suggested that denial of alleged abuse and statutory action were independently related to a negative attitude toward social services but that participation in the pilot areas was not. As stated previously, the removal of their child is the parents' greatest fear and the context within which ideas about equality within partnership must operate.

## Conclusion

The findings from the interviews with the parents confirm the largely favourable findings from other studies, that nearly all parents want to be at the conference and are pleased that they attended, although they find the experience emotionally difficult. The parents' positive feeling of involvement does not extend to a conviction that they have influenced the decisions of the conference, but their ongoing relationship with their social worker is less likely to be impaired where they have been invited and attended.

However, this research suggests that the parents' involvement does not, in itself, affect their feelings about registration or make them more cooperative with the child protection plan. The parents' greatest fear is not that their child will be registered, but that he/she will be removed. Where parents do not agree that abuse has taken place, and where they have experienced the heavy end of social services intervention involving removal of the child and statutory action, their attitude to the intervention is negative, irrespective of whether they attended or not.

The numbers of parents in this study who were invited and did not attend was small; they probably needed particular help from the social worker before the conference to address their apprehensions, correct misunderstanding and provide practical support, such as child care. There was also evidence to suggest that particular care should be paid to how the family is defined and who gets invited and to the fact that many mothers attend alone. The differences in the experiences of the families who were and who were not invited are significant. Almost all the parents from the control groups wished to have been invited and felt a sense of injustice which affected their relationship with their social worker adversely. The important difference between the pilot and control groups was not in their understanding of what was happening, which was sound, but their feelings about it.

### Summary of main findings

*Parents' preparation for the conference*

There was no difference between the parents in the pilot and control areas in the information they received or their feelings about the intervention in the time leading up to the conference. The small group of parents who had been invited but did not attend knew less about what was going on and felt more negative. Reasons for non-attendance were mainly late or inaccurate notification, practical difficulties and fear.

In half of the cases the social worker had gone through the procedures with the parents. Parents were rarely invited to put their views in writing, even when not attending. Most felt they had been able to put their point of view at this stage, half felt to some effect. Only 27% of the parents reported that other sources of help, such as a solicitor, had been suggested. At this stage there was no evidence of a generally more positive attitude to the professionals in the pilot than in the control areas.

*Parents' knowledge of the professionals' concerns and remit*

Three-quarters of all the parents said they knew what the social service department was worried about; in most cases the parents had an accurate perception. However, only a third shared these concerns, and only 43% thought it right to call a conference. Over three-quarters knew that the child's name went on a list, that the child protection conference could recommend statutory action and the implications for monitoring. However, less than one-third had any idea what happened to the list, how to deregister, or about the complaints procedure.

*Parents' experience of the conference*

Over three-quarters of the parents invited said they were pleased to be asked and the rate of attendance was 72%. Nearly all the parents who went were glad they had gone, but found the experience difficult. Eighty per cent of these parents believed that the information reported in the conference was largely accurate, although some questioned the relevance of information which related to their family background or lifestyle, rather than the incident.

Parents thought the meetings were too big. The police presence was not welcomed, nor was that of other professionals who appeared to the parents not to have had a direct connection with the incident. The way in which the chair made them welcome, handled introductions, and managed the meeting helped. Only 4% said that the case conference had been unhelpful to them.

Overall two-thirds of these parents felt that they had not influenced the decisions of the conference, and most did not like being asked to leave at the decision making stage. However, three-quarters of them felt they had been listened to and felt fairly treated.

Their experiences contrast with those of the parents in the control group, 91% of whom wished to have been invited. Over three-quarters of these parents said they had no idea what had been said about themselves or their child or whether it was accurate. They share with the parents in the pilot a sense of impotence in the decision making process, but differ dramatically in feeling an overwhelming sense of injustice.

*Parents' experience after the conference*

Half of the parents in the total sample received the letter informing them of the decisions taken at the conference. Nearly all had a clear idea what had been decided. In cases where the child had been registered, over one-third said this would be helpful, and half welcomed social work intervention. The important difference between the pilot and control groups was not in their understanding of what was happening but their feelings about it. Parents in the control group were more likely to feel unfairly treated and to report that their relationship with their social worker was worse. Parents in the pilot area were not, however, more likely to have a favourable attitude to the Social Services Department than those in the control areas, nor were they more likely to say that the plans made for them were helpful.

*Other factors*

Other factors which were strongly and significantly correlated with parents' negative attitudes were the removal of the child before the conference and the recommendation to take statutory action (Sec.47). In all cases where statutory action had been taken or was recommended, parents felt unfairly treated throughout the course of the investigation. Positive attitudes were connected with cases in which the child had disclosed abuse and the parents were not denying that it had happened. They were also associated with a sense of fair play and justice which the parents in the pilot attest to, even where they express negative views about specific aspects of the process or the outcome.

In summary, these findings were favourable to the involvement of parents. However, they raised questions about the extent to which parents had been given information that would genuinely empower them and about the extent to which involvement in the conference of itself could be expected to have a major impact on opportunities for working in partnership.

**Discussion and practice points**

The research findings commonly underline the need for parents to be carefully supported throughout the initial investigation. They throw some light on what effective partnership practice in child protection work might consist in. Providing information that is accessible to all racial and class groups, for example, attention to the detail of reception facilities, and the skills of the chairperson in managing the business and effect of the meeting are important factors in communicating respect and a sense of fairness. Access and contribution to the available information is a critical starting point for establishing a partnership in which the parents' expertise is acknowledged and the basis laid for collaborative work. Hearing what is said in the conference allows the parent to hear how the diagnosis of abuse has been constructed. They can then share their perceptions of what they understand to be the problem and ways of resolving or mediating it.  In cases where the diagnosis is not disputed and where the parents feel blameless the professionals and the parents should be able to agree on a common goal - to protect the child - and the means of achieving it. As Cleaver and Freeman (1995) suggest, where instrumental intervention coincides with concord between parents and professionals, outcomes such as the safety of the child are more likely to be satisfactory.

This research has suggested that there are situations in which the benefit of full participation and the open sharing of information is in doubt. Over a third of the conferences were attended by the mother alone, and a number of the parents experienced the open sharing of information about their family background as oppressive, yet they had no control over what was said at the conference. It seems reasonable to assume that the child would have even less control.  Leaving aside the issues for the child and the child's protection, for parents who are separated and have secrets from one another, or for parents who disagree about the childs' welfare, or for mothers within a violent relationship who fear retribution, some information could be damaging to themselves or the child.

Further, while the parents interviewed here were helped to and did contribute to the open sharing of information about the abuse, they did not receive information about how to deregister, how to complain, how to access the legal system, or the conference minutes - information essential to any empowering process. Neither were the parents who did not attend encouraged to put their views in writing; again an essential prerequisite of partnership practice. The research points up the need for workers who wish to genuinely empower their clients to  provide information in a user friendly way and to spend time enabling the parents, key carers and children to find a way of presenting their views.

This part of the study forges new ground by analysing the relationship between conference attendance and attitudes to intervention. The finding that the client-worker relationship is less likely to be impaired where parents have attended the conference than when they have not lends support to the view that, at least in those cases where parents and professionals agree about the abuse, a partnership approach should be encouraged. However, the research also suggests, as does Thoburn et al's (1995), that optimism about partnership practice, even in these best scenario cases, should be tempered. The parents in this study were fully aware that their expertise was the subject of close scrutiny in the conference, and, in a number of cases, was found wanting. While they valued hearing and being heard - and this contributed to a sense of fair play which was empowering - they did not believe (and they were correct in this belief) that they influenced the registration decision. Farmer and Owen (1995) also found that parents and children experienced the intervention as powerful, and yet one over which they had little control. This belief must feed into a sense of disempowerment which is further nurtured by the unequal power balance in the social work relationship, and by the parents' knowledge and fear that their child could be removed.

Marsh and Fisher (1993) suggest, as has been determined here, that forming a partnership presents fewer problems when the parents agree with the judgment of the conference as to the nature and cause of the problem. This research goes further in providing evidence that such "agreement" is not straightforward and depends upon many variables. For the professionals, partnership practice is built upon assessments and plans constructed on the basis of concepts of family and relationship dysfunction which are not necessarily shared by their clients. Parents may not agree that the situation as described is abusive and may feel that the solution to their problems is an adequate income, better housing, and employment. The parents we interviewed did not share the professionals' view that family history and family dynamics contributed to the abuse; while professionals did not have access to the resources that parents felt they needed. Since, collaborative discussions about what is helpful and possible begin from the professionals' interpretation of events and are limited by inadequate resources, there are clear limitations to the parents negotiating powers within the relationship.

The research findings demonstrate that, however well the meeting is managed and prepared for, many of the disempowering elements identified by the parents are inherent in the potentially contradictory tasks that are being pursued within the initial conference. No favours are done to parents by ignoring this, and good partnership practice would begin by acknowledging that tensions do exist, that there may be conflicts of interest and that the dilemmas for practitioners are encapsulated within the concept of partnership practice rather than solved or made easier by it. In the following chapter the experiences of the investigating social workers will be explored in detail.

# 8 The Investigating Social Workers: their experiences and practice

Will you, won't you, will you, won't you, will you join the dance?
The Mock Turtle (1865), Alice's Adventures in Wonderland, Carroll.

The last chapter explored the experience of the parents and other family members of their involvement in the investigation of the allegation, the preparation for the conference, their attendance at the conference and the immediate aftermath. Overall, the parents were pleased to be involved, and when they had been their relationship with their social worker was less likely to be impaired than when they had not. However, their feeling of involvement did not extend to a conviction that they had influenced the decisions of the conference. Attendance at the conference per se was not a significant determinant of attitude to the overall intervention.

This chapter examines in more detail the content and process of the social work undertaken by the local authority social worker carrying out the investigation, preliminary assessment and work with family members before, during and after the conference. A primary objective is to explore the ways and means by which the social workers carry out their assessments. It has been suggested that social workers' assessments consist principally in collecting information about the incident which is then pieced together, added to by the other professionals and presented to the conference as an accumulation of concerns. A suggested consequence (see Stephenson, 1995) is that, since the conference is more interested in what has happened than why, short shrift is given to theoretical considerations. Within this model social workers describe what has happened and identify factors in the family background that are material to the consideration of risk, such as a history of drug abuse; but they do not offer a theoretical explanation for the connections. In many cases, of course, background information is crucial to the assessment of risk. As well as confirming the allegation already made and providing further evidence of risk, background material can provide an explanatory theory about the aetiology of the abuse. For example, if a parent has been brought up in residential care, reference to attachment theory could enhance an understanding of present parent/child relationships, and suggest therapeutic interventions. This chapter therefore aims to explore what priorities the social workers accorded different elements of their assessment, particularly in relation to family background. Further, it explores the degree to which they thought this task achievable. Other research studies have suggested that the shortness of time between the allegation and the conference means a full assessment is not a realistic objective. Yet conference agendas and the participants operate as if a full assessment were possible. King and Trowell (1993) have drawn attention to the impossibility of providing an instant assessment of parenting capacity for courts, and the same applies here.

This chapter also looks in more depth at the views of the social workers on participatory practice and whether this objective is compatible with the inquisitorial stance outlined above. Thoburn et al. (1995) have suggested that there is relationship between social worker's attitudes to partnership and their agencies policies and procedures. Social workers were therefore asked what they know about agency policy and procedures and an attempt is made to explore the congruence between individual principles and agency policy and the impact this had on practice. The importance of procedures to workers in child protection work in managing anxiety has been previously discussed, and here it is explored again with particular reference to the inter-agency dimension.

Finally, this chapter takes further the debate about consensus by exploring crucial aspects of social work practice, such as whether the social workers went to the conference with a preformed view about registration. As we have seen, the cases professionals find difficult are those where parents disagree about the abuse and the need for a conference, and where certain characteristics previously identified exist. (Bell, 1996) An objective here is therefore to understand more about how social workers viewed the management of conflict and how this tied in with their views on rights and justice.

# Method

Twenty two local authority social workers based in the four neighbourhood teams involving parents were interviewed by trained interviewers in the last six months of the project using a semi-structured questionnaire. Sixty three per cent of the interviews took place three weeks after the conference, and the remainder between one and three weeks after it.

The questionnaire followed the chronology of the investigation and was designed to acquire quantitative and qualitative data in three main related areas;

* *worker profile*, such as age, ethnic origin, experience of child protection work, and knowledge of agency policy and procedures on parental involvement;

* *the nature of the investigative work*, such as which family members and professionals were seen before the conference, time allowed for the assessment, and the preparation of parents;

* *experience of the conference itself*, addressing issues about the influence of the parents' presence on information sharing and the ongoing social work relationship, and the related partnership skills.

The intention was to pursue in greater depth, and in relation to individual cases, a number of the issues that had been raised by other parts of the research. For example, to discover whether the social workers judged that they had undertaken a full assessment before the conference some questions pursued the nature of the direct work with the family - how the family was defined, how the views of family members not present, including the child - were represented. Other questions asked what partnership skills were used. The inter-agency component of the social work practice was examined by asking how was conflict managed and whether consensus prevailed.

# Reliability

The means for ensuring reliability were the same as those employed in the family interviews. The completed questionnaires were checked against each other to ensure the answers made sense and were similar. Additionally the data was cross-checked against other interview schedules: fifteen of the families concerned here had also been interviewed, and all of the cases were included in the survey on the professionals' views and the monitoring study. Regular meetings were held with the interviewers to review their approach and address problems as they arose. The interviewers deemed two thirds of the completed questionnaires to be reliable. In some cases the social workers were rushed and occasionally called away or failed to turn up at short notice. Many appreciated the opportunity to reflect upon their practice in this area of work which they saw as being key to partnership work. As one of the principle social workers interviewed said, "if they get it right here, its downhill all the way".

## Analysis

The interviewing data was analysed quantitatively and qualitatively and the results were informed by the qualitative material from the observation study and by data collected from the families and the other professionals. Nine of the conferences involving these families were observed and fifteen of the families had also been interviewed.

## Results

### The sample

The sample comprised twenty two social workers who had carried out a child protection investigation and attended the initial conference with parental involvement in the last six months of the research project. Some of the social workers had acted in more then one case. Half of them had attended between one and three conferences with parents present, and some had attended four. These included three conferences from which a parent had been excluded, and four where the parents had not turned up. Two thirds of the social workers were female (15), two thirds were white European, two were African-Caribbean, one African and the remaining four of mixed racial origins. Two thirds were aged between twenty five and forty, the remainder being over aged forty. All were qualified social workers, 85% of whom were trained in the last ten years. The majority (81%) had over three years experience of child protection work and carried predominantly child care workloads. Fourteen percent were principal social workers, the rest being basic grade fieldworkers. These findings are similar to Thoburn et al.'s (1995). In her study the majority of social workers included were also female, white British, aged over thirty, qualified and with substantial experience of child protection work.

*1 Preparation and agency policy*

Discussion in previous chapters has drawn attention to the relationship between good social work practice and the agency's management of its fieldworkers (Hallett, 1995; Bingley-Miller, 1992; Mcluskey, 1995). The work of Lyth-Menzies, for example, illustrated the way nurses use organisational structures in the hospital as a means of managing the emotional content of their work. The social workers were, therefore, asked about their knowledge of their agency's policy on participation across the continuum of meetings in which parents might be involved, as well as related issues such as open access to records and complaints procedures. As can be seen from Table 8. 1, nearly all the respondents were aware of the agencies policies on open access to records and on planning and review meetings with parents and children. A third of the respondents were not aware of the policy on complaints procedures, a finding also established in the interviews with parents, the majority of whom were not aware of the authority's complaints procedures. The implications of this for empowerment will be discussed later.

**Table 8.1   What social workers knew about agency policy**

| Social workers' knowledge of agency policy | No. | % |
|---|---|---|
| On planning meetings, reviews and conferences | 20 | 91 |
| On access to files and records | 20 | 91 |
| On complaints | 14 | 63 |

Total No. = 22

Table 8.2 illustrates the documentation received and the opportunities available to discuss it. While nearly all the respondents had seen Working Together, 1991, and the letter sent to parents inviting them to the conference, fewer had seen the policy guidelines issued by the agency on report writing or the explanatory leaflet sent to parents. This is surprising since 91% of the respondents reported having attended team meetings where these issues were discussed and where the opportunity to peruse them would, one would have thought, existed. This finding supports the hypothesis in Chapter 5 that training is seen as an avenue for addressing matters that should also be addressed by management.

**Table 8.2  Which documents were seen by social workers**

| Agency documents seen by social workers | No. | % |
| --- | --- | --- |
| Working Together (1991) | 19 | 86 |
| Policy guidance on attendance at conferences | 10 | 45 |
| Policy guidance on report writing for conferences | 15 | 68 |
| Leaflet to parents about conferences | 17 | 77 |
| Letter of invitation to parents | 20 | 91 |

Total No. = 22

The social workers' general view, where they had seen the policy guidelines, was that they were helpful and good, although they would have preferred a clear format for report writing, such as was provided to the nurses. Of those who had seen the literature sent to the parents most rated it, generally, as good. Some thought the language could have been simplified but did not suggest any concrete improvements. One did not know what languages it was available in.

*Agency policy and views on partnership and parental involvement*
In exploring the factors that support partnership practice, Thoburn et al. (1995) identified a relationship between the agencies' policies and approach to partnership issues and the social workers inclination and ability to engage in partnership practice. Where the agencies approach was seen as supportive the social workers' practice was more likely to be participative, along specified dimensions. As in Thoburn et al.'s (1995) study, all the respondents in this research were aware of their agency's policy on involving family members in the conference. 68% of them (60% in Thoburn et al.'s) considered there were no differences in principle between their own attitudes and those of the agency. The differences that did exist were in relation to the policy of sending parents out at the

decision making stage - the social workers disagreed with this - and many thought the parents should receive a copy of the minutes.

*Agency support*
Findings from the research reported in Chapter 5 suggested that structures in the agency for managing, supervising and supporting the fieldworkers within their teams were important determinants of the workers' experience of and capacity to involve parents. Other work has been cited which emphasised the importance of agency structures to the quality of the work - especially the child protection task. The social workers were therefore asked to describe ways in which they felt the agency facilitated their task. In the first instance they mentioned support services, such as paying for interpreters, child care arrangements, and sending out the letters.

> We're all in agreement that the parents should be there...I've had interpreters at the conference and the department has paid for the service - no questions asked.

When practical arrangements fell down it was the social workers who had to pick up the pieces, or who were faced with the impact of inadequate or poor resources or facilities. A number mentioned their discomfort about the dreadful accommodation which they saw as communicating contradictory messages to the parents:

> ...out of date furniture, run-down, shabby - doesn't go with the importance of the issues...I felt ashamed. Also there were no creche facilities available.

The respondents clearly felt that their managers and the Area Child Protection Committee were attempting to address these practical matters, and that they were all moving in the same direction. Ideologically they were as one. The problem was that the resources to meet the families needs simply did not stretch, and the social workers had no control over these.

The administrative and secretarial support provided to the workers was also seen as important, both for them and for the families. In some cases the families had not received the letter inviting them to the conference, and this made the preparatory social work more difficult. They, like the respondents in Hallett's (1995) study, also reported that the lack of administrative back up for their own work meant they had less time to spend in direct work with the families for the conference attendance, and this was a source of concern.

A number of the social workers (63%) mentioned the value of supervision in preparing themselves for the conference. Their managers, like those in Thoburn et al.'s (1995) study, were closely involved in decisions about who should be invited and in the inter-agency work, especially where a joint investigation was being undertaken with the police. Discussions in team meetings were also used as forums for exchanging and acquiring information and reinforcing policy directives. Training events also served that function. In many cases the social workers had discussed the management of the case with the chairperson. Usually the discussion was about concrete matters, such as the time and location of the conference, but more complex issues, such as how to handle confidential information were also resolved between the social worker and the chairperson. Indeed, as reported previously, where issues had not been resolved prior to the conference, difficulties were more likely. The social workers also took the opportunity to tell the chairperson of any anticipated difficulties. In one difficult case:

> The office where we had the conference did not have any security - only a Yale lock. We had to make plans for if Dad turned up.

It was striking that what the social workers most frequently took to supervision and team discussions were, again, management and procedural matters - especially in cases where the police were involved and where they feared aggression. This finding is supported by other studies. Cleaver and Freeman (1995) also found that social work managers were key in making decisions about how the investigation should be handled by the authorities. The professional respondents in Hallett's study (1995) more commonly used procedures and guidelines in resolving inter-agency disputes and only rarely reported that the existence of procedures helped them in their direct work with families. Hallett (1995) suggests that the social workers welcomed the structure and safety afforded by procedures. She finds this significant since previous studies have suggested that social workers perceived guidelines as compromising their professional autonomy. Her suggestion is that in child protection work procedures are used as a means of allaying anxiety in this stressful area of work, a point to which we will return.

*Training*
Three quarters of the social workers interviewed had received training on parental participation. This included the Area Child Protection Committee inter-agency events previously described, and additional in-house training offered by the child protection co-ordinators to the neighbourhood teams. Two thirds of the respondents rated the training they had received as good or very good. This group of social workers valued the same elements as were valued by the respondents to the attitude survey, described in a

previous chapter. They mentioned, in particular, the opportunity to share their experience with other professionals. They wished for more help with how to prepare parents, guidance on writing reports and greater opportunities to review their practice afterwards. The respondents saw the conference as a key point in their child protection practice, and wanted more training on broader child protection issues, as well as on the handling of matters specific to the conference. Again, how to manage aggressive parents was high on the agenda.

## 2 Profile of work with the family

Three key aspects of the work undertaken with the family were pursued to explore the nature of the partnership with parents. Firstly, did social workers believe they had undertaken a thorough investigation of the incident and had they involved the family members in this? Thoburn et al. (1995) for example, found that the child had frequently contributed, whereas Cleaver and Freeman (1995) found that few relatives were involved in decisions about the investigation. Secondly, did the social workers consider they had carried out a meaningful assessment of the family background, and had they made contact with the significant adults in the child's life in preparation for the conference? Thirdly, what direct work was undertaken with the family which they believed helped to build a relationship based on participative principles, and was the inquisitorial stance required for the assessment of risk compatible with this?

### The assessment
Some of the difficulties involved in undertaking assessments in these circumstances have been suggested, including shortage of time and high levels of anxiety. Other studies have demonstrated that a variable in both process and outcome is whether the family is already known to social services. Cleaver and Freeman (1995) found that the social workers' assessments of families who were already known were less complete than those conducted on new referrals. Further, the children of families already known were more likely to be registered than those newly referred. Thirteen (59%) of the families in this part of the research were new to the social workers interviewed and there were both similarities and differences in the time taken and the nature of the assessments with these two groups of families.

### Time between referral and conference
Cleaver and Freeman (1995) quote thirty four days as the mean number of days between referral and conference in their sample. In this study, in just

over half of the cases contact had been made with the family either on the same day or within a week of the allegation. Half of these cases were conferenced between two and four weeks of the first contact. The rest - mainly those already known to the social worker - were held within, or sometimes even after six weeks had elapsed. There was a longer time between referral and contact where the family was already known.

*Was a thorough assessment carried out?*
Three different elements form the social work assessment, and the format of the conference is built around these: a) the incident, b) the family background, and c) significant adults in the child's life.

*a) The incident*
Overall, one third of the social workers believed they had undertaken a full investigation of the incident, one third thought it reasonable and one third thought it inadequate. There were differences between the new and the known cases, the social workers feeling less confident of their assessment of the new referrals although they reported finding them easier "to like". Of the known families they judged that they knew two thirds of them well and, in most cases, had been able to undertake a thorough, or reasonably thorough, investigation of the incident. In all cases this was described in terms of gathering information, with a heavy reliance on contributions from other professionals.

Of the nine families already known to the social workers, seven had been known for between one and three years, and the remaining two for a year. The social workers judged that they knew five of these families well or very well, and one not at all. Six of the social workers reported that they liked the families, although even in those cases they had not always been easy to engage. So, while the social workers did not express confidence about their knowledge of these families - even where they knew them already - they felt satisfied that their investigation of the incident was reasonably thorough.

*b) Family background*
Again, one third of the social workers replied that they had been able to undertake a full investigation of the family background, 22% judged this part of their assessment as only reasonable and the remaining 48% said they were unable to assess the family background. The main reasons they gave for this related to particular features of the family, not to shortage of time. In the main, this was that they were uncooperative, or that attempts to gain this information would put family members at risk.

I could not carry out a full investigation because the father might have punished the children by putting them in the lift. They were very hostile to me, and would not let me in.

Again, the social workers reported less confidence in their assessments of the family background of the new referrals which they judged lacked depth in all but two cases.. Where social workers already knew the families, seven said they had a reasonably thorough knowledge of the family background. As one social worker commented on a mother she knew well:

Yes, I knew her already; she's a lovely person. Otherwise the time constraints make it impossible to be thorough, and  it is important not to delay.

However, in most cases the assessment described already existed in the sense that workers relied on information on file - and did not attempt to undertake a fresh assessment. Given what we know about shifting alliances and the reconstitution of families that have a history of involvement with social services, relying on such information might be risky. Moreover, Thoburn et al.'s (1995) research revealed that files were unreliable sources of information on family circumstances in the year prior to referral. Half of the parents in her study described a serious loss by death or divorce in the preceding year and a quarter told of serious illness or accidents.

*c) Significant adults in the child's life*
Only three of the respondents thought they had seen most of the child's primary attachment figures, and twelve replied that they had not. The remainder did not know. In some cases there were particular reasons for this, such as that the father was violent, or had not lived in the household for some time. In two cases, the fathers had gone abroad; in another the mother was mentally ill, and in another had severe learning difficulties and was unable to cooperate. In others - especially in relation to grandparents - it did appear not a great deal of thought had been given, or importance attached. As one social worker said;

If the relatives had been around I might have wanted them to attend.

In another case, the social worker felt responsible for not letting damaging information seep out to the extended family;

I think the maternal grandmother should have been involved, but she is unaware of the marital violence so this would have caused problems in the conference and after it.

Quinton and Rutter (1988) identified positive support from a partner as a key factor in preventing the inter-generational transmission of parenting problems. It is therefore alarming that family support figures were so rarely seen. Thoburn et al.'s (1995) research identified more family members as having been seen. However, on her broader definition of involvement (being informed and consulted) only 42% of the main parents and 10% of the non-resident parents were rated as involved.

In summary, this analysis reveals some interesting similarities and differences. It seems that, where families are already known, more time elapses between the first contact and the conference. This is understandable in terms of the uncertainties and anxiety around a new referral. These findings also suggest that the focus of the investigation is on the incident, and that the approach is forensic - on gathering information on risk factors for the conference, not on helping the family with their welfare needs. Where families were already known to the social worker, there was a heavy reliance on what the worker already knew about the family. Where the social worker liked the family, collecting information from the family posed less problems. In the new referrals, there were also difficulties in exploring the family background and in seeing other significant adults. Here, also, the reasons given were not shortage of time, but that the difficulties that presented themselves could not be addressed at the time.

## 3 Contact with other professionals

All the respondents had consulted other professionals as part of their investigation. In most cases at least two professionals were mentioned. Frequently as many as four or more were listed, sometimes leading to an informal gathering before the conference. The social workers said that information shared at these meetings was also discussed with the parents in all but two cases. There was no evidence that such meetings were generally used to circumvent the open sharing of information in the conference, and in some cases meetings were cancelled when the decision was taken to hold a full conference. The quote that follows is from a social worker engaged in an investigation of child sexual abuse that had been going on for two years:

> Police, Paediatrician, health, school...I did the works. We had a strategy meeting with the police, but no information was shared which was unknown to the parents.

This quote is highly representative of the social workers' reliance on working with other professionals. In all cases the level of inter-agency consultation was very high.

## 4 The conference

*a) Who should be invited, and how was the absence of family members managed?*
The pattern of the child protection work focusing on the mother emerges further here. All the respondents thought the mother should be invited to the conference although only two thirds thought the father should be invited. In 68% of the conferences the mother attended, compared to 13% where the father was present. As suggested previously, it seems factors other than family composition are at work, supporting Farmer and Owen's (1995) suggestion that social workers chose the mother as the focus for their pre-conference work.

Turning to how the absence of family members was managed, the social workers did not see this as an essential part of their work. In only one of the cases where a parent had not been invited were the reasons explained to the parent. Likewise, in only one case were the views of an absent parent or family member specifically represented at the conference. Only three thought, with hindsight, that another adult, for example a grandparent, should have been invited. The views of this social worker are reasonably representative:

> Grandmother lives with the family but the question of her attendance did not occur.

In contradiction to the findings reported earlier, only 28% thought a friend should have accompanied the parent. Again, there were a number of quite specific situations where the practice presented problems and social workers, understandably, chose the safe option for them.

A similar picture emerges in relation to the attendance of children. Although in principle half thought older children should be invited, only one thought the child should have been included in the conference in question.

> You are talking about children and they have a right to participate. The fact that they actively contribute towards any decisions and recommendations that are made means they are more likely to stick to them.

Table 8.3 provides a profile of the work done with children in preparation for the conference.

**Table 8.3    Did social workers obtain the views of the child?**

| Views of the child | Yes | | No | | Not Applicable | |
|---|---|---|---|---|---|---|
| | No. | % | No. | % | No. | % |
| Were they obtained from the child beforehand? | 6 | 27 | 6 | 27 | 9 | 43 |
| Were they represented to the conference? | 7 | 32 | 6 | 27 | 7 | 32 |

Total No. = 22

As can be seen, the views of the child were only obtained in just over one quarter of the cases (27%), and specifically represented to the conference in under a third of the cases. Fifty three percent of the children were aged over four, an age at which communication is possible. In most cases the reasons for not seeing the child separately were not given; where they were it was usually "mother would not allow it". This social worker was investigating an allegation of child sexual abuse over two years;

> Mother would not allow me to see the child on her own. I was only able to see her with her mother or another sister.

Some differences exist between these findings and those of Thoburn et al. (1995). The workers she interviewed were strongly committed to involving children, although less sure that they should attend conferences, and this commitment did translate into action in 59% of the cases in their study. The difficulty she identified was that social workers were interviewing children without asking their parents' permission, and this also raised ethical problems and difficulty in the ongoing work. In this study, a small number of the social workers (18%) experienced conflict between the interests of the child and the parents. On the whole, they chose to avoid it by not seeing the child. Overall, only three of the workers judged that the parents' presence would help their relationship with the child, and the majority believed it made no difference.

These findings suggest that the factors that we have previously identified as creating problems in practice, such as the absence from the household of key parental figures and the presence of intimidating adults do act as barriers to partnership practice, notwithstanding ideological principles. This is also true when we look at the social work engagement with the child which was not regarded as a priority by the social workers in this study.

*b) The preparation of the families for the conference*
The interviews with the parents conveyed the deep sense of shock and bewilderment following the allegation and in the run up to the conference. Other parts of the research have shown that social workers are, also, anxious and feel threatened; if they get it wrong they risk damage to the child as well as to their professional integrity and status. Farmer and Owen (1995) found that the social workers they interviewed handled the investigation differently. They noted that some sensitive workers were aware that the feelings of the family were raw, and that for them the families experience was not a side issue - it was actually part of the story:

> What needed to happen in the time between investigation and conference, and often did not happen, was that the social workers understanding should move beyond a simple familiarity with events and circumstances - beyond the mere collection of evidence, in other words - to encompass the feelings experienced by child and family (p.91).

The findings from this research revealed that the social workers practice did go beyond the collection of evidence, but fell short of encompassing the feelings experienced by the child and family. Forty percent of the social workers said that they had worked with the family in preparation for the conference. Mainly, this consisted in an explanation of the process, and rehearsing the detail of the arrangements. Two mentioned that they had gone through their report with the parents;

> I told the parents there would be a conference, explained who attends and the procedures for using an interpreter.

> I did no other work with the parents other than the call to stress the importance of attending.

> I went through the purpose of the conference, the reasons for it, and the procedure.

Where work of even this level had not been engaged in, the main reason given was that the parents were uncooperative. In two cases the preparation had been left to other professionals, such as day nursery staff. None suggested time was a factor. The level of direct work described seems limited, in the main, to giving information. Seventy one percent of the social workers, nevertheless, believed that they had helped the families to engage in the child protection work, and half believed the families were more cooperative as a result of their inclusion in the conference. Their view is supported by some of the parents who, it will be remembered, reported that they felt well prepared for the conference. In some cases, they described a broader base of work than did the social workers.

A possible explanation of this discrepancy in accounts is that the social workers placed a high value on the sharing of information and under rated other supportive aspects of their work which parents valued. This is in line with Farmer and Owen's (1995) suggestion that social workers see the primary purpose of the conference as information sharing. In their study, and in Thoburn et al.'s (1995) for many of the workers the social workers rated information sharing as a crucial part of their contribution. However, from the parents' perspective, the way that information is given and the sensitivity of the workers approach seems equally important for establishing a partnership.

*c) Experience of parents' presence in the conference*
Consolidating findings from the other parts of the research all but one of the social workers thought that involving parents was a good thing, the reasons being generally from the rights and effectiveness arguments.

> Having parents at conferences is positively good. They are aware of how decisions are arrived at and by whom. It helps in working with the parents because they have a better understanding of the multi-disciplinary way of working.

Seventy-one percent of the social workers reported that the conferences did feel different with the parents there. They judged that in 54% of the cases the conference went well or very well, the reasons given echoing those reported earlier: discussion was more focused, careful use of language forced people to be precise, and an inter-agency perspective was fostered. The difficulties of involving parents were also the same as those previously presented, most predominantly the inhibiting effect on the professionals in the conference, particularly in the presence of intimidating parents. Picking up on the discussion of difficult cases in Chapter 6, aggression was mentioned by a number of the social workers. Additionally, just under half of the respondents were worried about the effect on parents, fearing it would be difficult for them. Concern was also expressed about particular types of case, including those with a police investigation ongoing, families with mental health problems and families from an ethnic minority background - especially where language was a problem and interpreters were present. The difficulties in involving parents where the child had been sexually abused raised more concerns in this part of the study, especially where the evidence was thin and/or the abuse was denied by the parents.

More concrete detail also emerged from this focus on the social workers' experience of particular conferences about the complexity of the logistical problems created. For example, what to do when the parents are expected but do not turn up; or, how to manage situations where the conference went on longer than expected, and the parent had to leave to collect a child from school. The role of the chair in managing these situations sensitively was seen as crucial.

*d) Participatory practice*
One aim of these more focused interviews was to explore whether the social workers' experience in particular cases led them to believe that the positive benefits they described translated into more participatory practice. Forty one percent of the social workers said that involving the parents in the conference made for more cooperative practice. In this they included the inter-agency component of their work as well as their direct practice with the parents. With regard to the parents, they mentioned in particular that there was less secrecy and that it promoted a greater sense of responsibility in the parents. Overall, one third of them thought that the parents' presence in the conference had a beneficial effect on their ongoing relationship, and one third that it made no difference.

Seventy two percent of the social workers believed they needed particular skills in developing participative practice in this arena. The most frequently mentioned skills that would be associated with participatory practice were communication and negotiating skills. Openness and honesty were referred to several times. Also mentioned were holding on to their own judgment, allowing disagreement and presentation skills - abilities associated with good practice, but not necessarily key to partnership practice. In many respects, the social workers relied on the chairperson to set a style and atmosphere that would engage parents and gain their trust. For a number of the social workers, he provided a role model and did the job.

> The chair was very approachable. He was good at not patronising and at explaining things...He made the parents focus on the child, and made them feel comfortable and good about themselves...He helped them to participate.

*e) Registration decision*
The decision to register is the key purpose of the conference. While data

from the monitoring study provided evidence that registration rates and categories were not affected, other parts of the research have suggested that the process of decision making was effected by minimising conflict. The social workers were therefore asked whether they went to the conference with a view on registration and whether they thought the presence of parents had influenced the decision to register. Finally they were asked to rate the degree of consensus on the decision in the conference.

As can be seen from Table 8.4, over three-quarters of the social workers believed that the child should be registered and they had formulated this view before the conference. Vernon and Fruin (1986) believe that this demonstrates that the conferences are not really decision making fora; rather their purposes are instrumental. Two thirds of the social workers here thought that registration would offer some protection to the child by reinforcing the gravity of the concerns and by highlighting the case for other professionals. Farmer and Owen (1995) also found that social workers believed registration would raise the status of the case.

**Table 8.4  Social workers' views on registration**

| Views on registration | Yes | | No | | Don't know | |
|---|---|---|---|---|---|---|
| | No. | % | No. | % | No. | % |
| Should the child be registered? | 18 | 81 | 2 | 9 | 2 | 10 |
| Would registration protect the child? | 14 | 64 | 4 | 18 | 3 | 14 |
| Would registration achieve family cooperation? | 15 | 68 | 2 | 9 | 4 | 18 |
| Would registration achieve agency cooperation? | 12 | 54 | 4 | 18 | 5 | 23 |
| Was there consensus? | 20 | 91 | 1 | 4 | 1 | 4 |
| Did the parents' presence influence the decision? | 5 | 23 | 10 | 45 | 7 | 32 |

Total No. = 22

Slightly less said inter agency cooperation would be achieved, but as we have seen, ongoing inter-agency work (apart from meetings) rarely takes place after the conference anyway (Hallett, 1995; Thoburn, 1995). All but one of the respondents reported that there was no disagreement over the registration decision and that consensus prevailed. In Farmer and Owen's (1995) research, dispute about whether registration was advisable was extremely rare. In this study there was less agreement about the influence of the parents on the decision, with half saying they had no effect, a third were not sure, and the remainder thought they had influenced the decision. It will be remembered that none of the parents thought they had influenced the decision.

Other issues were also pursued here. Discussion of the child protection plan was not given high priority (half thought it adequate), and only three of the respondents believed registration would result in more resources being made available to the family. This implies that, contrary to what some writers suggest, the social workers do not see registration as the gateway to resources.

*f) Contact with the family after the conference*
Interviews with the parents revealed that they generally knew what had been decided at the conference but that the level of social work support after the event was low. Further, and in line with what has been discussed above, the thrust of the contact after the conference was to ensure information had been received rather than to consolidate or progress a practice aimed at modifying or changing the way the families related to their children. Twelve of the social workers interviewed reported telling the parents the conference decision immediately, and that the families understood. This method of communication was preferred to visiting the families at home. Only six of the social workers reported visiting the families at home in the week after the conference. However, most (17) believed the families had received the follow up letter reporting the conference decisions. After the conference four social workers saw the child alone. The social worker mentioned earlier who had not been allowed by the mother to see the sexually abused eight year old before the conference reported at this stage that:

> I have not seen the child yet, but I've arranged an appointment for the children to be seen by other professionals - psychologists and paediatrician. I am due to see them shortly.

Farmer and Owen (1995) suggest that this lack of follow up after the conferences is because "many parents were left feeling disaffected and alienated" (p.185). A further possibility is that social workers lack clarity about interventions which, on the one hand, require them to exercise control, while on the other do not provide the legal authority to manage this effectively.

## Conclusion

The views of the investigating social workers on involving parents in the child protection investigation and conference are in line with those recorded in other parts of the research. Ninety one percent of the social workers interviewed welcomed the inclusion of parents within the conference, reporting that it focused discussion on the issues, enhanced a multi-disciplinary approach and promoted a sense of partnership. In some cases they reported difficulties in information sharing, particularly where the evidence for sexual abuse was thin, or where the abuse was denied by the parents. Aggressive parents, or parents whose ethnic origin was non-European, raised particular difficulties.

Over two thirds of the social workers believed their views on family participation accorded with agency policy, excepting that many believed parents should be present throughout and receive the minutes of the meeting. They felt the agency supported their practice by providing back up services, and most received supervision and welcomed team discussions and training events. Discussions here were used largely to ensure the structures and procedures for managing the investigation and conference were being followed, and for addressing particular problems. The role of the chair in facilitating the process both before and during the conference was important for the social workers.

Nearly two thirds of the investigations were of families not previously known to the social worker. Two thirds of the social workers felt able to undertake a reasonably thorough investigation of the incident. However, only one third expressed confidence that they had done a thorough assessment of the family background. The reasons given were not shortage of time - 50% of the conferences were held within four weeks, and the rest sometimes six weeks or more - but generally related to characteristics of the family which made them uncooperative. Where families were already known to social services, the social worker relied largely upon information they already had about the family background. Only a few of the social workers had seen all the relevant family members, and this was not a priority for them. Only 27% had seen the child alone both before and after the conference. The views of these absent family members were rarely presented to the conference. In comparison, a strikingly high proportion (90%), consulted other professionals before the conference.

Only 40% of the social workers reported that they had worked with the parents in preparation for the conference. Mainly this was to provide information about what would happen. Afterwards they also ensured parents knew what decisions had been made, but did not embark on an intensive social work plan in the immediate aftermath. Nevertheless, they described their work as participatory in character, for example requiring negotiation and openness. About one half said they thought involving parents in the conference would lead to more cooperative work, but only 23% felt their relationship with the child directly benefited. Most thought the child should not attend, except possibly some adolescent children whose interests clearly conflicted with their parents.

The views of the social workers on the conferences were that a third benefited from the parents' presence, that in a further third it made no difference, and that there were some difficulties in the remainder. Three-quarters of them went to the conference with a predetermined view about the registration, and in nearly every case they said the decision was based on consensus. The social workers were confident the families knew and understood the conference decisions, but there was no evidence that they had much direct contact with the families in the immediate aftermath.

**Summary of findings**

*Workers' profile*

Two-thirds of the twenty two social workers were female, mainly white European, aged between twenty five and forty. All were qualified social workers, the majority of whom had over three years experience of child protection work and they carried predominantly child care workloads.

*Preparation and agency policy*

Nearly all the social workers were aware of their agency's policies on participation in meetings, but a third of them were not aware of the policies on complaints procedures. Most had seen the literature sent to the parents, whereas less than half had seen the guidance on conference attendance. All were in agreement with the agency's policy on involving parents, although the majority thought parents should not be sent out at the decision making stage and that they should receive a copy of the minutes.

*Agency support*

The management, supervision and support of the social workers were important determinants of their experience of and capacity to work with parents. Management and procedural matters - especially relating to inter-agency issues - were most commonly taken to supervision, and discussed with the chairperson before the conference. The administrative resources were seen as important, but were not always available. Training was valued as providing the opportunity to talk to other professionals, and for help with preparing parents and dealing with aggression.

*Profile of work with the family*

The time between referral and conference varied from two to six weeks. The gap was longer where families were already known to the Social Services Department. The social workers found the newly referred families easier to engage than those already known. Two thirds judged that they had not undertaken a full assessment of the incident or of the family background. Where families were already known a heavy reliance was placed on the information on file. The investigation consisted largely in collecting information from other professionals and from the family. In a number of cases only the mother was seen, whereas commonly up to four professionals were consulted. The social workers reported a number of difficulties in engaging with the families, including aggressive fathers, missing relatives and uncooperative mothers.

All the respondents thought the mother should be invited to the conference, whereas only two thirds thought the fathers should be. Little attention was paid to the role of the extended family. The views of absent family members and of the children were rarely represented at the conference. Only 27% of the social workers saw the child before the conference, the main reason being that the parents did not want them to.

The focus of the social work practice during the investigation was on collecting evidence about the allegation, following procedures and providing information. Social workers rarely attempted to work with the feelings of the family members during the investigation. 71% believed they helped the family to engage in the child protection work and 40% believed families were more cooperative as a result of their inclusion in the conference.

*Partnership practice*

The social workers believed they had been successful in promoting a greater sense of parental responsibility. The skills they associated with partnership practice were communication and negotiating skills, and being open and honest. They placed a high value on sharing information.

The social workers judged that conferences with parents present went well in 54% of the cases. The role of the chairperson in managing anxiety and setting a role model was seen as key. They also believed that conferences were improved by more focused discussion, careful use of language and a shared inter-agency perspective. There were specific difficulties in a number of the conferences, especially where a police investigation was ongoing, where the families were from an ethnic minority background, and where the evidence to support the allegation was thin or denied by the parents. Aggressive parents also aroused anxiety and created situations which were difficult for the chair to manage.

With regard to the registration decision, most of the social workers went to the conference with a pre-formed view. There was little overt disagreement in the conferences. Consensus was maintained by the chairperson and a consensus view generally prevailed. The social workers believed that registration would reinforce the gravity of concerns to the parents and highlight the case for other professionals. However, they did not believe registration would result in more resources being made available to the family, or that the inter-agency work fostered by the conference would continue afterwards.

*After the conference*

In the weeks after the conference there was not a high level of social work visiting to the families. Generally, the purpose of visits was to ensure that the families knew what had happened, not to engage in therapeutic work. The level of inter-agency work with the family fell off sharply after the conference.

In summary, social workers valued the opportunities provided for working with the parents, but in a number of cases they experienced specific problems in putting the principles of partnership which they adhered to into practice. The difficulties in operationalising their values were caused in some cases by the characteristics of certain families. However, the social workers also were required to perform sometimes contradictory tasks. The enquiry was conducted largely with the mother, and a heavy reliance was placed on gathering information from other professionals and on following procedures. There was little attempt to work with the families' feelings, or to involve the child, and the focus was on giving information.

**Discussion**

In line with the other research studies cited (Thoburn, 1995; Farmer and

Owen, 1995; Cleaver and Freeman, 1995; Hallett, 1995), most of the social workers interviewed here were committed to the philosophy of partnership and believed their practice to be more participatory at all stages of the process. However, this study has suggested that they found these ideals could be difficult to achieve and has revealed some of the limitations of the extent and degree to which partnership principles can be put into practice. The social workers themselves generally expressed the prohibitions on participative practice with reference to the family: they were uncooperative, they were difficult to engage, they weren't there, they prevented access to the child, there was a police investigation ongoing, the mother was mentally ill, the father was violent, there was a language barrier. In many of these cases these characteristics were present. As we have seen from the interviews with the parents, for their part they are extremely unlikely to genuinely engage in a partnership arrangement if they disagree with the judgments made and disagreed on the need for a conference in the first place. It takes two to tango, and clearly these factors must be a major determinant as to whether a partnership arrangement is feasible in terms of achieving change and protecting the child. However, as previously suggested, the difficulties are also endemic to the ambiguous nature of the task social workers are being asked to perform. These ambiguities are as follows:

*Ambiguity number one: Information gatherers versus expert assessors*

Social workers are employed by the authority undertaking the investigation to assess the risk to the child and to present a full assessment to the conference. As we have seen, in approximately half of the cases a full assessment was not possible in the time and because, for a number of reasons, the families would or could not cooperate. Notwithstanding, the social worker has to operate as if these conditions did not exist. Lynch (1992) has pointed out that the rules are written as if parents are reasonable and the authorities always get it right. It is possible, as Thoburn et al. (1995) suggest, that more determined and more skilful practice might engage some of these extremely difficult families and result in better assessments which would lead to more cooperative practice. The findings reported here, however, suggest that the task of undertaking an assessment which includes, as full assessments properly should, a detailed analysis of the aetiology of the families problems is, in many cases, very difficult under these conditions and within the present resource constraints.

*Ambiguity number two: Tell-tale-tits versus advocates*

To do the investigation efficiently, social workers must undertake a forensic investigation, uncovering information that, in their professional judgment, is relevant to the consideration of risk and that, in their moral judgment, constitutes acceptable or unacceptable parenting behaviour. If the families disagree with these 'facts' and moral judgements it is difficult to see, firstly, how a relationship of trust can be maintained and secondly, how such a position marries with the advocacy role the social worker occupies in the conference. An understanding of such a sharp conflict of role offers a possible explanation for the reluctance of the social workers to gather different family members' views and to find ways of representing them in the conference. It may also explain the reluctance of social workers to provide families with the wherewithal to complain since there is a clear conflict between acting as an advocate for the family in the conference and acting as a representative of the agency investigating the complaint. There may often be a conflict between being an advocate for the parent and being a representative of the local authority, and in practice there seems to be some reluctance to relinquish power when disagreements surface.

*Ambiguity number three: Adjudicators versus representatives*

Although there are a number of conflicts of interests and rights, there is no guidance as to how the social worker should adjudicate between them. At the same time there is an expectation that one social worker can represent the views of all family members. Where there is a conflict of interest- for example between parent and child - good practice would entail that they had different social workers. However, it would clearly be impossible to operationalise the principle that parties in disagreement have different social workers. Apart from the logistical problems, a decision making process relying upon consensus judgements would be rendered unmanageable. Other questions of principle and practice are raised. This part of the research has revealed that social workers were likely to resolve conflicts of interest between children and parents by not seeing the child. In Thoburn's (1995) study, the child was more frequently seen but this made the parents angry and had a negative impact on future relationships. If the language of rights is widely regarded as setting absolute principles, what of the rights of the parents to refuse access to the child? Equally, if parents are the experts on themselves, on what principle can their judgement be questioned?

*Ambiguity number four: Managers versus therapists*

Procedures exist to help social workers to provide a better service to families and to ensure the protection of the child. The research has demonstrated that social workers and their managers do pay careful attention to procedural regularity, particularly with regard to inter-agency matters. However, as the findings relating to the social workers preparation of the family for the conference suggests, working in accordance with procedures conflicts with the families needs for a service based on the principles of crisis intervention, and which addresses their feelings. The narrow focus on information sharing and on procedural regularity is not unhelpful, but does not address the families' wider emotional and social needs. The question arises whether it is possible within this system for social workers to case manage for the authority and be therapists to the family, and to address the requirements of different systems and networks.

*Ambiguity number five: Empowerers versus restrainers*

A partnership arrangement, by definition, is based upon reciprocity and entails negotiation. This research has demonstrated that families have very limited power within the relationship for negotiating. They see the cards as being stacked against them and their cooperation is, in many cases, based on a sort of voluntary coercion. Many of the studies cited have suggested that families do not welcome ongoing social work involvement but go along with it to gain brownie points which can be cashed in later to stop it. For their part, as we have seen social workers are cautious about giving parents information about complaints procedures, how to deregister, and so on. So, social workers are themselves creating a framework in which some of their practice is empowering, while some is not.

*Ambiguity number six: Decision makers versus instrumentalists*

Child protection conferences are set up as if they are decision making. Much of the research evidence, however, is that the decisions are already made. The social workers reported that they came with their decision preformed, and the parents - apparently quite correctly - believed this to be the case. Further, consensus prevailed and preformed judgments were not changed as a result of discussion in the conference. Farmer and Owen (1995) concluded that judgments in the conference were not challenged because social services is seen as possessing actual and dispositional power. This research suggests that the presence of parents gives a further push in this direction because the professionals choose not to challenge consensus decisions and wish to present a united front.

*Ambiguity number seven: Spokesman for the needy versus social controller*

One effect of involving parents in the conference was to highlight the adversity of the social conditions in which a number of the families lived. At the same time, resources to meet the families ongoing welfare needs were found to be inadequate. This research has demonstrated that these factors disempowered the social workers involved. The findings have also demonstrated that, and explained why the social workers focus was on procedural matters. These factors combine to reinforce the control function of the social work in child protection work, and to make it more difficult for social workers to balance this with their caring function. At the same time, their employment by the authority responsible for the conference makes it difficult for them to be critical of the authorities provision. The capacity for social workers to act as spokesmen for the needy is thus compromised by their policing functions.

In the next and concluding chapter, these issues will be further explored.

# 9 Conclusion: social policing or social welfare?

This study has evaluated the effect of involving parents in eighty three initial child protection conferences on the conference process, on the decisions and recommendations made and on the views and experiences of the professionals and families involved. Generally, the findings are positive but they also highlight the potential for conflict within the conference task and the trauma of the experience for the families. The parents prefer to be there than not, but there are limitations to the degree to which working in partnership with them is possible and to the extent to which the process could be described as empowering. The implications are that, wherever possible, other routes should be found for addressing the welfare needs of children and families; that, where a conference is held, the task, guidelines and procedures should be less ambiguous; and that other models for involving families in planning their child's protection should be tried. There are implications for how the conference should be run, for practice and for the agencies involved.

In this concluding chapter, I will discuss the issues raised by this study and suggest some implications. The findings reported here are largely in line with those of the other studies cited although they offer some new understandings, for example by identifying features of the most difficult cases and suggesting those where partial exclusion should be an option. They are also more broadly based in that they address the wider network of family support and because they take into account more recently published research as well as the subsequent developments in policy and practice and in the conceptual analysis of partnership.

Although this study evaluated only one model of family involvement in initial child protection conferences at a time when the policy was new there have not subsequently been substantive changes in policy, procedures or practice either in the authority studied or elsewhere. Now family members are more likely to stay for the duration of the meeting and they generally take a friend – often their solicitor. Some authorities occasionally include adolescent children. Some have experimented with family group conferences and mediation meetings. More are employing independent chairpersons. However, the problems identified here remain, as illustrated in Messages From Inspections, 1992-1996:

> In 1996 - Some workers showed a lack of skill, confidence and clarity of role - resulting in a drift of focus away from the child's needs toward adult concern. Most assessments were incomplete with no systematic evaluation of information already available, and variable practice across SSD areas. Case records did not reflect the views of parents and children. Child protection plans were not always very clear. The commitment of all members of the core group was not always high and procedures were not always adhered to Management systems had weaknesses, inaccuracy and variations in providing good management information. Staff supervision lacked a sufficiently rigorous approach.
>
> (Messages from Inspections, 1997, pp.1-38)

The consultation paper, Working Together, 1998, represents an attempt by Government to address some of these policy, procedural and practice issues. For example, it is made clear that decisions about registration should remain in the hands of professionals and that family group conferences should be supplementary to child protection conferences. The need to develop community based, preventive services to provide family support for children in need is acknowledged. The position on partnership is also helpfully clarified:

> There should be opportunity for separate professional discussion to take place between professionals. Evidence from the field indicates that partnership with parents has been interpreted to mean that professionals should never engage in analysis of the parents' situation without the parents present. This was never the intention.
>
> (Working Together, 1998, p.49)

However, other issues, such as the focus on mothers, the preoccupation with risk assessments, the tension between producing a comprehensive assessment and holding the conference at an early stage and the inherent difficulty of constructing a detailed child protection within the conference remain. More seriously, there is no attempt to reconsider the legal base of the intervention or to locate it alongside changes in the court system. The following discussion will further highlight these issues before drawing out policy and practice issues that are specific to the initial child protection conference, as well as reviewing the implications for the broader area of child care social work.

## Discussion

### *Introduction*

The requirement to involve parents in the conference was initially controversial: some professional groups, particularly social workers, were in favour; others, such as the police and Doctors, were concerned that the children's safety would be put at risk. It is now accepted that involving parents in decisions that are made about their children is an essential component of effective child protection practice and that their involvement in the conference has brought some benefits. In attempting to fulfil the conference tasks, however, new conflicts for the professionals have been created and existing ones made more difficult to manage. The other research studies cited had identified these issues but concentrated their conclusions on the benefits of involving parents. This study suggests that the way forward is to openly acknowledge and address the conflicts that are endemic to the conference tasks. In this concluding chapter I will consider the implications of this analysis for the debate on partnership and empowerment, discuss the ambiguities and the conflicts as outlined above and then suggest the main implications for policy and practice.

### *Partnership*

Child protection conferences were originally designed to protect children by ensuring that the professionals met and communicated their concerns. The emphasis was on partnership between professionals. The response to new concerns, particularly the requirement to work in partnership with parents, led to their inclusion in the process. The research has shown how the tasks the social workers face in setting up partnerships with families who have or may have abused their children involve conflict. In some cases, especially where there is an agreed perception between the professionals and the families on what has happened, it makes sense to talk about partnership. In others, for example, where families deny the abuse or, as in cases of neglect or emotional abuse, do not share the professionals judgment of their parenting behaviours, working in partnership seems an unrealistic goal. Attempts to define partnership arrangements by suggesting they are based on a separation of the care and control functions, such as is proposed by Marsh and Fisher (1993), seem naive. In contrast, Thoburn's (1995) conceptualization of partnership with parents as taking place on three levels is helpful. The findings reported here also suggest that opportunities for working in partnership vary along three dimensions - from providing information, through a more active involvement such as consultation, to participation in decision making.

The next stage is to determine which level of partnership is appropriate in individual cases. Full partnership is only likely to be appropriate in the few cases where there is certainty about the child's safety. In families where the risk factors are low and perceptions about the abuse are shared, such as in cases of sexual abuse where the perpetrator is no longer in the household, a full partnership in which the protective adults and the child are empowered to protect themselves may be achievable. Walton (1996) provides an example of empowering practice in describing a group work initiative for mothers whose children have been sexually abused. She sees group work as allowing mothers the opportunity to deal with the traumatisation, stigmatisation, betrayal and powerlessness that are commonly described as being the mothers' response to their children's sexual abuse (see Hooper, 1994).

Alternately, the most appropriate intervention in a family scoring high on identified 'risk factors' –such as those suggested here - may be intensive and careful monitoring, a daily family aid and provision of extensive day care for the children. My findings imply a relationship between 'high risk' families and difficult conferences. It seems likely, then, that achieving partnership in the conference with families having these characteristics is also likely to be extremely difficult. In providing information about which conferences the professionals find difficult this research suggests some clear criteria for determining intervention strategies and for alerting the chairperson as to which conferences are likely to be problematic.

Whatever level of intervention is undertaken, however, it is clear that it is the way the interaction is handled - the messages the parents are given about being respected as people - rather than their feeling influential, which was empowering to them. It is the human qualities of the professionals and their commitment to partnership that are valued by the parents. They feel respected as people if they are listened to, given information, engaged in the task and treated fairly. In that respect, in creating partnerships the process is more important than the outcome. Further, the role of all the agencies involved in supporting and facilitating partnership practice after the conference should be promoted.

*Empowerment*

Are parents empowered by this process? The comparative nature of the research design helped to answer this question by pointing up the differences in attitude between parents who had and had not attended the conference. Those who attended found a number of things helpful. They gathered information which they said would help them to protect their child. They liked being invited and, where they had been invited and had attended, they felt more positive toward the social worker. Most importantly, they felt fairly treated. At the same time, the parents we interviewed, like those described in a similar study by Corby et al. (1996), did not feel they had influenced the decisions. In my study, in most cases the families had not received information about other sources of help or about complaints procedures. Within the context of the power imbalance described above it is questionable whether, in any event, having access to written procedures would encourage parents to complain. A report from the National Consumer Council (1993) quotes one person as saying 'the sense that we do not have a right to services raises fears that we will lose what we have got, as a punishment for making a fuss'.

Aspects of the meeting also served to disempower the parents. A number expressed concerns about their lack of control over the membership of the conference and about information brought into it that they considered irrelevant to the abuse. They were concerned that information about the abuse would seep into the extended family and valued social networks, thus further stigmatizing them and damaging relationships. As we have seen, in some cases parents had no prior warning of the 'bombshells' that were dropped, the emotional impact of which was paralyzing.

Corby suggests that the process of removing conflict from the conference, added to the parents' belief that the decisions had already been made, is more likely to alienate parents and make them apathetic than to empower them. He believes the process is inevitably disempowering. The comparative data in my research, however, demonstrated that the parents who had been to the conference had a more positive attitude to the social work intervention than those who had not. The strong sense of having been fairly treated seemed to lessen feelings of anger and allow for a more rational response to develop. These factors combined to allow for a more positive social work relationship to be maintained. So, while the parents did not feel powerful in terms of influencing the important decisions, their involvement in the process seemed to lay a firmer base from which to proceed. This is likely to be enabling, if not empowering, in terms of their negotiating power within the social work relationship. Further, it is reasonable to assume that in some cases the knowledge gained in the process will increase those parents' ability to protect their children from further abuse. The contribution made by the parents' presence, both regarding additional information and in reassuring the workers, will also make the child protection plan more relevant to the families' needs.

In summary, this discussion suggests that, for parents, being involved in the conference is better than not, that they are helped by hearing of the risks their child has been exposed to and that they may be more inclined to cooperate with the social worker. The way in which their involvement is handled is key to the parents' experience. I have also identified a number of ways in which parents feel disempowered, particularly within the context of inadequate support service provision. Is the term empowerment helpful in this context?

Like user involvement, empowerment is a contested concept with a range of meanings. Banks (1995) suggests there are three main approaches: the consumerist approach, within which users would be given some limited choices; the citizenship approach, which involves power sharing; and the radical approach, whereby people are encouraged to realize their own power and take action for themselves. These three approaches are strikingly similar to the three levels of partnership already defined in that they carry with them aspects of empowerment, in varying degrees. Within the consumerist approach, providing information can be empowering. For example, people should be given information about their rights, about the procedures that will be used in the investigation and about what will be shared in the conference. This may offer them some limited choices and some limited control. The citizenship approach is more likely to embrace opportunities for consultation. Katz, (1995) for example, suggests that parents could be given more say in how the assessment is carried out. In his study, parents and children who were consulted felt more powerful as the assessment progressed. Of course, consultation will only be real when a choice is offered and when it can be refused without negative consequences. As we have seen, neither of these conditions may exist. In any event, choice is more likely to be offered at the treatment stage than before or during the conference when uncertainties about risk prevail. Lastly, from the radical approach, there are few opportunities for power sharing because of the overriding need to protect the child. In seeking ways forward we need next to look more closely at the conflicts identified.

## The conflicts

Generally, the conflicts can be grouped into three main areas. They arise from the muddiness surrounding the basis of the intervention, from the requirement on professionals to consult the interests of different people and from their having to perform contradictory tasks.

## The basis of the intervention

### Legalism

My findings have suggested that the conference is serving a quasi -judicial function. The present system feels legalistic – yet it has no base in law. Parton (1991) and Stevenson (1995) have described how the recent emphasis on risk and culpability and the closer working relationship between the police and social services has rendered the discourse socio-legal rather than socio-medical. Concern that investigations are now dominated by the evidential requirements of criminal prosecutions have been heightened by unhappiness with the low levels of prosecution in the court system. The way the courts operate is a contributory factor. To render the intervention less legalistic would require changes in the court system running alongside, a point to which I shall return.

Three issues arise from the legalism that is endemic to the conferences, as follows: that culpability has to be addressed; that the social and legal implications of the findings of abuse take precedence over discussions of aetiology; and that the relationship between professionals and families is not a voluntary one.

### Culpability

At the beginning of this book I suggested that the guidance on the conference purpose fudged the issue of culpability, so presenting the conference with an ambiguous task. Working Together, 1991 describes the function of the conference as being to identify abuse, while at the same time saying the meeting must not make "a formal decision that a person has abused a child". The consultation document, 1998, continues to duck this dilemma. What continues to happen in the conference is that information is presented as evidence and then used to construe the parents' responsibility or culpability for the alleged abuse. In determining risk, the conference has to determine what acts of commission and omission by which responsible adults place the child at risk.

Culpability, therefore, has to be addressed. In the conference arena this is outwith the trappings of the legal system. The parents told us that they feel judged and the analysis of the conference process suggested a number of ways in which the parents' capacity to speak for themselves was undermined or non-existent. Habermas' work on the way power effects communications and relationships was used to explain the dynamics of this process. Further, we have seen how the parents' position without legal representation in the conference could be said to be potentially unjust. In my view, the quality of representation and fact disputation that actually takes place in the conference does not accord with the principles of natural justice.

At the same time, the importance to parents of fairness in determining their attitude to the ongoing intervention has been established. Issues relating to justice as fairness, and the relationship between empowerment and whether people feel they have been fairly treated are important. This study has suggested that, while natural justice does not exist in this arena, procedural justice is a more useful concept for understanding the conference process. Although the balance of power did not change when parents were present they nevertheless felt that, procedurally, they had been fairly dealt with. Provided that children are not removed from home it is the way the process is managed, rather than simply the outcome of, for example, whether children are registered or not that determines the parents' experience. This has important implications for practice to which I will return.

*A jigsaw of information*
As we have seen, the focus of the social work intervention at this stage of the investigation was on collecting information. Against the background of the Inquiries, which have castigated professionals who have 'missed' key bits of information, the focus on information gathering can be seen as an important way of managing professional and personal anxiety. I have also suggested that the conference is instrumental in managing anxiety, for there information is shared and the responsibility for addressing it becomes a collective one. The findings demonstrated that sharing information is accorded the bulk of the time and that its collection and presentation preoccupied the professionals. The emphasis of the investigation and its presentation is on what people said and did, rather than on theoretical linkages which could provide an understanding of the connections between the disparate bits of information. There was also evidence to suggest that professionals were wary about making judgments and about owning their expertise. This is worrisome if interventions and the child protection plan are to address the complexity  and interconnectedness of the dynamics underlying the abuse. It is also important that in this area of uncertainty the expertise of professionals is not undermined.

*Voluntary or not*
The interviews with the parents revealed that they did not appreciate that their cooperation after the conference was voluntary and that the

registration had no legal basis. A more recent study, comparing parents' understanding of registration decisions in England and the U.S.A. (Bell, 1997), supports this finding. A factor contributing to the parents' misconception was that few were given information about how to deregister, how to appeal or how to complain. Any debate about the nature of partnership practice and the opportunities for empowering parents within that must address the power imbalance that is endemic to a relationship which is in part coercive.

At the same time, it has been suggested that social workers are also disempowered by the unsatisfactory basis of an intervention which on the one hand requires them to exercise control while on the other does not give them the legal authority to manage this effectively. Cooper and Hetherington's study (1996) of seven European child protection systems is helpful here. They found that in countries other than England the system is frequently organised so that the transition from "confidential" to compulsory intervention is made easier. In France, for example, as in Scotland a "hearing" with a judge who is as available to children and parents as to professionals can be requested simply on the basis of concern about a child's welfare. Cooper and Hetherington found that the backing of authorities freed social workers to use their authority more confidently with uncooperative parents in the voluntary domain. All the continental social workers felt that there was an emphasis on "control" by their English colleagues combined with lack of support from the authorities which disabled them from confronting abusing parents and engaging them without the backing of the courts. This research adds weight to mine in highlighting the difficulty of balancing care and control within a pseudo-voluntary arrangement. It also highlights the disabling effects - both on social workers and on the families - of the way that entry and exit to the system is currently negotiated.

*Power and justice*
Power has been seen to be a key feature in the relationship between different professional groups and in relationships between professionals and family members. Power has also been seen to be instrumental to the decision making process, operating as it does on different levels. For example, the chairperson uses power in determining whether some bits of information are confidential; the social workers have power in determining which information they will present; doctors have power because of the status invested in their knowledge and expertise. At the same time, we have seen that social workers in the conference were disempowered when the parents contextualised the abuse because they could not do anything about it; teachers were disempowered because they did not consider their

contribution to be of key importance in the context of child protection; and parents had no effective source of power.

The sharing of power between professionals and families is clearly problematic. Parents have power which, if exercised, may prove to be detrimental to the child's welfare: power to appear to cooperate, to refuse permission to see the child, to withhold information. Professionals also have power which they exercise at all stages of the investigation. Before the conference the professionals hold the power by defining which family members will be invited, during it they maintain power by suppressing disagreement and avoiding conflict and after it the social workers maintain power by controlling the families' parenting behaviours. The interviews with the families revealed that, for them, the ultimate threat is the removal of their child and this hangs over them like a hawk over chickens.

## Consulting different interests

In an ideal world it might be assumed that legal, professional, social and moral rights and duties would complement or coincide with those required by the agency. In complying with its statutory duties, the agency requires that social workers perform duties to society, duties to the profession, duties to users, as well as duties to themselves. As we have seen these duties conflict - yet social workers are given no guidance as to how to manage or prioritise them. Social workers have to manage conflicting interests in the following ways:

### The family and the agency

The findings have pointed up a number of difficulties for the professionals, particularly for social workers, in working in the close partnerships prescribed with two different systems - the professional system and the family system. Family systems theory (Satir, 1964; Minuchin, 1974) has enabled us to understand why it is difficult to work with some abusing families where boundaries are impermeable or fragmented. The interviews with the social workers well demonstrated the difficulties they experienced in engaging with sometimes chaotic and often uncooperative family systems. A systems approach to working with professional networks (see Vickery, 1976) also facilitates an analysis of the dynamics, such as those involving power, that operate within the inter-agency system. The interviews with the social workers and the attitude survey revealed the degree to which the workers felt bound by procedures and inter-agency collaboration during the investigation and the effect this had on their engagement with family members and children. Working within and across the professional system and the family system engendered a number of conflicts for the professionals, as will be discussed below. Within the time constraints available it is questionable whether effective work with both systems can be achieved by one social worker.

Systems theory also provides a helpful way of exploring a related issue - that of the conflicting role demands placed upon the social workers. In conducting the investigation social workers are acting for the system that employs them. The needs of the members of the family system may well diverge, however. The interviews with the families showed that in some cases there was congruence between what they believed and wished for and what the social worker believed and recommended. In other cases there was not. In explaining how perspectives may come together or may diverge, Cleaver and Freeman's term, the operational perspective, was found to be useful. Where congruence existed, the social workers roles within the family and the employer systems were complementary. However, there were a number of situations where such congruence was absent and the roles conflicted. The nature of that conflict was evident in 'the most difficult cases' group, and was graphically described by the mother in Case 3 presented in Chapter 6.

*Different family members*
Social workers also experienced role conflict in acting for different family members. The monitoring study revealed that the identification of key family members or adults the child was attached to was not straightforward. Additionally, some attachment figures - such as separated fathers - were difficult to access, or their views on the child's welfare differed from the mothers. Difficulties of definition and access were further compounded by the hostile response of some parents to the intervention, as well as by differences in language, culture and class.

The involvement of extended family members was also problematic. The interviews with the social workers vividly demonstrated the difficulties they faced in engaging with all family members and that they managed this, generally, by working with the mother. For many, this was only a partial and temporary solution and they were left feeling concerned about the limitation of their focus but without the power, time or resources to change it.

*The child*
The social work role in relation to the child was a further area of conflict. While the attendance of children at the conference is advocated in Working Together 1991, this authority was not including them at the time of the study. Social workers therefore had a particular responsibility to act as advocates for the child in the conference and therefore to find out

beforehand their needs and wishes. It became clear in the interviews that the social workers did not engage with the children and that to do so would have (in their view) engendered conflict in their role with other family members. In my study, workers responded to this role conflict by not seeing the children. It will be remembered that, in Thoburn's study the social workers did engage with the children, but in cases where this had not been discussed with the parents their relationship was adversely affected.

Direct work with children is skilled and specialised. In child protection work, there are additional complexities, for example where a criminal prosecution is also on-going (see Lynch, 1992). The social workers we interviewed did not seem confident in engaging with the children either before or after the conference or in undertaking such work within the family environment. Their difficulties in doing this were exacerbated by the need they felt to maintain the mother's cooperation. The implications for practice of this analysis will be suggested later.

*Performing contradictory tasks*

An early hypothesis was that social workers are required to perform a number of contradictory tasks. The chapter reporting on the interviews with the social workers described these in detail. I have suggested that these contradictions are a product of the history. The primary task for professionals at the conference is to classify children as being at risk and to implement the means for reducing future risk. This function is a policing one. In evaluating the impact of involving parents in initial conferences, the monitoring study demonstrated that this primary purpose - to assess risk to the child and to decide whether or not the child's name should be placed on the 'at risk' register - was probably not affected. There were no differences in the proportions of children registered as between the conferences where parents were present and where they were not. (It is interesting, within the context of discussions about empowerment, to note that this finding allayed professional anxiety!)

The analysis of the history of the initiative to involve parents explained that the conference had acquired a secondary purpose - to involve parents in the decision making process by working in partnership with them. The primary task, here, is for the professionals to be helpful to the parents by setting up a relationship which would, firstly, engage the parents in the conference and secondly enable the ongoing work to be cooperative. This function is a welfare one. Findings from all parts of the research have demonstrated that this enabling and helping task conflicts with the primary objective - to classify risk. The conflicts were apparent in the process of making and presenting assessments, in balancing the care and control functions of the work and in the way the decision making is managed. These will be addressed in turn.

*Making an assessment: classifying risk and assessing need*
There are a number of problems for social workers, in particular, in undertaking a full assessment of the family for the conference. Clearly within the time available and with the difficulties revealed a full social work assessment is rarely possible. Yet the guidance is written as if, and the nature of the decisions made by the conference are such as to suggest a presumption that a family assessment can be presented to the conference. As we have seen, even in cases where the families have been known to Social Services Departments for some years, the up to date information necessary for an assessment is often absent. The interviews with the social workers also demonstrated the difficulties they had in accessing key family members and gaining the cooperation necessary to do the work. The underlying assumption - that a meaningful assessment can be made in the time available is, in many cases, unrealistic. Doing this according to inter-agency procedures, while at the same time setting up a partnership with families who are traumatised and frightened, is conflict ridden and may be experienced as de-skilling. A full social work assessment of risk or need is, as we have seen, unlikely to be achieved.

*Presenting the assessment in the conference*
The research has suggested that, when parents are present, the professionals are more rigorous in presenting accurate information. At the same time, they are less confident about interpreting, formulating and expressing judgments in front of parents. Various factors seemed to be operating here. One was the difficulty in balancing a therapeutic intervention with a forensic investigation. This was revealed by the attitude survey and the interviews with the social workers and the parents, as well as by the observations of the conferences. 'How to say nasties nicely' preoccupied a number of professionals, some of whom struggled with the imperative to be 'up front' about their concerns while fearing that this might endanger their capacity to protect the child. Their fear was that, if the parents heard 'what they really thought' they would be alienated and deny access to the child. At the same time, parents objected to information about their family background being shared in the conference, as well as to the professional interpretation of some events or behaviours as abusive.

A further difficulty for the social workers in presenting their assessment in the presence of parents was revealed in the analysis of the 'most difficult' conferences and by the observations. These drew attention to the disempowering experience the social workers faced when hearing from the families about the severe deprivation they faced. The presence of parents in the conference seemed to exacerbate the 'mismatch' in assessing risk and in addressing need and this undermined the professionals' expertise and made them feel helpless because they had few resources to offer. Similarly, the families - especially the mothers - felt ground down by the relentless concentration on risk factors without resources being offered which would relieve their often dire material circumstances.

## Balancing care and control

This book has attempted to explore and evaluate the conflicts raised for the social workers by trying to work in partnership with families and with their professional colleagues within the context of the child protection procedures. It has identified a number of difficulties, central to which is the conflict between policing the intervention and acting as a welfare agent to the families involved. Social workers in this capacity are agents of social welfare as well as agents of social control and we have seen that holding the balance is extremely difficult.

While the assessments made focused on risk, the decisions the conference took focused on control. Spelling out the care function of the child protection plan was largely left for a further meeting held after the conference. However, if families are to experience the investigation as helpful the care element of the work has to be balanced from the outset with that of control. While the social workers in the study were aware of the families' distress at the investigation, their primary preoccupation was to 'get at the facts' by gathering information. Managing the balance between care and control was made more complicated by the requirement to work in partnership. Additionally, the professionals were not confident how to do it. Their preoccupation with procedures and with inter-agency communication can be seen as strategies for managing the balance in a professionally safe way. There remained little capacity for them to, at the same time, work with the families distress. The effect of this on their sense of integrity as well as on the lack of therapeutic help offered has been described.

For the parents, the interviews revealed that the control element of the intervention was invasive and ultimately pervasive. Their abiding fear was not that their child would be registered but they he/she would be removed - and they felt they had little control over that. The study suggested that, while the partnership dictat enabled the professionals to, at least theoretically embrace the care aspect of their intervention, the families experience was different. Their quite understandable difficulty in understanding the legal basis of the intervention and negotiating within that context is related to this.

*Family support*

The lack of service provision to support families in need is a further factor. This study strongly supports the view which the Government now holds, that the separation between child protection and family support services is both false and unhelpful. Both the families and the professionals lacked the resources needed for effective family support and this impacted in a variety of ways on their relationship. The families expressed the need for concrete support services and its relationship with positive outcomes has been discussed. Additionally, family support means the families find the investigation less traumatic. In Cleaver and Freeman's research outcomes on all aspects studied improved when material support for the families coincided with the parents and professionals holding corresponding perspectives on the events. Achieving congruent perspectives was seen to be an important component of effective partnership practice.

The professionals were also disempowered by their inability to meet the families' needs with appropriate services. The parents' expression of material deprivation in the conference was discomforting for the social workers who see themselves as being there to help. One effect of the parents' presence was to bring to their attention the structural nature of deprivation and its relationship with abuse. Social work practitioners generally are not in a position to counter structural issues, (see Banks, 1995). Adding this factor to the lack of theoretical input to the judgments made about risk increases the likelihood that social workers will perceive their professional integrity and expertise as being undermined. It seems likely, therefore, that workers as well as families would be empowered by easier access to and greater provision of material resources.

*Achieving consensus*

Performing contradictory tasks has other implications for the process and management of the conference. The findings have suggested that the presence of parents in the conference may progress and harden unhelpfully the move to consensus. The professionals told us that they thought it important to present a united front to the parents. In some cases disagreement was suppressed; in others the negatives were diluted or not shared openly. Parents were also inhibited from disagreeing with assessments as the power dynamic mitigated against their appearing to be awkward or difficult.

Corby et al.'s (1996) more recent work on one hundred and ten initial conferences provides support for this perspective. He concluded that parents had little opportunity to disagree with assessments either during or after the conference. "They felt unable to challenge professional views or put forward their own concerns and had no say in the final decision making." Echoing my comparison with a theatrical performance, Corby goes on to describe conferences as being "carefully stage managed to avoid conflict in the presence of parents - who were carefully groomed and moulded into the process". Corby concludes:

> The very absence of obvious conflict may itself be symptomatic...It is not necessarily a sign of consensus, but may be an indication that the power of the conference is working to define problems and solutions for parents, precluding alternative views.

My study also suggests that the drift toward consensus may be furthered by the presence of family members in the conference. The findings demonstrated the ways in which disagreement was suppressed and that decisions were made beforehand. The chairperson had a key role in encouraging and supporting the expression of differences of view in the conference and in managing the ensuing conflict constructively. Farmer and Owen (1995) suggest that they are "groomed" to improve their theoretical competence and in the management of conflict. While such grooming can only help - and the move toward using independent chairpersons may counter the dominance of social services - a more pragmatic and effective way forward would to build flexibility into the system so that space is available for the professionals to talk privately when necessary. In my study the parents understood this.

**Implications for policy and practice**

This analysis has implications for the development of child care policy and practice and for the organization and management of the child protection system by the agencies involved. Some of the implications are practice specific, some address the legal and procedural base of the intervention and some concern the wider context of service provision within which the conference takes place. In considering the implications for the initial conference I also question whether other types of meeting would enhance the benefits while diminishing the difficulties.

This study has suggested that there are benefits to be gained by supporting and improving certain aspects of the present system while radically changing others. There is evidence that initial child protection conferences fulfil an important function in the investigation and classification of children at risk and that involving families throughout the process is an essential ingredient of participative practice. This research has identified some of the ways in which the conference and social work practice can be improved, for example by ensuring the views of the child are represented - if necessary by an advocate. It has also suggested that there are some conferences where partial exclusion may be in the best interests of the child. The professionals were in agreement about the features of some of these cases and the analysis of the 'most difficult' cases provides the means by which these can be identified at an early stage of the investigation. Such information could be acted on by Social Service Departments and incorporated into their existing models of running and managing the conferences.

At the same time the studies have demonstrated conclusively that the experience of the present system is traumatising for the families. There is now general agreement that other ways of addressing the needs of a number of children who currently fall within this system should be found. A more flexible system of referrals should be developed so that, wherever possible, families can be diverted away from the present conference arrangement to a support structure which more appropriately meets their welfare needs. Directors of Social Service Departments and Area Child Protection Committees could usefully supplement the formal conference by having family group meetings where a more detailed child protection plan is considered and negotiated by the families. This would serve to emphasise the role of the family in the decision making and in the future protection of the child.

I have identified a range of difficulties for professionals in addressing the needs of children and families within the present system. The research is consistent in revealing the distress caused to families by the investigation and that the difficulties are compounded by the lack of resources. One of the sad ironies arising from the recent Rikki Neave case was that it was Rikki's mother who made some of the clearest statements as to the risks at home, yet she felt unsupported. Protecting children is as much about supporting parents and carers to prevent abuse from happening in the first place as it is about erecting procedures to prevent it from happening again. Child protection is about family support and the systems in place to enable children to live free from abuse are - or should be - on one continuum. The first implication to consider therefore relates to pathways into the child protection system. If there is some other means of classifying risk and meeting the needs of families it should be found. The second and related implication is the need for more community based child care services.

*A more flexible response to referrals*

In order to reduce the number of families who are subject to child protection procedures  tighter criteria for child protection referrals should be developed. Gibbons believes there are opportunities to develop more flexible responses to child abuse allegations within the existing statutory framework of  The Children Act. She points out that the rigid response currently operating may not be the intention of the legislation and supporting guidance. 'Expressions of concern', she suggests,  should not be treated in the same way as a definite suspicion that a child is at risk of or suffering significant harm. The opportunity to offer support under Section 17 of The Children Act could be used more widely. Such shifts are advocated in the Working Together, 1998, consultation paper and reflected in the Children's Services Plans now required from every authority. This shift in focus has the benefit of ensuring a more positive response from the parents and families while at the same time more appropriately addressing their welfare needs by developing preventive services.

There are various ways forward within the existing system to develop more appropriate responses to the wide range of referrals received. While the use of risk factors as screening tools is controversial because it can lead to false positives  (Corden, 1995), there is a strong argument for using them judiciously.  Jones (1996) recently surveyed seven hundred and one decisions in 'child protection' and 'child care' cases within one local authority and found that major risk factors could be identified at four different levels in the decision-making process. At the end of the process he found that workers were appropriately discriminating between child protection and child care cases based on the risk factor weightings given by independent auditors.  Thoburn (1995) and Farmer and Owen (1995) also identified cases which they believed could have been filtered out of the child protection system at an early stage. Thoburn, for example, mentions "some very needy families who had been crying out for help for some time, and others whose children had been harmed by an acquaintance or partner who had promptly been ejected" (p.235). The criteria identified with the difficult conferences in my study also includes factors commonly associated with the likelihood of child abuse, such as the high incidence of domestic violence. If, as seems likely, there are common features between high risk families and difficult conferences agencies should be cognisant of this in planning their intervention and in channeling referrals appropriately.

## The development of family support

I have argued that the potential for conflict between care and control that is endemic to the child protection conference in its present form would be lessened by the development of a broader based child care system. Such a system would require Government funding for resource provision, enabling preventive services to be developed on a community basis as well as providing for more effective post conference services within an inter agency framework. Within this framework a more flexible response to referrals and clearer, more workable and more effective intervention strategies could be developed.

The development of community based preventive services funded by voluntary and statutory agencies seems essential. One example is Easterhouse, Glasgow, where lead staff help local people to establish services and activities which meet the needs of disadvantaged families, such as credit unions, community shops, babysitting circles, toy libraries and after school clubs. The importance of such locally based activities in supporting families where abuse is likely was also illustrated in a study in Leeds on service provision for children and young people who had witnessed domestic violence (Bell, 1997). The incidence of domestic violence in families who abuse children is high (Mooney, 1994). However, the violence is often hidden and its effects on children not immediately recognised as abusive. Professionals in Leeds consequently identified the need for different levels of prevention and support. Primary preventive work was most likely to be undertaken by the voluntary sector, for example by providing information and support to local community groups. Secondary prevention was seem as being provided by, for example, school nurses, teachers and home carers, well placed to identify problems at an early stage and refer on. Tertiary prevention was undertaken primarily by social services and health agencies, who react to identified need - especially where it is couched in terms of risk.

This programme illustrates the link between supportive activities, inter-agency initiatives and child protection. It highlights the key role that parents can play in developing and supporting services. Further, it provides a sharp focus for discussions about partnership practice. In such arrangements as those outlined above, partnership is voluntary, it is reciprocal and it is based on negotiated agreement both with families and with other key professionals in the community. Service provision on these different levels is likely to mean capable and disadvantaged families mixing and therefore offers a non-stigmatising approach to families with a social service label. Reducing the stigma associated with a social services intervention may result in earlier referrals and greater opportunities for preventive intervention. It also requires the involvement of all the child care professionals in a community which, as was demonstrated by my and Halletts' (1995) research, is essential for effective inter agency work in child protection. Hearn's (1995) description of family support is helpful here because it includes the range of agencies involved with children.

> Family support is not solely the province of social workers and social service agencies nor simply a partnership between them and local people. It is enhanced by, and enhances the work of all primary professionals including adult and community education, community police and nursery staff. So head teachers can contribute space, parents groups and parent education programmes throughout the school; health visitors can lead health education programmes for young people and parents; youth workers can pay special attention to the 'difficult' young person.
>
> (Hearn, p.24)

## Clarifying the basis of the intervention

The contradictions inherent in the secondary purposes the conference has now acquired should be acknowledged and addressed. As things stand, the conference is instrumental in managing professional anxiety and in formally progressing the registration of children at risk. Research evidence suggests the conference largely achieves this primary task. The basis on which parents are involved in the process is, however, unclear and this was seen as being unhelpful to all parties. Being more explicit about the power base of the intervention and developing some structures to formally validate that seem important. The family group conference offers a model here.

Family group conferences were developed in New Zealand following the implementation of the Children, Young Persons and their Families Act 1989. The essence of Family Group Conferences (see Connolly, 1994) is that the family meet without the professionals to construct a plan which the professionals feel confident will protect the child from future harm. Before their meeting, the family are told the professionals concerns and acceptable parameters for a family constructed protection plan are laid down. A facilitator is on hand for the family. The meeting culminates with an agreement between the family and the professionals about action which the professionals consider will ensure the safety of the child.

While further research needs to be done, this model, as the Government has recognised, has advantages in that families are given a real opportunity to make proposals about their children's future based on clear reasons for professional concern. The professionals' power is made explicit by the fact that they can reject the families proposals if they consider them inadequate and can then apply to the courts to resolve the issues. Corby (1996) believes that family group conferences explicitly acknowledge the potential for conflict between the different parties and provide for a clearer negotiation process. However, it is acknowledged in the consultation document, 1998, that risk to the child may not adequately be addressed within this forum. It seems unlikely that family group conferences will replace the formal inter-agency meeting where registration is decided, although they may well provide further opportunity for formulating a more detailed child protection plan.

A different model, but having similar advantages, was that researched on the continent by Cooper and Hetherington (1996), and described above. There, when control had to be kept in the hands of the professionals the authority is provided by the court. The court system would need to develop procedures to enable civil and criminal actions in child abuse hearings to be heard earlier and in a less formal context, such as happens in Scotland. Responsibility for assessing culpability and for determining the threshold of significant harm might then be placed more properly within a judicial system where the interests of all parties could be properly represented. An additional benefit would be that the child protection conference could then concentrate on assessing need and on the construction of the child protection plan.

## Agency support

The relationship between good practice and agency support has been spelt out by this research. Where agency support structures existed, staff found their task more manageable There are a number of policy, management and training implications for local authority social service departments and for the other key agencies.. Support needs to be provided in the following areas.

### *Supervision*

It is evident from the findings that effective child protection work depends upon good supervision. Supervision offers a means of developing reflective practice and of addressing a number of the practice dilemmas identified. Within supervision, ways of diminishing conflicts of role could be considered. Developing the role of advocacy could also be discussed. This would be helpful in enabling the interests of different parties to be represented and presented. Involving more than one social worker in the family may also reduce conflict and should be considered in supervision after the conference. The therapeutic needs of the child should be routinely addressed. Due care should be given to aspects of personal safety, including acknowledging the impact of working closely with people who are aggressive and violent. Supervision also has an important function in ensuring that social workers address the emotional impact of the investigation on families, as well as following procedures. The preparation of families for the conference and their care afterwards were important aspects of the users' experience. Supervision should ensure and encourage good practice in this regard – especially for more inexperienced workers. Finally, the maintenance of accurate up to date records and written agreements is a clear area where supervision can assure quality.

*Management*

The findings revealed a number of ways in which practitioners and users were disadvantaged because they had not seen key documents. Management should take the primary role in ensuring procedures are known to staff and that they have been followed. By owning this responsibility for providing accessible information and by taking responsibility for streamlining procedures and ironing out some ambiguities, fieldworkers may feel less exposed and freed to address the families' fears (as well as their own).

Management has a clear responsibility to understand and address the ambiguities inherent in the practitioners' role, especially where these are now further complicated by the purchaser/provider model of case management. They should also be seen as effective in addressing issues of time management and resource development. Time and space are basic to good practice and it is management's responsibility to ensure workloads are manageable and that the quality of the supervision available is of a high standard.

The conference was stressful for the professionals as well as the families. Effective support structures for staff are essential. Structures within the agency should provide supports at different levels within the organisation, including for black staff. Lines of responsibility and accountability should be transparent and located appropriately within the hierarchy. All agencies need to ensure that debriefing is available to all staff after the conference. Special arrangements will need to be made for staff who do not work in the core protection agencies, such as schools. Team meetings, where experiences were shared, were also valued and experienced as supportive and these should be promoted by management. The training needs of practitioners should also be monitored and addressed by management in consultation with Area Child Protection Committees.

## Administration

The need for good administrative support was mentioned by the social workers and the families. Social workers and families are dependent upon administrative and clerical backup for the arrangement of the conference and good record keeping. Administrative staff should ensure parents are provided with accurate information about the conference, as well as the steps they can take to deregister their child and with complaints procedures. They should also ensure accurate minutes of the conference are made and sent to the parents afterwards. Minute tickers need training and support.

## Facilities

The interviews with the parents and the social workers demonstrated that the environment in which the conference was held communicated messages about how they were viewed as people. Social Service Departments need to provide adequate facilities for the reception and accommodation of family members attending the conference, including attending to language and race. They also need to provide support services, such as child care.

## Running the conference

The observation study provided insight into the importance to professionals and families of how the conference process was managed. Where people sit, how introductions are made and the way in which parents are welcomed into the meeting makes parents feel supported and respected as people. Parents should be encouraged to take a friend and, if necessary, an advocate and/or interpreter. In structuring the meeting, the chairperson should take account of the different interests of family members, including what they know about each other, their language needs and any gender issues. Agendas should contain a discrete place where the views of the child and absent key family members are made known. All participants should be clear about the way confidential information will be handled and whether there is likely to be a need in the conference for the professionals to have a private discussion. The chairperson should ensure that parents have had access to all written reports before the meeting. The Area Child Protection Committee procedures for the conferences should address the matter of exclusion, so that clear guidance is given with regard to situations where it may be appropriate for some family members to be excluded for all or part of the conference. The situations identified here included cases of sexual abuse where one or both parents were the perpetrators and cases where the child had made an allegation not known to the parents. Consideration should also be given to the membership of the meeting with a view to restricting the numbers present and to encouraging GPs to attend.

The advantages of using independent chairpersons should be further explored.

*After the conference*

In considering the ongoing intervention the continuing involvement of agencies other than social services should be required, as appropriate. While many professionals gather for the conference the evidence suggested that the interagency support fell away afterwards. In some cases, it may be appropriate to nominate a professional other than the social worker as the key worker.

A number of parents were not visited for some weeks after the conference. Social workers wait for the planning meeting before engaging with the families in therapeutic work. They should be encouraged to and supported in making earlier interventions. Holding family group meetings soon after the protection conference may encourage formulation of the protection plan.

Particular attention should be paid to the child's therapeutic needs and services developed to ensure their availability. Social work help should be offered before and after the conference and not left until the planning meeting.

In response to the finding that mothers are the primary target for the intervention, social workers should develop methods of working with fathers, and ensure that, wherever possible, they are encouraged to participate. The role of extended family members in protecting the child needs to be acknowledged, as does the importance of listening to neighbours.

Some families direct their anger at the investigating social worker. In those cases a new worker should be considered as a positive measure and not as a failure.

*Training*

The training needs of professionals from all agencies were identified by the attitude survey. Training should provide all participants with an awareness that their emotional reactions can be unhelpfully brought into play by parents' attendance at the conference and this should be addressed in supervision. Training needs to take into account the impact of cultural factors on the assessment and definition of abuse and on the experiences of the families concerned.

Inter-agency training was valued and should be maintained and developed. Each agency has special needs - especially those not closely identified with the core agencies - and these should be acknowledged and addressed.

Social workers should receive training to develop their confidence in working with children, in family work and in working with men.

The role of advocates should be developed and appropriate training and support provided.

### Area Child Protection Committees

In determining and writing local procedures, the Area Child Protection Committees should be cognisant of the amount of skilled professional time that is taken up with the requirements of bureaucratic regularity and that this can get in the way of good practice. Other models of conference meetings are being explored and the Committee could encourage some trials of these, for example on the Family Group conference model. The Committee has a role in initiating and supporting inter-agency training, in allocating resources to support the use of the procedures and to pay for training events and in monitoring service provision, taking into account the users perspective. Making closer links with voluntary agencies, such as domestic violence fora, should be encouraged.

### Resources

The research has demonstrated that resources need to be provided to support initial conferences, and to provide services that can help families before and after the conference. As stated above, for the conference there has to be adequate accommodation, administrative and child care facilities. Community based family support services should be developed in both voluntary and statutory agencies, in particular therapeutic services for children after the conference.

## Conclusion

Is the conference, with parents as members, the best way of protecting children from further abuse? This study suggests that the primary purpose of the conference should be reinforced. As things stand the conference achieves its primary purpose - of protecting the child from future harm - as well as any other system (Stevenson, 1995). Although more longitudinal studies of outcomes are needed, Farmer and Owen's (1995) research was positive in suggesting that most of the children registered were not reabused. Further, the development of 68% of these children had been enhanced during the follow up period. It seems, then, that the conference is effectively meeting its primary purpose. However, there are intrinsic dilemmas in attempting to meet the secondary purpose of working in partnership with families in the conference to empower them. Involving parents has brought some benefits - these can be enhanced; but the policy initiative raised some false expectations. One implication of this analysis is that there should be an explicit acknowledgement that there are power differentials and there are constraints on what it possible to offer or achieve. Some of these constraints are external to the conference process. Others are encapsulated within it.

The initial conference does not and should not be regarded as a one off event standing in isolation from other essential children's services. That this has happened is partly a product of its history and partly due to the previous government's policy on the family. Recent research by the Joseph Rowntree Foundation (Utting, 1996) has shown how, despite political rhetoric emphasising the importance of family life, the years of Thatcherism witnessed a policy shift away from recognising the costs and demands of parenthood. The present Government is beginning to redress this drift by supporting parental responsibility within a broader based framework of children's services and family support. The early years initiative and the requirement on authorities to produce children's service plans represent moves in this direction. Entry to the child protection system should be narrowed and reserved for cases of serious abuse.

Some ways forward, both for the initial conference as it now stands, as well as for alternative models, have been identified in this concluding chapter. It is within the power of social service Departments to implement some immediately; others require changes in policy and procedure which will take time; others require a substantial input of resources.

# Appendix 1 Parental involvement in case conferences Policy guidelines: October 1991

1       **Introduction and clarification of terms**

1.1     These guidelines have been drawn up to enable those involved in convening and chairing child protection case conferences to implement the policy of the Area Child Protection Committee to involve parents in case conferences wherever possible.

1.2     The guidelines are intended to take into account the duties imposed on local authorities and other agencies by the Children Act 1989: and also to follow the guidelines and regulations issued by the Department of Health in "Working Together". Both the Act and the regulations require all agencies to ensure that the interests of the child are paramount, but they also recognise that this is normally most likely to be achieved by establishing a working partnership with parents and other carers.

1.3     **Definitions**

1.3.1   The term "case conference" is used in these guidelines to refer only to the formal meeting convened in the course of an investigation of alleged child abuse or neglect, in which a decision is taken about the need to register a child, and, if the child is registered, recommendations are made about any action necessary to protect the child, the appointment of a key worker, and the establishment of a multi-disciplinary core group.

1.3.2   Where parents are invited to attend case conferences, it is assumed in these guidelines that they will also be invited to attend subsequent planning meetings and reviews, unless the circumstances of the case change dramatically.

1.3.3   The term "parent" is used to refer to any adult who has parental responsibility for the child as defined by the Children Act 1989. Other carers who have played a major role in the care of the child may also be invited. Grandparents, step-parents and others may be included in this category. The chairperson of the case conference will have the power to decide how widely to extend the invitation, taking into account any difficulties which might arise in the case conference.

## 2   The decision to issue an invitation

2.1   The decision on whether or not parents should be invited to attend a case conference needs to be taken at the earliest opportunity. Once the decision to call a case conference has been taken, it is essential that close consultation takes place between the agencies directly involved in the investigation, and the chairperson of the case conference, wherever there is any doubt as to the wisdom of inviting a parent. Otherwise the presumption will be that parents are invited to attend all case conferences.

2.2   If after consultation the chairperson decides that a parent's presence will prevent a case conference from taking a decision which is in the best interests of the child, a letter will be sent to the parents explaining the decision, in the name of the chairperson of the ACPC. There will be no appeal or complaint procedure against this decision.

2.3   Parents who are, at the time of the conference, primary suspects or the partners of primary suspects in a criminal investigation should be excluded if the police consider that their presence may inhibit the thorough and effective investigation of the crime. This is most likely to occur in situations where a conference has been called to consider an incident of sexual or serious physical abuse. The decision to exclude a parent in these circumstances should only be applied where the suspect is likely to be alerted to information implicating him/her which will not already have been disclosed. Where the parent is in custody or on bail with conditions attached, an invitation will not normally be issued.

2.4    There are certain other situations in which it is anticipated that the need to exclude parents must be seriously considered. These might include:

i) situations where there are grounds to believe that a parent might be violent, or might intimidate workers, either at the case conference or subsequently, as a result of statements made at the case conference.

ii) situations where a parent is suffering from a serious psychiatric disorder or some other condition which prevents them from meaningful participation in the meeting.

In situations of this kind (and other circumstances) a decision to exclude a parent should only be taken when there are good grounds to believe that the presence of that person would prevent those attending the case conference from acting in the best interests of the child.

2.5    All parents will be notified of a decision to convene a case conference. A written invitation will be issued, accompanied by a simple leaflet outlining the procedures to be followed at the case conference. Where a decision is taken not to invite a parent, this decision, together with the reasons for it, will be recorded and attached to the minutes of the case conference.

2.6    Parents will not normally be permitted to bring anyone else with them to the case conference. However, particular consideration must be given to parents for whom English is not their first language, and to parents with special needs such as a sensory disability or a learning difficulty. Any exemption will be at the discretion of the chairperson.

3      **Before the meeting**

3.1    Agencies holding information of a confidential nature which may need to be presented to the case conference, but which cannot be shared with parents, must inform the chairperson at least two working days before the meeting, and discuss with the chairperson whether and how that information can be shared at the meeting without breach of confidentiality.

3.2     The worker from the agency which has had lead responsibility for the investigation prior to the case conference will prepare a written report, the contents of which will be shared with the parents before the case conference takes place.

3.3     The chairperson will arrange for the parents to be invited to the case conference 15 minutes before the time when it is scheduled to begin. The chairperson will use this time to explain to the parents the procedures involved in the case conference.

## 4     During the meeting

4.1     All agencies which have information to contribute to the case conference will put this in writing using the agreed format. A copy of their report will be handed to the chairperson immediately before the start of the meeting. Information agreed beforehand by the chairperson to be confidential will be set out on a separate sheet, and handed to the chairperson immediately before the start of the meeting.

4.2     The case conference will proceed with each agency speaking to their written report, and providing clarification where necessary. There will also be an opportunity to provide supplementary information which may only have become relevant as a result of hearing the other reports. All participants including the parents will have an opportunity to clarify factual information and to correct any errors.

4.3     The chairperson will then provide a resume of the factual position, including any issues on which there is substantial disagreement. Discussion will then take place with the parents present as to the nature and extent of any concerns based on the factual information already presented. The parents will be given the opportunity to put their views at each stage on the matters before the case conference.

4.4     The chairperson will ask parents to leave the meeting if, at any time, their behaviour prevents a reasonable discussion from taking place. The use of this power should normally be preceded by an informal and a formal warning that their behaviour is becoming unacceptable.

4.5     The parents will have a final opportunity to express their views on the issues before the case conference before they are asked to withdraw. Further discussion will then take place about the necessary decisions and recommendations. Information agreed beforehand by the chairperson to be confidential will be presented at this stage.

4.6 The parents will be invited to remain behind in the building to be told the decisions and recommendations of the case conference. The chairperson of the meeting will always be available together with other appropriate workers including at least one who is already known to the parents. Normally all decisions and recommendations will be shared with the parents at this stage, but where the chairperson considers that full disclosure at this stage is not in the best interests of the child, certain recommendations may be withheld until they can be implemented. Parents will also be informed at this stage of their right to seek a review of a decision to register their child.

## 5    After the meeting

5.1 Parents will be sent a letter from the chairperson of the case conference whether or not they were invited, informing them of the decisions and recommendations made by the case conference, and informing them of their right to seek a review of a decision to register their child. They will not be sent a copy of the minutes of the meeting.

# Appendix 2 A brief guide for parents and guardians attending case conferences

**What is a case conference?**

A case conference is a special meeting organised by the Social Services Department. It is only called when there are genuine reasons to think that a child has been, or might be, abused or neglected. It brings together people who know the child and their family, as well as people who are experienced in working with children and families in general.

**What is the point?**

The point of this meeting is to make sure that all the people working with a child and family know what has happened so far. They will also consider what the broad plan for any future work might be as well as deciding who will do that work.

**Who else will be invited to this meeting?**

The main services; social worker, health, police, education, probation and the NSPCC are all invited to each case conference. They will usually send along the person most directly involved with you and your child. Often more than one person from each service will attend. For example, invitations to the Health Services would normally go to your family doctor, your health visitor (if you have one) as well as any doctor who might have examined your child at the time when the concerns first came to light.

## How will I be involved in the case conference?

Everyone who attends the case conference is asked to make written notes of their involvement with your family. You may also find it helpful to write down your thoughts before the meeting. The Social Worker can help you with this, or you could get help from an advice centre or solicitor.

Generally the conference first hears details of the events leading up to the meeting, then goes on to hear more general information about your family before reaching any decisions. You will be given the chance to talk about what has happened, and to question or correct anything said by other people, as well as give your opinion about what should happen now. You will not, however, be able to take part in making the final decisions and will be asked to leave the meeting before this point.

## What decisions can they make?

The meeting can decide that there is no real reason to be concerned for the well being of your child and that nothing more needs to be done. It sometimes happens that the people at the meeting find they do not have enough information to make a proper decision. In those cases they may well decide to hold another meeting at a later date when more information will be available.

If the people at the case conference think that there are grounds for serious concern they can decide to put the name of your child on the Child Protection Register. They can also suggest other steps, such as court action, when that seems necessary.

Whenever a case conference decides to put a child's name on the Child Protection Register a Social Worker will be named as the person responsible to bring together all the information about that child. They will also be expected to keep in touch with the other people who may be involved with the family and let them know about any changes or developments.

**What is the child protection register?**

It is a list of children who have been or are thought to be at serious risk of being abused or neglected. The list is kept secure by the Social Services Department and is not open to the public. It can only checked by professional people who are responsible for working with children and families. The main point of having such a register is to make sure that any professional person worried about the safety of any child, has a quick way of checking if anyone else is involved with the child and their family or has had similar worries in the past.

**After the case conference**

Immediately after the conference you will be invited to meet with the person who has chaired the meeting, together with the Social Worker and perhaps other workers that you know. They will tell you the decisions and recommendations of the conference and what happens next. You will also get a letter that confirms the decisions later.

**How long will the child's name be on the register?**

If your child's name is placed on the Child Protection Register this means that all the agencies involved have agreed on a plan to protect your child and offer you help. This plan will be reviewed every three months. Part of this review will be concerned with checking that it is right for your child's name to stay on the register. As soon as it becomes clear to all the agencies involved that the reasons for the original concerns are no longer there, your child's name will be taken off the register.

**What can I do if I think that the decision is wrong?**

If you feel that the wrong decision has been made in putting your child's name on the Child Protection Register, you can ask for the decision to be reviewed by writing to Director of Social Services, Selectapost 9, Sweet Street, Leeds LS11 9DQ, within 28 days of getting the written details of the case conference decisions. A review will then be arranged, unless court proceedings are underway, in which case the review will not start until all those proceedings have finished. Reviews will usually be completed within three months of receiving your request.

# Bibliography

Access to Personal Files Act, 1987.

Ahmed, S., Cheetham, J. and Small, J. (eds) (1986), *Social work with Black children and their Families*, Batsford, London.

Aldgate, J. (ed) (1990),*Using Written Agreements with Children and Families*, Pitman, Family Rights Group, London.

Allen, N. (1991), 'Editorial; PCLB considers the need for statutory regulation of case conferences and child protection registers', *Practitioners Child Law Bulletin*, Longman, 4, 5.

Allsopp, L. (1994), *Concepts of Partnership and the Protection of Children*, unpublished paper, Nottingham.

Archard, D. (1993), *Children, Rights and Childhood*, Routledge, London.

Aries, P. (1973), *Centuries of Childhood*, Penguin, Harmondsworth.

Aristotle (1954), *The Nichomachean Ethics of Aristotle*, translated by Ross, Oxford University Press, London.

Atherton, C. (1992), *Child Protection Procedures: What they mean for your Family*, Family Rights Group, London.

Atherton, C. and Ryburn, M. (1996), 'Family Group Conferences: Partnership and Practice', *Adoption and Fostering*, 20, 1, pp.16-20.

Audit Commission (1994), *Seen but not Heard*, HMSO, London.

Baglow, L. (1990), *A Multi-Dimensional Model for Treatment of Child Abuse: a framework for cooperation*, Child Abuse and Neglect, vol. 14.

Banks, S. (1995), *Ethics and Values in Social Work*, Macmillan, London.

240 *Child Protection: Families and the conference process*

Barclay Report (1982), *Social Workers - their Roles and Tasks*, Report of a Working Party under the Chairmanship of Peter Barclay, Bedford Square Press, London.

Barn, R. (1990), 'Black Children in Local Authority Care: Admission Patterns', *New Community*, 16, pp. 229-246.

Bedford, A. (1986), 'An Alternative View', in Brown, T. and Waters, J. (eds), *Parental Participation in Case Conferences*, BASPCAN, pp. 30-33, Rochdale.

Bell, M. (1993), 'Partnership with Families: Unequal Partnership', *Community Care*, 28.10.1993, pp. 2-3.

Bell, M. (1995), 'A study of the attitudes of nurses to parental involvement in the initial child protection conference, and their preparation for it', *Journal of Advanced Nursing*, 22, 250-257.

Bell, M. (1996), 'An account of the experiences of 51 families involved in an initial child protection conference', *Child and Family Social Work*, vol.1, January.

Bell, M. (1996), 'Why some conferences are difficult: A study of the Professionals Experience of some initial child protection conferences', *Children and Society*, February.

Bell, M. (1997), *A survey of the needs of and service provision for children and young people in Leeds who have witnessed and/or experienced domestic violence*, Department of Social Work, University of York, York.

Bell, M. (1999), 'Working in Partnership in Child Protection: The Conflicts', *British Journal of Social Work*, June, Blackwells, Oxford.

Bell, M. and Sinclair, I. (1993), *Parental Involvement in Initial Child Protection Conferences in Leeds; an External Evaluation*, Nuffield Summary Report, University of York, York.

Bentovim, A. (1992), *Trauma Organised Systems; Physical and sexual abuse in families*, Karnac, London and New York.

Beresford, P. and Croft, S. (1992), *Citizen Involvement: A Practical Guide for Change*, Macmillan, Basingstoke.

Berry, L. (1988), 'The Rhetoric of Consumerism and the Exclusion of Community', *Community Development Journal*, Vol.23, No.4, pp. 266-72.

Besharov, D.J. (1990), *Recognising Child Abuse: A Guide for the Concerned*, The Free Press.

Biesteck, F. (1957), *The Casework Relationship*, Unwin University Books, London.

Birchall, E. (1992), *Report to the Department of Health: Working Together in Child Protection: Report of Phase Two: A Survey of the Experience and Perceptions of Six Key Professions*, University of Stirling, Stirling.

Blackburn, C. (1991), *Poverty and Health*, Open University Press, Buckingham.

Bradshaw, J. (1972), 'The Taxonomy of social need', in Mclachlan, G. (ed), *Problems and Progress in Medical Care*, Oxford University Press, Oxford.

British Association of Social Workers (1980), *Clients are Fellow Citizens*, BASW, Birmingham.

British Association of Social Workers (1985), *Policy on the management of child abuse*, Report of a project group, etc., BASW, Birmingham.

Brown, T. and Waters, J. (eds) (1986), *Parental Participation in Case Conferences*, BASPCAN, Rochdale.

Browne, K. (1994), 'Child Abuse: Defining, Understanding and Intervening', in *The Child Protection Handbook*, 43-66, Balliere Tindall, London.

Browne, K. and Saqi, S. (1987), 'Parent Child Interaction in abusing families: possible causes and consequences', in Maher, P. (ed), *Child Abuse: An Educational Perspective*, pp. 83-89, Blackwell, Oxford.

Bullock, R., Little, M. and Milham, S. (1993), *Going Home*, Aldershot, Dartmouth.

Bullock, R., Little, M. and Taylor, K. (1995), 'Balance of power', *Community Care*, 27, August, 2-3.

Burns, L. (1991), *Partnership with Families: a Study of 65 Child Protection Case Conferences in Gloucestershire to which the family was invited*, Gloucestershire Social Services Department.

Butt, J. (1994), *Same Service or Equal Service*, HMSO, London.

Carroll, L.D. (1865), *Alice's Adventures in Wonderland*.

Cheetam, J., Fuller, R., McIvor, G. and Petch, A. (1992), *Evaluating Social Work Effectiveness*, Open University Press, Milton Keynes.

Children Act Report 1992 (1993), Department of Health, HMSO.

Cleaver, H. and Freeman, P. (1995), *Parental Perspectives in Cases of Suspected Child Abuse*, Studies in Child Protection, HMSO, London.

Cleveland (1988), *Report of the Inquiry into Child Abuse in Cleveland*, HMSO, London.

Connolly, M. (1994), An Act of Empowerment: the Children and Young Persons and their Families Act (1989), *British Journal of Social Work*, 24.

Cooper, A. and Hetherington, R. (1997), *Protecting Children: Messages from Europe*, Russell House Publishing, London.

Corby, B. (1987), *Working with Child Abuse*, Milton Keynes, Open University Press.

Corby, B., Millar, M. and Young, L. (1996), 'Parental Participation in Child Protection Work: Rethinking the Rhetoric', *British Journal of Social Work*, 6, 4.

Corby, B. and Mills, C. (1986), Child Abuse Risks and Resources, *British Journal of Social Work*, vol. 16, 5.

Corden, J. (1995), personal communication.

Corden, J. and Preston-Shoot, M. (1987), *Contracts in Social Work*, Gower, Aldershot.

Cousins, C. (1987), *Controlling Social Welfare*, Wheatsheaf, Brighton.

Daines, R., Lyon, K. and Parsloe, P. (1990), *Aiming for Partnership*, Barnado's, Essex.

Dale, P., Davies, M., Morrison, T. and Waters, J. (1986), *Dangerous Families: Assessment and Treatment of Child Abuse*, Tavistock, London.

Data Protection Act, 1981.

Day, A.T. (1981), *Social Work and Social Control*, Tavistock, London.

Department of Health (1989), *The Care of Children: Regulations and Guidance*, HMSO, London.
Department of Health (1991), *Patterns and Outcomes in Child Placements*, HMSO, London.
Department of Health (1991), *Working Together under the Children Act 1989: A guide to arrangements for inter-agency cooperation for the protection of children from abuse*, HMSO, London.
Department of Health (1992), *Children Act Report 1992*, HMSO, London.
Department of Health (1995), *Child Protection: Messages from Research*, HMSO, London.
Department of Health (1995), *The challenge of partnership in child protection: Practice Guide*, HMSO, London.
Department of Health (1996), *Messages from Inspections: Child Protection Inspections 1992 – 1996*, HMSO, London.
Department of Health (1998), *Working Together 1998, Consultation Document*, HMSO, London.
Department of Health and Social Security (1974), LASSL (74), 13.
Department of Health and Social Security (1983), *Code of Practice, Access to Children in Care*, HMSO, London.
Department of Health and Social Security (1985), *Social Work Decisions in Child Care*, HMSO, London.
Dingwall, R., Ekelaar, J. and Murray, T. (1983), *The Protection of Children: State Intervention in Family Life*, Blackwell, Oxford.
Education Act, 1981.
Edwards, D. (1996), 'Life in the Balance', *The Guardian*, 13.11.96.
Eisenhardt, K.M. (1993), 'Making Fast Strategic Decisions in High Velocity Environments', *Academy of Management Journal*, Vol.32, No.3, pp.516-542.
Etherington, S. (1986), *Social Work and Citizenship*, BASW, Birmingham.
Etzioni, A. (ed) (1969), *The Semi-Professions and their Organisation*, The Free Press, New York.
Everitt, A., Hardiker, P., Littlewood, J. and Mullender, A. (1992), *Applied Research for Better Practice*, BASW, Macmillan, Basingstoke.
Fairclough, N. (1989), *Language and Power*, Longman, London.
Fantuzzo, J.W. and Lindquist, C.U. (1989), 'The effects of observing conjugal violence on children: A Review and analysis of research methodology', *Journal of Family Violence*, 4 (1), pp.77-94.
Farmer, E. and Owen, M. (1993), *Decision-Making, Intervention and Outcome in Child Protection Work*, Report to Department of Health, University of Bristol, Bristol.
Ferguson, H., Gilligan, R. and Torode, R. (eds) (1993), *Surviving Childhood Adversity: Issues for Policy and Practice*, Social Studies Press T.C.D., London.
Finklehor, D. and Brown, A. (1985), 'The Traumatic Impact of Child Sexual Abuse; a conceptualisation', *American Journal of Orthopsychiatry*.
Fisher, M. (1990), *Parental Participation in Case Conferences*, University of Bradford, Bradford.

Foucault, M. (ed) (1977), *Discipline and Punish*, Allen Lane, London.

Furnis, T. (1991), *The Multi-Professional Handbook of Child Sexual Abuse: Integrated Management, Therapy and Legal Intervention*, Routledge, London.

Geach, H. and Szwed, E. (1983), *Providing Civil Justice for Children*, Edward Arnold, London.

Gibbons, J. (1995), *The Child Protection System: Objectives and Evaluation*, Paper read at Lancaster University, 11.1.95.

Gibbons, J., Conroy, S. and Bell, C. (1995), *Operating the Child Protection System*, HMSO, London.

Gil, D. (1970), *Violence Against Children*, Harvard University Press, Mass.

Goffman, I. (1963), *Stigma: Notes on the Management of Spoiled Identity*, Penguin, Harmondsworth.

Gough, D. (1993), *Child Abuse Interventions: A Review of the Research Literature*, HMSO, London.

Habermas, J. (1977), *Legitimisation Crisis*, Heinemann, London.

Hallett, C. (1995), *InterAgency Co-ordination in Child Protection*, HMSO, London.

Hallett, C. and Birchall, E. (1992), *Co-ordination and Child Protection: A Review of the Literature*, HMSO, Edinburgh.

Hallett, C. and Stevenson, O. (1980), *Child Abuse: Aspects of Inter-professional Cooperation*, London.

Harre, R., Clarke, D. and De Carlo (1985), *Motives and Mechanisms*, Methuen, London.

Hearn, B. (1995), *Child and Family Support and Protection. A Practical Approach*, National Children's Bureau Enterprises Limited, London.

Hobbs, C. (1994), 'Could it have Happened when he Fell, Doctor?', *Child Abuse Review*, vol.3, 148-150.

Hohfield, W.N. (1923), *Fundamental Legal Conceptions*, Yale University Press.

Hollis, F. (1966), *Casework: A Psychosocial Therapy*, Random House, USA.

Home Office, Ministry of Health and Ministry of Education (1959), *Joint Circular on Children Neglected or ill treated in their own Homes*, 31 July.

Hooper, C.A. (1992), *Mothers Surviving Child Sexual Abuse*, Routledge, London.

Housiaux, S.T. (1984), *Parental attendance at child abuse case conferences*, Coventry: NSPCC Child Protection Unit.

Hugman, R. (1991), *Power in the Caring Professions*, Macmillan, Basingstoke.

Jones, D.N., Pickett, J., Oates, M. and Barber, P. (1987), *Understanding Child Abuse*, Macmillan, Basingstoke.

Jones, R. (1996), 'Decision Making in Child Protection', *British Journal of Social Work*, 26, pp.445-446.

Jordan, B. (1990), *Social Work in an Unjust Society*, Harvester, Hemel Hempstead.

Kaganas, F. et al (1995), *Legislating for Harmony*, Jessica Kingsley Publishers.

Katz, I. (1995), 'Approaches to Empowerment in Child Protection', in Cloke and

Davies (ed), *Participation and Empowerment in Child Protection*, Pitman, London.

Kempe, R.S. and Kempe, C.H. (1978), *Child Abuse*, Fontana.

Kendricke, P. and Mapstone, E. (1989), 'The chairperson and child care reviews in Scotland, Implications for the role of reviews in the decision-making process', *British Journal of Social Work*, 17, pp.277-289.

King, M. and Trowell, J. (1993), *Children's Welfare and the Law*, Sage, London.

Korbin, J. (ed) (1981), *Child Abuse and Neglect: Cross-cultural Perspective*, University of California Press, Berkeley.

Leeds Area Child Protection Committee Report, 1991/2, Leeds.

Leeds Area Child Protection Committee Report, 1994/5, Leeds.

Lewis, A. (1992), 'An Overview of Research in Child Protection Work', in *Participation in Practice*, University of East Anglia, Norwich.

Lewis, A. (1994), *Chairing Child Protection Conferences*, Avebury, Aldershot.

Lieberman, S. (1979), *Transgenerational Family Therapy*, Croom Helm, New York.

Lishman, J. (1988), 'Social Work Interviews: how effective are they?', *Research, Policy and Planning* (2), pp 1-5.

London Borough of Brent (1985), *A Child in Trust*, The Report of the Panel of Inquiry into the Circumstances surrounding the Death of Jasmine Beckford.

London Borough of Greenwich (1987), *A Child in Mind: The Protection of Children in a Responsible Society*, The Report of a Commission of Inquiry into the circumstances surrounding the death of Kimberley Carlile.

London Borough of Lambeth (1987), *Whose Child*, The Report of the Panel Appointed to Inquire into the Death of Tyra Henry.

Lonsdale, G. (1991), *A Study of Parental Participation at Initial Child Protection Case Conferences*, Wiltshire Social Services Department.

Lynch, M. (1986), 'The International Society for the Prevention of Child Abuse and Neglect; the Future', *Child Abuse and Neglect*, 10, 451-563.

Lyth, I.M. (1988), *Containing Anxiety in Institutions*, Free Association Books, London.

Maluccio, A., Fein, E. and Olmstead, K.A. (1986), *Permanency Planning for Children; Concepts and Methods*, Tavistock, London.

Maluccio, A. and Sinanoglu, P. (1981), *The challenge of partnership; working with parents of children in foster care*, Child Welfare League of America, New York.

Marsh, P. and Fisher, M. (1992), *Good intentions: developing partnership in social services*, Joseph Rowntree Foundation, York.

Mattinson, J. and Sinclair, I. (1979), *Mate and Stalemate*, Blackwells, Oxford.

Mayer, J.E. and Timms, N. (1970), *The Client Speaks*, Routledge and Kegan Paul, London.

McCluskey, U. and Bingley Miller, L. (1995), 'Theme Focused Family Therapy: The Inner Emotional World of the Family', *Journal of Family Therapy*.

McDonnel, P. and Aldgate, J. (1984), *Reviews of Children in Care*, Department of Social and Administrative Studies, Oxford.

McGloin, P. and Turnbull, A. (1986), *Parent Participation in Child Abuse Review Conferences. A Research Report*, London Borough of Greenwich.

Menzies, I., *A Case Study in the functioning of Social Systems as a Defence against Anxiety*, Human Relations, 13.

Merchant, A. and Luckham, S. (1991), *A Study of Parental Participation in Child Protection Conferences in Mid-Essex*, Essex Social Services Department, Essex.

Meyer, H., Borgatta, E. and Jones,W. (1965), *Girls at Vocational High: An Experiment in Social Work Intervention*, Russell Sage Foundation, New York.

Milham, S., Bullock, R., Hosie, K. and Haak, M. (1986), *Lost in care; the problems of maintaining links between children in care and their families*, Gower, Aldershot.

Mill, J.S. (1972), *Utilitarianism: On Liberty and Considerations on Representative Government*, Dent, London.

Miller, L.B. and Fisher, T. (1992), 'Some Obstacles to the effective investigation and registration of children at risk. Issues gleaned from a worker's perspective', *Journal of Social Work Practice*, vol.6, no. 2.

Minuchin, S. (1974), *Families and Family Therapy*, Tavistock, London.

Moore, J. (1992), *The ABC of Child Protection*, Arena, Aldershot.

Morrison, T. (1990), in NSPCC Occasional Paper Number 8, *Child and Parental Participation in Case Conferences*, NSPCC, London.

Morrison, T. (1992), 'The Emotional Effects of Child Protection Work on the Worker', *Practice*, 4, 253-270.

Mullender, A. and Morley, R. (eds) (1995), *Children Living with Domestic Violence*, Whiting and Birch, London.

Murphy, M. (1995), *Working Together in Child Protection*, Arena, Aldershot.

National Health Service and Community Care Act, 1990.

Newson, J. and Newson, E. (1969), *Patterns of Infant Care*, Penguin; (1976), *Four Years Old in an Urban Community*, George Allen and Unwin; (1989), *Seven Years Old in the Home Environment*, Allen and Unwin; (1998), *The Extent of Parental Physical Punishment in the U.K.*, Approach.

O'Hagan, K. (1986), *Crisis Intervention in Social Services*, Macmillan, Basingstoke.

Ovretviet, J. (1986), *Improving Social Work Records and Practice*, BASW, Birmingham.

Pardeck, J., Murphy, J. and Chung, W. (1994), 'Postmodernism and Social Work: A Response to Professor Parton', *Social Work and Social Sciences review*, 5(2), 128-9.

Parents against Injustice (1992), *Child abuse investigations; the families perspective*, Pain, Essex.

Parker, R., Ward, H., Jackson, S., Aldgate, J. and Wedge, P. (eds) (1991), *Looking After Children: Assessing Outcomes in Child Care*, HMSO, London.

Parkinson, J. (1992), 'Supervision versus Control; Can Managers provide both Managerial and Professional supervision', in Cloke, C. and Naish, J. (ed), *Key Issues in Child Protection for Health Visitors and Nurses*, Longman.

Parton, N. (1991), *Governing The Family: Child Care, Child Protection and The State*, Macmillan, Basingstoke.

Parton, N. (1994), 'The Nature of Social Work under Conditions of (Post) Modernity', *Social Work and Social Services Review*, vol.5 (2), 93-112.

Parton, N. (ed) (1996), *Social Theory, Social Change and Social Work*, Routledge, London.

Paterson (1864), Waltzing Matilda.

Peace, G. (1991), *Interprofessional Collaboration, Professionals and Personal Perspectives, Part 2*, Manchester: Boys' and Girls' Welfare Society.

Phillips, J. and Evans, M. (1986), *Participating Parents*, ADB Publications, Bradford.

Phillips, M. and Butt, J. (1996), 'Enquiries into Allegations: A Black Perspective', in Platt, D. and Shemmings, D. (ed), *Making Enquiries into Alleged Child Abuse and Neglect: Partnership with Families*, Pennant Professional Books, Brighton.

Police and Criminal Evidence Act,1984.

Pope, A. (1744), *Moral Essays.*

Potter, J. and Wetherell, M. (1987), *Discourse and Social Psychology: Beyond Attitudes and Behaviour*, Sage, London.

Quinton, D. and Rutter, M. (1988), *Parenting Breakdown: The Making and Breaking of Intergenerational Links*, Avebury, Aldershot.

Rawls, J. (1971), *A Theory of Justice*, Harvard University Press, Cambridge.

Regina v Harrow LBC, Ex Parte D (1988), The Guardian, 29 November.

Rowe, J. and Tunnard, J. (1991), *The Children Act 1989; Working in partnership with families*, HMSO, London.

Sainsbury, E. (1989), 'Participation and Paternalism', in Shardlow, S. (ed), *The Values of Social Work*, Routledge, London.

Satir, V. (1964), *Conjoint Family Therapy*, Science and Behaviour, Palo Alto.

Satyamurti, C. (1979), 'Care and Control in local authority social work', in Parr, N., Rustin, M. and Satyamurti, C. (eds), *Social Work, Welfare and the State*, Edward Arnold, London.

Saunders, R. and Thomas, N. (1997), *Area Child Protection Committees*, Ashgate, Aldershot.

Secretary of State for Social Services (1974), *Report of the Committee of Enquiry into the Care and Supervision provided in relation to Maria Colwell*, HMSO, London.

Secretary of State for Social Services (1985), *Report of the panel of enquiry into the circumstances surrounding the death of Jasmine Beckford: A Child in Trust*, London Borough of Brent.

Secretary of State for Social Services (1987), *Report on Kimberley Carlile. A Child in Mind: Protection of children in a responsible society*, London Borough of Greenwich.

Secretary of State for Social Services (1988), *Report of the Inquiry into Child Abuse in Cleveland 1987*, Cm 412, HMSO, London.

Shemmings, D. (1991), *Client Access to Records: Participation in Social Work*,

Avebury, Gower.

Shemmings, D. (1991), *Family Participation in Child Protection Conferences - Report of a Pilot Project in Lewisham Social Services Department*, Norwich, University of East Anglia.

Sinclair, R. (1984), *Decision-Making in Statutory Reviews on Children in Care*, Gower, Aldershot.

Sinclair, R. and Webb, A. (1983), *Decision Making in Statutory Reviews on Children in Care*, Loughborough University.

Smart, M. (1992), 'Professional Ethics and Participation - nurses, health visitors and midwives, in Thoburn, J. (ed), *Participation in Practice*, University of East Anglia, Norwich.

Smith, G. and Cantley, C. (1985), *Assessing Health Care*, Open University Press, Buckingham.

Smith, M. and Grocke, M. (1995), *Normal Family Sexuality and Sexual Knowledge in Children*, Royal College of Psychiatrists, Gorkill Press.

Smith, N. (1990), *Learning From Parents*, Cumbria Child Protection Unit, Cumbria.

Social Services Inspectorate (1990), *Inspection of Child Protection Services in Rochdale*, Department of Health, London.

Social Services Inspectorate (1995), *The Challenge of Partnership in Child Protection: Practice Guide*, Department of Health, HMSO, London.

Steel, B. (1976), 'Experiences with an inter disciplinary concept', in Helfer, R. and Kempe, C. (ed), *Child Abuse and Neglect: The family and the community*, Ballinger, Cambridge, Mass.

Stein, M. and Ellis, S. (1983), *Gizza Say? Reviews of Young People in Care*, National Association of Young People in Care.

Stevenson, O. (1994), 'Case Conferences in Child Protection' in *The Child Protection Handbook* (eds. Wilson, K. and James, A.), 227-241, Balliere Tindall, London.

Stevenson, O. and Hallett, C. (1980), *Interprofessional Cooperation*, Allen and Unwin, London.

Tattersall, P. (1992), 'Communicating Assertively to Protect Children in Nursing Practice', in Cloke,C. and Naish, J. (ed), *Key Issues in Child Protection for Health Visitors and Nurses*, Longman.

Taylor, S. and Godfrey, M. (1991), *Parental Involvement in Child Protection Case Conferences: An Evaluation of the Pilot Project*, North Tyneside Social Services Department.

Tennyson, A.L. (1989), *The Works of Alfred Lord Tennyson*, Macmillan, London.

*The Convention on the Rights of the Child*, Adopted by the United Nations General Assembly (1989), HMSO, London.

Thoburn, J. (ed) (1992), *Participation in Practice - Involving Families in Child Protection*, University of East Anglia, Norwich.

Thoburn, J., Lewis, A. and Shemmings, D. (1995), *Paternalism or Partnership? Family Involvement in the Child Protection Process*, Studies in Child Protection, HMSO, London.

Thoburn, J., Shemmings, D. and Lewis, A. (1993), *A Study of Client Participation in Child Protection Work*, Report to Department of Health, Social Work Development Unit, University of East Anglia, Norwich.

Thorpe, D. (1993), *Evaluating Child Protection Programmes*, Paper read at Lancaster University, 11.1.95.

Thorpe, D. (1994), *Evaluating Child Protection Programmes*, Open University Press, Buckingham.

Tunnard, J. (1983), 'The Whole Family as Client', *Adoption and Fostering*, vol.7, no.3.

Vernon, J. and Fruin, D. (1986), *In Care: A Study of Social Work Decision-Making*, National Children's Bureau, London.

Vickery, A. (1976), 'A Unitary Approach to Social Work', in Olsen (ed), *Differential Approaches to Social Work with the Mentally Disordered*, BASW, Birmingham.

Walton, P. (1996), *Partnership with Mothers in the Wake of Child Sexual Abuse*, Social Work Monographs, University of East Anglia, Norwich.

Waterhouse, L. (1993), *Child Abuse and Child Abusers*, Jessica Kingsley.

Wattam, C. (1989), *Teachers Experiences with children who have, or may have, been sexually abused*, Occasional Paper No.5 NSPCC, London.

Wattam, C. (1992), *Making a Case in Child Protection*, Longman, Essex.

Wattam, C. (1995), *Developing Risk Assessment Work in Child Protection Practice*, Paper read at Lancaster University, 12.1.95.

Weiss, J. (1981), 'Substance vs Symbol in administrative reform: the case of human services co-ordination', *Policy Analysis*, 7.1, 21-45.

Westcott, H. (1995), 'Perceptions of child protection casework: views from children, parents, and practitioners', in Cloke, C. and Davies, M. (eds), *Participation and Empowerment in Child Protection*, Pitman, Wiltshire.

Wilcox, R., et al (1991), *Family decision making: Family group conferences: Practitioners' views*, Practitioners Publishing, Lower Hutt, New Zealand.

Wilde, O.F. (1946), *Complete Works*, ed. Maine, G.F., London.

Woodhouse, D. and Pengelly, P. (1991), *Anxiety and the Dynamics of Collaboration*, AUP.